Fantastic Adventures In Trusting Him

An Odyssey of Faith, Fire and Forgiveness

Faith and Joshua Alexander

This book is copyright. Enquiries should be addressed to the authors, care of
faithandjoshua@yahoo.com

"Fantastic Adventures In Trusting Him: An Odyssey of Faith, Fire and Forgiveness."
Copyright © *Faith and Joshua Alexander* 2004

The right of Faith and Joshua Alexander to be identified as the authors of this work have been asserted in accordance with the Copyright, Designs and Patents Act 1988.

ISBN 0-9548281-1-9

Published by Fourstreams Limited
203 Broad Walk, Blackheath, London, SE3 8NG
t: +44(0)2088562952 – e: *sales@fourstreams.co.uk*

All rights reserved. No part may be reproduced, stored in a retrieval system or transmitted, in any form or by any means, electronic, mechanical, photocopying, recording or otherwise without the prior written permission of the authors and publisher. This book is sold subject to the condition that it shall not by way of trade or otherwise be lent, re-sold, hired out or otherwise circulated without the publisher's prior consent in any form of binding or cover other than that in which it is published.

Unless otherwise noted, Scriptures are taken from
THE HOLY BIBLE, NEW INTERNATIONAL VERSION,
Copyright © 1973, 1978, 1984 International Bible Society.
Used by permission of Zondervan Bible Publishers.
Scriptures taken from the King James (Authorised) Version are denoted 'KJV'.
A catalogue record for this book is available from the British Library.

Fantastic Adventures In Trusting Him

Contents

	Map	iv
	Dedication	vi
	Preface	vii
	Acknowledgements	xi
Prologue	An Imaginary Audience in Heaven	xii
1	The Precious Pearl	1
2	Prophetic Gifts	18
3	Crystal Clarity	32
4	Silver Linings	45
5	Roman Holiday	54
6	The Treasure House	69
7	The Good Shepherd	85
8	Golden Prospects	98
9	Diamonds in the Rough	118
10	Father's Heart	133
11	The Refiner's Fire	156
12	His Glorious Riches	177
Epilogue	Another Imaginary Audience in Heaven	201
	Frequently Asked Questions	203

Fantastic Adventures In Trusting Him

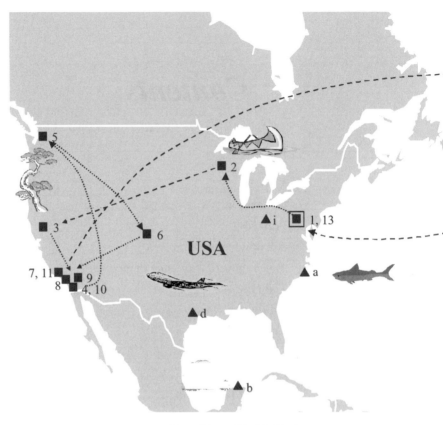

■ = **PLACES LIVED IN:**

1 Gaithersburg, Maryland (Chapter 1)
2 Eau Claire, Wisconsin   (6)
3 Santa Rosa, California   (7)
4 San Diego California   (7)
5 Seattle, Washington   (9)
6 Denver, Colorado   (10)
7 Pasadena, California   (11)
8 San Juan Capistrano, Calif.   (11)
9 The Ranch near Hemet, Calif. (11)
10 San Diego California   (11)
11 Los Angeles, California   (11)
12 Stevenage, England   (12)
13 Gaithersburg, Maryland   (12)

Fantastic Adventures In Trusting Him

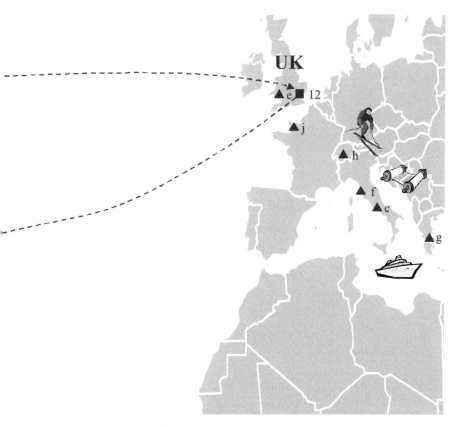

▲ = PLACES VISITED:

a Emerald Isle, North Carolina (Chapter 1)
b Chicxulub, Yucatan, Mexico   (3)
c The Vatican, Rome, Italy   (5)
d Flight from Houston, Texas   (10)
e Swansea, Wales (UK)   (10)
f Genoa, Italy   (10)
g Cruising the Aegean (Greece)   (12)
h Crans-Montana, Switzerland   (12)
i Columbus, Ohio   (12)
j Normandy, France   (12)

Move to new home by car ┈┈▶
by air ╌╌▶

Dedication

**'To HIM
who is able to do immeasurably more than all we ask or imagine,
according to His power at work within us,
to Him be glory...'**
(Ephesians 3:20)

AND

To His children, young and old,
who desire to know the true and living God
and to experience His abundant life.

Preface

"Without faith it is impossible to please God, because anyone who comes to Him must believe that He exists and that He rewards those who earnestly seek Him."
(Hebrews 11:4)

This book is about learning to walk and talk with God. It is not a biography, so all specific information that identifies the authors - including their real names - has been purposely omitted. [Some background details, however, have been included in this preface.] The authors prefer the spotlight in these dramatic stories to illuminate the main character, God Almighty, as if He were visible.

Faith in God is a mystery. It often comes unexpectedly to ordinary people (like the Alexanders), producing unexpected and extraordinary results. Jesus Christ said, **"I tell you the truth, if you have faith as small as a mustard seed, you can say to this mountain, 'Move from here to there' and it will move. Nothing will be impossible for you.**[1]**"** Jesus was not referring to what most people these days think of as faith - a mere belief and affirmation that God exists (sometimes called 'head-faith'). Jesus meant something supernatural, a 'heart-faith' that goes beyond belief and that **earnestly seeks Him.**[2] He exercised supernatural heart-faith in everything He did and said, and worked miracles when He discerned such heart-faith in others.[3]

---

[1] *Matthew 17:20*
[2] *Hebrews 11:4b*
[3] *See the four Gospels, among many instances: Matthew 8:13, 9:2-7, 9:22, 9:27-30, 13:58, 15:28; Mark 2:5-12, 5:34, 10:52; Luke 5:20-25, 7:9-10, 7:50, 8:48, 17:19, 18:42; and John 14:12*

The Bible declares that faith comes as a free gift from Heaven[4], **"by hearing the message... through the word of Christ.**"[5] After faith takes root in our heart, God begins to transform our thoughts, words and actions, even our character. To the natural mind these words make little sense. People who walk by faith appear to be cranks, fanatics, even lunatics. But once 'faithwalkers' are motivated by God's love, the world around them begins to change as others become infected by His love and also become faithwalkers.

A popular acronym for *FAITH* is *'Forsaking All, I Take Him'*. The authors' favourite (for reasons that will become obvious) is *'Fantastic Adventures In Trusting Him'*. Both of these aspects are illustrated in this book.

God Himself orchestrated these adventures of faith, fire and forgiveness. Each story seems to force Joshua and Faith right up against a wall of helplessness before a divine deliverance is offered. (This pattern in their life has prompted a catch-phrase, *'It's so the story might be better!'*) Above all, the stories record the interventions of the One who is trustworthy and true, who encourages, chastises, guides, provides and rescues His own.

These fantastic adventures serve to explore the mystery of heart-faith by illustrating the faith process: (1) God gives us a measure of faith, hope rises in our hearts and so we begin to pray. (2) God answers our 'faith-prayers', so we trust Him more and begin to obey what He tells us. (3) God responds to our trust and obedience and gives us more faith from Heaven (just as the Scriptures say). Thus, heart-faith can grow almost without limit - unless we shrink back in unbelief and disobedience.

Faith works rather like a muscle: the more it is exercised, the stronger and more durable it becomes. When God becomes real to us through faith, He invites us to surrender one area of our life after another into His loving care. He then carefully crafts the circumstances of our life so that we will become more attentive to Him, more dependent on Him and more obedient to Him - as this book so clearly illustrates.

The Alexanders seem to be on a roller coaster of spiritual and physical 'ups and downs', but by the end of the story God sets them totally free, both spiritually and financially, in order to display His great love, goodness and faithfulness. Follow in their footsteps through 15 years of laughter, tears, defeats and triumphs. They learn to trust, to obey, to know and to love a

---

[4] *Ephesians 2:8*
[5] *Romans 10:17*

personal, intimate (yet all too invisible) God, who never lets them down - although it appears that He does so every once in a while.

Joshua was born in England during World War II, his parents and sister having emigrated from Central Europe just before war broke out. This talented family included engineers, doctors and musicians, most of them agnostics or atheists. Joshua was sent to a very academic private school where the Bible was read, hymns were sung and prayers were offered each morning before classes. In spite of the daily liturgy, Joshua finished his schooling even more sceptical and resistant than when he started. He worked hard at his academic subjects and also prepared for a possible career as a concert pianist. After winning a place at Cambridge University to study physics, Joshua abandoned his musical ambitions to pursue a scientific career. He moved to the USA after his graduation and earned a doctorate from Massachusetts Institute of Technology (MIT). This book begins a couple of years later, when he is the supervisor of a laboratory for an American 'high-tech' company and manages several of their international research and development (R&D) contracts.

Faith was born in the same month as Joshua but on the other side of the Atlantic Ocean in the USA. Her parents also had emigrated from Europe before the War and also highly valued education. Unlike Joshua's parents, however, they also valued the Ten Commandments, the Golden Rule[6] and the Lord's Prayer. Faith was the fourth of five children all of whom were encouraged to develop their various academic and artistic talents. Her four siblings all became professionals: two university professors, a physician and a lawyer. Before Faith was born, her aunt, a Catholic nun, wrote to her parents with a prophecy: ***"This child belongs to God..."*** As it turned out, Faith's earliest desire was to know God and to hear His voice. She continually searched for Him, and after becoming a Catholic in her early twenties, she studied theology for her BA. When a priest encouraged her to pursue graduate work in clinical psychology, Faith took his advice and earned a master's degree - meanwhile dropping out of the Catholic Church - and finished her training at Harvard Medical School.

Joshua and Faith are a sober-minded, sceptical couple as this story begins. Self-sufficient and reliant on their education and experience, they are proud of their accomplishments. They have an extremely happy marriage, and have a baby daughter. They own a house just outside Washington DC, both their cars are paid for and they have almost no debts. Joshua enjoys a secure, well-paid

---

[6] ***"Do to others as you would have them do to you."*** *(Luke 6:31)*

job at the outset of a promising technical career. They love music and the arts, studying and reading, and they think of themselves as 'good people'. They have hardly a care in the world. Yet, like many of their generation, they have no spiritual life of any kind. Little do they suspect what lies in store…

Note: Each detail has been recorded as accurately as possible, but the name of nearly every living person mentioned in this book has been changed in order to protect his or her privacy. A section at the end of the book entitled 'Frequently Asked Questions' addresses several issues raised by readers prior to publication.

Acknowledgements

There are so many people - too numerous to thank individually - who came alongside the authors during their journey of faith and offered them God's hand of love. They comforted them when they were hurting and encouraged them when they were in despair. They provided their needs when they were helpless and sheltered them when they were homeless. They laughed with them, cried with them and (most important) corrected them when they were wrong.

The Lord knows each one by name and appreciates how much it cost to obey Him in reaching out to Faith and Joshua. He will surely provide an eternal reward in Heaven, which is far more precious than any acknowledgement by name here on Earth.

The authors especially acknowledge the patience, fortitude and longsuffering of their three children, Jacqueline, Richard and Andrew, who were captive yet willing participants during this oddest of odysseys through 15 years of childhood. Their excellent and hilarious company, wisdom, encouragement and unstinting love have been immeasurable blessings.

> "The LORD bless you and keep you; the LORD shine
> His face upon you and be gracious to you; the LORD turn His
> face toward you and give you peace."
> *(Numbers 6:24-26.)*

Prologue

An Imaginary Audience in Heaven

"Welcome, Guardian Angels of Faith and Joshua."

"Praise and thanks to You, our Sovereign Lord! We worship You. Thank You for calling us into Your Holy Presence. We are eager to learn our assignment and to do Your Majesty's will..."

"It is time to share with you My purpose for this couple. You must prepare them so that I can have their full attention. I want to reveal Myself to them and plant supernatural faith in their hearts. Then I shall show them the full extent of My Love.

"I have longed for the day when Joshua and Faith will open their hearts and allow Me to enter, so they might know Me as their Lord and Shepherd and listen to My voice, obeying everything I say. I want them to become My very own so that they will completely depend on Me as their Provider.

"You know how worldly they are and how completely they depend on their education and hard work for their security. But when - with your devoted help - they decide to turn around and trust wholeheartedly in Me, I will give them My Heavenly Treasure and teach them that real security on earth is enjoyed only by those who belong to Me and follow after Me, whatever their circumstances.

"Those who are hungry for truth, like them, must learn that everything of genuine value depends on My grace and mercy and is by faith from first to last - and that even the faith that they have comes to them as a free gift, by My Spirit.

"My plan for the Alexanders is to prosper them, not to harm them, but first I will bring them through severe and fiery trials so that I may become their refuge and their fortress, their God in whom they trust. Their hearts will

become fully committed to Me, they will learn to revere and fear Me, and they will put their hope in My unfailing love. My eyes will always be on them to strengthen them, to preserve their lives and to deliver them from death. I will protect them and be with them in trouble and will continually deliver them. Nothing will be too difficult for Me!

"I will put My law in their minds and write it on their hearts. I will be their God and they will be My people. They will know Me, the only true God, and I will forgive their wickedness and will remember their sins no more.

"Now for the plan. As you know, Joshua is extremely resistant to any conventional approach, so you must use signs and wonders to draw them. Here are the details, in this scroll...

"Now go, My faithful messengers, and minister to them!"

Fantastic Adventures In Trusting Him

"The God who made the world and everything in it is the Lord of heaven and earth...

"<u>He determined the times set forth for them and the exact places where they should live</u>. God did this so that man would seek Him and perhaps reach out for Him and find Him, though He is not far from each one of us.

"'For in Him we live and move and have our being... We are His offspring.'"

(Acts of the Apostles 17:24a, 26b-28)

1

The Precious Pearl
(September 1971 - October 1972)

"...The kingdom of heaven is like a merchant looking for fine pearls. When he found one of great value, he went away and sold everything he had and bought it."
(Matthew 13:45-46)

A Wake-Up Call

The baby's screams were piercingly loud, jolting Faith Alexander out of a deep, dreamless sleep. She jumped out of bed and hurried to Jacqueline's room to pick her up. Reaching down, she realised with a shock that her 18-month-old was quietly sleeping.

The screams continued, almost deafening her. Bewildered, Faith backed slowly into the hallway. *"If Jacqui isn't crying, who is? Where are those screams coming from? There's no other baby around here..."*

She turned on the light to make sure she was really awake. An urgent thought came into her mind.

"The pill... I forgot to take my PILL!" She checked her watch. *"Two o'clock... Oh, NO!"* With a sick feeling, she turned towards the bathroom to take her medication, but a second shock stopped her again: the house was now

completely silent. The screams had stopped the instant she remembered to take the pill.

The young mother went shakily to the medicine cabinet. She almost dropped the package but managed to swallow a pill. As she returned to the bedroom she wondered, *"Oh my God, did those screams just save my new baby? How could I have been so careless?"*

Faith was six weeks pregnant. The morning before, an obstetrician had given her an injection of progesterone to prevent her from miscarrying for the fourth time in only nine months. He had also given her a prescription for progesterone pills and warned her to take the first pill at bedtime - or else she would lose this baby also. Faith was so exhausted at the end of the day, however, that she fell asleep without remembering to take the critical overnight pill.

Had it not been for the screaming 'baby', she would have slept on until morning and almost certainly would have miscarried again.

Gratefully she flopped into bed, her heart pounding. Thanksgiving overflowed into prayer. *"I don't know who was responsible for those screams, but whoever you are, thank you, THANK you!"*

Incredibly, she heard an answer. **"You're perfectly welcome, Faith, any time! Just keep on taking your pills and your pregnancy will turn out fine. You will have a wonderful brother for Jacqueline."**

Her eyes popped wide open with astonishment. The words had just floated into her mind, distinct and light-hearted. She had never experienced hearing an internal voice like that.

Out of the corner of her eye she perceived the faint outline of a figure kneeling beside the bed. As she turned to face it, the apparition vanished. Things were getting weirder and weirder: screams, a voice and now a spirit being…

"Could that have been an angel?" she marvelled. She leaned over and shook her husband. "Joshua, please wake up!"

"Huh?" He turned over slowly without opening his eyes. "Waddisit?"

She told him as calmly as she could what had just happened and waited impatiently for his reaction. Eventually he roused himself. "Really? A BOY? That's greeeaaat…" he muttered. Moments later he was asleep again.

In the morning, Joshua found his wife bursting to tell him her bizarre experience for the second time. Faith was ecstatic at the possibility that God had actually spoken to her. It had been her lifelong desire to hear His voice.

Missing God

"My soul thirsts for the living God. Where can I go and meet with God?"
(Psalm 42:2)

Healthy and handsome, their baby boy came on his due date in May 1972. Thanksgiving was mixed with renewed curiosity about the mysterious cries and unusual encounter that had protected Richard's life and prophesied his safe arrival.

Faith's heart began thirsting again for the things of God. She missed the sacramental life of the Catholic Church and longed to return to it, but this longing was mixed with despair: Joshua was an avowed agnostic.

In bed one Saturday morning, Faith found her eyes filling with tears. Wrapped in grief, she didn't hear her husband come in.

"What's the matter, darling? Postnatal blues getting you down?" He sat down next to his weeping wife and cradled her head in his arms. His kind eyes caressed hers. "This isn't like my girl. What's wrong?" He stroked her long brown hair and encouraged her with a smile.

"You're going to think I'm so silly. I know you hate churches and don't want to have any part of them." She could hardly speak, choking on her words. "But... I miss the Church so much! I really do. Yesterday I was passing a Catholic Church and saw lots of cars parked outside. I decided to go in and find out what was going on. About 40 children were receiving their First Communion..." She sobbed aloud with another flood of tears.

"I wanted so badly to take Communion. Do you realise I haven't been to Mass in six years? As I sat there listening to the priest talking to the children about God's love for us, everything in me wanted to return to the Church."

Faith turned a teary face to her husband. "There's something missing in our life together, Joshua. I know we have everything anyone could desire - we love each other, we have a girl and a boy, we own a lovely little home - but there's something missing! I wish I could make you understand."

He pondered her words. "Well, I think I do understand. I've been wrestling with some questions myself. It does seem that we have everything, but I have no real answers about life - who we are, what we're doing here, where we're going..."

He took a deep breath and continued, "I've always detested religious things, going to church and all that stuff. It's just never been real or attractive to me (at least since I was seven years old). But if you can convince me somehow that it's true, I'll gladly become a Catholic or whatever... I just want you to be happy."

Joshua stood up with a grin. "I know what: you go to church tomorrow while I take care of the children."

His words brought great encouragement to Faith's heart. She got out of bed and gave him a warm hug. "You are so good to me!" Her heart sang as she began to go around the room, tidying up.

"By the way, before I go to Mass I'll have to go to Confession. A friend happened to tell me about a really 'liberal' priest. I think I'll make an appointment with him right now." She sat down to make the call while Joshua went out to play with Jacqueline.

"This time will be different," thought Faith with satisfaction as she waited to enter the Monsignor's office for her appointment. She had left Catholicism because she could not face confessing a serious sin. Ever since then she had tried repeatedly to confess in several churches, at the right time and with the right intention, but could not bring herself to step into that little confessional box. Now she was feeling quite proud of herself for having overcome her cowardice and for doing the 'right thing' at last. She entered the priest's office.

"I was at Mass a few days ago for the first time in several years, Monsignor. I wanted so much to take Communion, but I realised I had to go to Confession first..."

The priest fixed her with a penetrating look. "Do you love God?"

"Oh yes, I have always loved God."

"Then you could have taken Communion," he answered matter-of-factly.

She was aghast. "You're joking! How can I receive Communion with a guilty conscience?"

"But you said you were hungry to receive Communion. The Lord saw your heart: He was drawing you to His table. He has forgiven you. You didn't need to come here."

Faith reacted with anger and disbelief at his answer. Having been away from the Church all these years because she couldn't bring herself to confess her sins, now - finally face to face with a priest - she was being told she didn't NEED to confess. It was a cruel blow to her pride.

She argued vigorously using her knowledge of the Church laws, but the Monsignor was only interested in the mercy and compassion of God. The more they argued, the angrier she became; she still hadn't confessed her sins.

The priest suddenly interrupted Faith. "Say an act of contrition." He began to speak words of absolution over her.

Now she panicked. *"Oh dear God, this is sacrilege! How can I receive absolution when my heart is seething with anger? Help me!"* She was incapable of recalling any act of contrition. She left the office in embarrassment and confusion without saying another word.

Outside in the car, Faith exploded in rage. She shook her fist at heaven, shouting, *"What are You doing to me, God? Just look at my heart! Have you ever seen me this angry? That priest didn't even let me confess my sins - and I'm worse off than before! How can I go to Communion now?"*

She burst into tears as the full impact of the last question pierced her heart. She wept and wept. All her hopes of being restored to the sacraments had been dashed because she had neither received nor believed the priest's words of mercy and acceptance.

"I'll tell You this one thing, God. I'm not going to Confession ever again. Never, never, never! And don't You try and make me!"

Faith drove slowly home. The further she got from the church, the calmer she became as the fire of her anger and frustration died down. Then it dawned upon her that perhaps God did not want her to be a Catholic again. An unusual peace settled over her.

"Okay, God, I give up. You do it Your way. All I want is for You to be part of our life. We need You! Please, would You show us the way to find You? And, Lord, I am SO sorry I was angry with You."

Chinks in the Armour

A few days later, a friend loaned the Alexanders a book by a man calling himself Brother Andrew, who for years had been taking Bibles into Communist countries behind the Iron Curtain.

Joshua read *God's Smuggler* first and was deeply stirred, much to his wife's surprise. "Darling, you must read this," he urged, coming into the kitchen while she was preparing dinner. He held up the book and said with barely concealed excitement, "There are some INCREDIBLE things in here.

"Listen to this: Brother Andrew's ankle was badly crippled. He was desperate to know God's will for his life, but realised that his bad ankle was keeping him from saying an unconditional 'yes' to God. It was always a 'yes, but...'

"He finally surrendered to God with a real 'yes!' and took a step forward onto his bad foot. Instantly there was a sudden wrench and pain in his ankle, but then he realised it was completely healed! Isn't that amazing? There are lots of stories like that. It's hard for me not to believe them, I have to admit - the book is so utterly sincere."

He sat down at the table and spoke slowly and deliberately. "Brother Andrew's story somehow reminds me of my own leg, only in reverse. You remember how I told you that my thighbone snapped while I was running slowly along in a friendly game of softball? Everyone on the field heard the crack. They thought it was a gunshot. The doctors couldn't believe I'd broken my femur - the strongest bone in my body - when my foot wasn't even touching the ground." His wife nodded.

"But what I've never admitted to anyone is what happened later, after my operation. I was on painkillers, drifting in and out of consciousness, when a priest came into the ward. I was embarrassed and didn't want to talk to him (you know me). Yet when he came over to my bed I heard myself saying, 'That's okay, sir, you needn't spend your time with me because I know that this was an act of God, and that good will come of it.'"

Faith gasped. "You actually said that?" she marvelled.

"Yes, I did... I was shocked to hear the words come out of my mouth - it wasn't me speaking! Later on I decided it must have been all the codeine, and I tried to forget about it."

"But you said it was an act of God - I thought you didn't even believe in God." She paused. "Do you, Joshua?" she continued softly,

He frowned and rubbed his forehead. "Faith, I don't know what to believe any more. After reading Brother Andrew's book, I'm almost... well, I'm realising that there are so many things I don't understand. I'm a scientist; I've always looked for evidence before believing things, evidence that I could see, touch, or at least reproduce if I had to. But I keep being confronted by these things that go far beyond what's familiar or normal, things that seem impossible to explain."

He took his wife's hand as she came over and sat down next to him. "I've been thinking about that screaming baby that woke you up and saved Ricky's life, and recalling all those times when our lives were protected as we drove around Europe two years ago... and all those magical things that used to happen almost every Friday on our weekly anniversary. Remember how we used to joke that our 'Good Spirits' were helping us?

"I'm sure the probability of all these things happening to us simply by chance, or with some natural explanation, has to be effectively zero. I can't explain them, taken together or even taken one by one. But I know they happened! Why is our life so... so charmed, so MIRACULOUS?"

He stood up and began pacing the room in frustration. "I guess what's really beginning to bug me," he blurted out, "is that I'm nearly thirty years old and I STILL haven't a clue what life is all about. All I have are these questions I can't answer - about whether God exists, about what I'm doing here on earth, about all these things that keep happening."

He sat down again and looked guardedly at his stunned wife. "From time to time you've intimated that something important was missing from our life. I never wanted to discuss it because I knew you meant something religious and I hate anything that's religious. But now this book... this BOOK! It's making me think that... that maybe you're... right." Joshua flushed and drew a deep breath. "There's some kind of hunger or craving inside me, Faith. It bothers me a lot. I can't explain it. I've never known anything like it."

Nodding his head slowly and pensively, he muttered almost to himself, "But, IF there's a God, I wish... I really wish I could know Him the way Brother Andrew does."

A New Life

"For you have been born again... through the living and enduring word of God."
(1 Peter 1:23)

On a sunny Saturday afternoon in mid-September, Joshua and Faith were strolling along the sidewalk outside a large brick house in Washington DC. Joshua was scheduled for a most unusual consultation. Holding hands, they had absolutely no inkling of how radically their life was about to change.

"I can't believe you want to go through with this, Joshua. It's so unlike you."

"Why?" he retorted defensively. He stopped and faced her. "After all, Faith, if she's a fake we'll find out, but if she's for real then I'll have some evidence to satisfy me." His face clouded over. "Oh NUTS!"

"Whatever's the matter?"

"After all that time and effort last night, I've gone and forgotten my list of questions," he growled. "How can I test her answers if I don't ask her the right questions?"

Moments later the door opened and Joshua was invited in.

Faith found a rocking chair on the porch and moved it into the shade. She sat down and felt moved to pray: *"Dear God, thank you that Joshua wants to know more about You, but I wish I could be sure that it was Your voice that led us here. It did seem to be just like the voice I heard last year telling me about Ricky, but why would it... why would You lead us here?*

"Hmmm. Is it because Joshua refuses to step inside a church door? He wouldn't even let us get married in church. Yes, I suppose that's why we're here.

"I do so love You, God. It would be so wonderful if You became part of our life and we could worship You together. Please do a miracle in his heart and make him believe. And please, God, forgive us and protect us if we were wrong to come here..." She continued praying for her husband.

After about another half-hour the door swung open again. There was Joshua, beaming from ear to ear, beckoning her to come in. "I can't wait to tell you what happened," he exulted quietly, before introducing his wife to Deborah.

Faith looked her over. Deborah seemed pleasant and friendly and, above all, very normal as she said with a happy laugh, "You know, this session with your husband was so exciting! It was a pleasure, a real pleasure. Goodbye, and thank you!" She smiled broadly and waved as the couple ran lightly down the steps to their car.

Joshua was unable to contain himself as he began driving home. "I'm a different person, my darling," he laughed. "I feel completely different inside. My heart doesn't feel empty any more - there's no more hunger! And I've fallen in love with God!

"It's so wonderful to know - to really KNOW - that He exists, and that He loves me. I never imagined that I would ever be saying this, but for the first time in my life I really believe it. I know that it's true. You were so right about something being missing - GOD was missing!

"From her very first word, the things Deborah said were like arrows hitting a bull's-eye. She described me, my relationship with you, and even our children as if she knew us from the inside out. She said things about me that I've never thought about (let alone expressed) but that I recognised to be absolutely true.

"And then..." He paused, trying to control his emotions. "Then, I heard her giving me answers to the questions I'd been wanting to ask her. You know, those questions I worked out last night? Honey, I never even opened my mouth! It was utterly amazing. I'm overwhelmed - talk about 'convincing evidence'. And it's all on tape."

"Joshua, this is a miracle! And you're glowing like a light bulb. What exactly happened in there?" Faith was no longer sceptical. She was looking at a transformed man, totally converted and with a sudden passion for God.

"It's hard to put into words because it was... supernatural. At first I was shocked to hear things about myself that were so accurate and true. They were deep longings of my heart... things that only I (and of course God) could know. As I listened to her words, I began to sense this Presence around me. It was wonderful, and so full of love. It had to be God! The Presence came over me, and then it - or rather He - came INTO me. When He filled my heart I thought I would burst.

"That's when I knew that Deborah's words had to be coming from God, not just from her. He was speaking to me THROUGH her. It was a 'double-whammy', knowing the words were true and realising they were from God. I guess my mind and heart were working together to assure me that I was hearing from God.

"I decided then and there to give up my way of doing things, to give my life to Him, to just surrender to Him and trust in Him. Then I felt my whole world turn upside-down, or rather right side up. I felt brand new and fulfilled inside. What an amazing change! I'm a different person. I've never felt anything in my whole life like this. Not even close to it. It's as if I can see and hear and feel for the first time. I feel truly alive as never before..." Tears of joy were streaming down his cheeks.

Faith was dazzled at how completely God had answered her prayers. In fact she had never seen anyone so fired up about God, so completely transformed. All at once she exclaimed, "Joshua, that's it, that's IT! Deborah has obviously got a 'hotline' to God."

He laughed. "I'll say she has! She was hearing and even seeing from Heaven. It was so amazing, so…"

"Listen to me, Joshua, just listen a moment. If she can hear Him, why can't you and I hear Him too?"

He looked at her in astonishment. "What a fantastic idea! But Faith, you've already heard Him. I'm sure it was His voice that got us here today, and of course it must have been His voice that saved little Ricky."

"That must be true," she nodded. "But still, I want to hear Him as clearly as Deborah does, don't you?"

"Well yes of course, that would be incredible. But what grabs me is that less than an hour ago I wasn't even sure that God exists, and now we're talking about hearing His voice. That's awesome…

"Oh, what a love I'm feeling from God," he burst out. "And what a love He has for us. You know, all those things that happened to us since we got married were because of Him, because of His love. He was drawing us to Him - He was wooing us! It's all coming into focus now, at last making complete sense. Those 'Good Spirits'? They were God's ANGELS. They were protecting us, caring for us, guiding us to the right place at the right time.

"And sweetheart, He must have such a wonderful plan for our life." Unable to clear his eyes of tears, he slowed down and stopped the car by the roadside.

Faith was also weeping, and she murmured, *"This is wonderful, so wonderful. Oh God, You are incredible."*

After a long pause Joshua shook his head. "Darling, I need time: time to digest all of this, to talk with you about God and His Kingdom and to learn how to pray. Couldn't we go away for a few days, maybe back to Emerald Isle? I still have some holiday time left."

"Oh yes, I'd love to. But before we talk about that, did Deborah say anything else, something special?"

"Special? Hmm, well it's funny you should ask. I didn't understand this, but at the end she said very intently, **'May Jesus the Christ be always at your doorstep.'** What could that mean?"

The Shadow of Death

"If you make the Most High your dwelling... He will command His angels to guard you... They will lift you up in their hands."
(From Psalm 91:9-12)

The holiday on the Atlantic coast of North Carolina was everything they hoped it would be. The couple rested, reflected, discussed things endlessly and even prayed together. One day, after lunch, the little family was enjoying the sun's bright warmth as it came slanting in through the open windows. After some rainy days, the autumn sky had finally cleared. The afternoon was perfect for swimming.

The quiet time ended abruptly when 2½-year-old Jacqueline, a blonde little bundle of energy, put down her crayons and marched over to her dozing father.

"Daddy, Daddy," she chirped, "I want to go into the WABES. Come on, Daddy. Come ON." She fastened her hands around Joshua's bare knee and pulled and twisted his leg with all her strength.

"Not wabes - waves, sweetie," articulated her father as he stood up and stretched. He went over to his wife. "I'm sorry to leave you behind, darling. Try and come down as soon as you can, will you?" He leaned over and gave her a light kiss before crossing the room to open the screen door for their little girl.

Faith watched her husband and daughter running and skipping along the wooden-slatted walkway, past the little lookout with its green benches at the edge of the dune. They disappeared down a flight of steps leading directly onto the beach.

"How fortunate to have found this cottage," she thought. It had torn screens, peeling green paint and wrinkled floors, but it overlooked the beautiful sands of Emerald Isle.

The young mother stroked her baby's tiny face and smiled into his clear blue eyes as he sucked purposefully at her breast. Several minutes passed before Ricky's eyelids fluttered closed and he sank into a deep, peaceful sleep. Faith carefully settled him in his crib and tiptoed out.

Father and daughter had already finished their swim and were out of the water. They were kneeling on the sandy beach, busily poking long reeds down a crab hole and hoping for a response from the invisible occupant. When Faith appeared they waved. She greeted the crab-hunters with a laugh and ran the short distance down to the water's edge.

The tide was all the way up and the water was exceptionally calm, its colour matching the sapphire sky above. An on-shore breeze was gently rippling its surface. Faith stepped into the bright water and was surprised at how warm it felt. She waded out through long, shallow waves that were breaking slantwise to the beach because of the strong prevailing current flowing past the island.

Dropping into the water with a lazy sidestroke she swam out beyond her depth, more than a hundred feet from shore. She rotated slowly into an even lazier back-float. The sun seemed to do a graceful dance above her.

Everything within Faith rejoiced to be alive. She closed her eyes and lost herself in thankful prayer.

Moments later she felt a harsh scraping of sand under her legs. Blinking with surprise, she sat upright in about ten inches of water and looked around. She discovered with some irritation that she was back at the edge of the beach, exactly where she had entered the water only a few minutes before.

"This is bizarre... how on earth did I get here?" Faith rubbed her eyes. *"The current couldn't have done this, I was much too far out. Anyway, it would have carried me quite a way down shore. What is going on?"*

"Maybe Ricky needs me," she reasoned. *"Yes, that must be it. I'd better go and make sure he's all right."* She stood up and crossed the hot sand toward the steps.

"Where are you going, Faith? You've only been swimming a couple of minutes," called Joshua, catching sight of his wife climbing the wooden stairway.

"I think I'll just check on Ricky and be right back," she replied from the top, projecting her voice over the inviting splash and tinkle of the surf. "Perhaps he's woken up."

"That's silly, you should go back in the water," he exclaimed as he approached the steps. "It's so beautiful today. We may not have another afternoon like this. Please, can't you just enjoy yourself and stop worrying?"

"Well, I WAS enjoying myself." She smoothed her long dark wet hair behind her ears. "I just can't understand what happened out there: I was quite far from shore, almost up to the sand bar, and the next moment I was back on the beach. I would have stayed out there otherwise. I don't really know what's going on... I'll be right back."

Joshua saw a trace of confusion in her eyes, quite uncharacteristic of his self-assured wife. He shrugged and turned back to Jacqueline who was totally absorbed by the sand-crabs.

Faith was perplexed to find their baby fast asleep. She retraced her steps slowly. As she came to the lookout on top of the dune, something bright caught her attention. The sea was glittering and flashing under the sun and she shaded her eyes.

"What is that?" she thought. *"Can it be a fin? That's exciting. And there's another one - they must be dolphins! Why, it looks like they're just about where I was swimming a few moments ago."*

She called out and waved her arms to get her husband's attention.

He looked up and cupped a hand to his ear. "What is it?"

"Look, Joshua, look," she cried. "Look out there - sharks, SHARKS!" Faith started with surprise and clapped a hand over her mouth. *"Good heavens, did I really say that?"* she wondered to herself. *"Did I really say 'sharks'? I was thinking 'dolphins'!*

"Just a moment... could they be sharks? Could they be SHARKS?" Fear gripped her heart.

Joshua climbed up the steps and put an arm around his wife's trembling shoulders. He tried to make out what she was staring at so intently. Jacqueline scampered up after her father, not willing to miss any excitement.

"Look, there," Faith pointed. "Do you see them? The fins? Look how many there are now! There were only two or three when I called to you. I thought they were dolphins, and I meant to say dolphins - but 'sharks' just slipped out of my mouth. Do you think they ARE sharks?"

Her face suddenly froze and her voice dropped to a whisper. "And what if I were still out there, in the water?"

Joshua held her tight and stared out at the ocean, unable to speak. There were now dozens of huge black fins darting around in the water, criss-crossing the precise area where his wife had been floating just minutes before. Their number kept increasing. He remembered how he had reproached her for leaving the water.

"I see them, I see them. Wheee!" Jacqui was jumping up and down, holding her parents' knees.

Joshua found his voice. "There must be fif... no, more like a hundred fins out there. They certainly look like sharks, but maybe they're dolphins." He tried to reassure her. "Didn't our friends say dolphins often come in close to shore?"

"Yes they did, Joshua, but I'm almost sure they're sharks. Those are shark fins, aren't they?" Both of them shielded their eyes and studied the creatures.

"Hey! Look what they're doing now," exclaimed Joshua.

They watched with morbid fascination as the huge number of fins moved as if on command into a great circular formation, slowly rotating. The circle began to move faster and became tighter. All at once the water in the middle of the circle erupted with a shock. Enormous fish tumbled and leaped over one another, frothing the water with furious thrashing.

"Joshua, that's a feeding frenzy!" gasped Faith. "Did you see them attack the fish in the middle? Now they're eating it - one of their own kind." She clenched her teeth and hunched down onto the bench. "How horrible! Those ARE sharks, not dolphins." She wrapped her hands around herself, eyes riveted to the scene.

The victim was consumed in seconds. The frenzy passed quickly and the black fins resumed their slow circling. A dark patch and some white foam remained as the only sign of the savage attack.

Joshua anxiously scanned the beach to look for other vacationers in order to warn them, but there were none. The season was over and the Alexanders were the only ones there.

He sat down slowly by his wife and settled Jacqui onto his lap. In shock he reflected, *"What if Faith had been attacked and maimed... or worse, eaten alive? What would I have done? What could I have done?"* He imagined her screaming for help while he and little Jacqueline watched helplessly from the beach. Waves of nausea passed over him. He tried to swallow, and offered a silent prayer of thanks that his beloved wife was still with them, unharmed.

The hideous black wedges continued to slice through the water exactly where Faith had been so recently. Within a few minutes they began moving faster again, chasing each other. The water boiled up a second time and the sickening slaughter was repeated. A hundred hungry predators tore apart their second victim and again left nothing behind but the telltale discolouration and foam.

"Joshua, I can't believe this is happening. Look at how many of them there are... I wouldn't have had a chance. You realise why they came here? For me! I started menstruating this morning and they must have smelled my blood," declared Faith, horror-stricken. "It's a miracle I was taken out of the water! I just can't imagine how it happened, how I was 'beached'. Those sharks would have eaten me alive, right in front of your eyes."

Ashen-faced, she turned to her husband and stammered, "An angel must have lifted me out - God saved my life."

Joshua put his arms around her. "I'm so grateful! But do you realise," he went on sombrely, "if Jacqui hadn't dragged me outside, we would all have gone into the water, and all three of us would have been attacked and probably killed - leaving our baby in his crib, alone and helpless..."

"No, darling, don't! It's too dreadful to think about..."

The sharks had settled into a much larger, slower-moving circle, centred on the same spot in spite of the strong sideways current. They seemed content to wait for the possible return of their human prey.

The young couple remained on the bench, mesmerised by the predators. Eventually there was a rapid crescendo of noise and a helicopter came clattering into view, flying a few feet above the water. "Don't go in the water!" blared a megaphone on board as the craft followed the shoreline. "Danger of sharks! Don't go in the water! DANGER, SHARKS!" The craft hovered opposite their cottage. The pair stood up and waved their acknowledgement, and Jacqueline ran over to join them from where she had been playing in the sand. The chopper continued into the distance.

They looked out over the water. The sharks had dispersed, presumably driven away by the noise, after circling for nearly two hours.

A Matter of Surrender

On returning home, Faith quickly made an appointment to see Deborah, the woman who had prophesied so accurately to Joshua. After praying, Deborah uttered some unforgettable words: *"Many a preying fish has swum over your head - sharks, with blood around their necks!"* Faith froze in her seat as she remembered her recent deliverance from death.

"So then," Deborah continued, *"what is the power that has kept you safe? It is the power of God! He has intervened in your life to save you, in all, seven times."*

Any doubts that Faith was still harbouring about God's part in her recent rescue were now banished. Deborah had known nothing about her and certainly knew nothing about her escape from sharks.

She listened intently as Deborah continued to prophesy for God. The words were sobering and blunt: that Faith's life did not belong to her but, rather, it belonged to God because He had repeatedly saved her from death. He was asking her to surrender. Faith was being asked to give up her education, her plans, her ambitions, her judgement, her will, even her children, to Him.

That evening she shared this unexpected call for surrender with her husband. "Oh Joshua," she wept, "how CAN I let all this go? I've been brought up to be independent and self-sufficient, and I do take pride in being able to rely on myself. And I think I'm a good mother, and I've spent years training to be a psychotherapist. Now God wants me to throw away all my plans and rely completely on Him. I don't think that's fair! I've always heard people say that 'God helps those who help themselves'..."

"But darling, our life has shown us so clearly that's not true," he responded gently. "Could you help yourself in the face of the shark attack? And all the other times you were in danger?"

"That's just the point!" she groaned. "That's what makes me so miserable... I NEED His protection but I WANT my own way."

"Surely God has a better idea of what's best for our lives than we do? He made us; we didn't make ourselves." Joshua held her face lovingly in his hands and looked into her eyes. "You know all that from your study of theology, don't you?"

"Yes of course," she stammered, "but it never prepared me for this dilemma. I was hungry to know about God but that didn't..." She paused.

"...Didn't change your life?" he finished. "But God is telling you now quite clearly that HE wants to change it, and even to take charge of it." He put his arms around her.

"So what would you do in my place?" whispered Faith.

"What I've already done. Give in and surrender! Your life belongs to Him many times over - and I'm so thankful that you're still here with me. In fact, I think we should both let God have His way with us, and we should do whatever He says from now on." His eyes were shining.

She shook her head in torment. "Honey, I know you're right, but it's really hard for me to surrender. I just can't get my own will out of the way. I'm simply being honest. Would you pray for me, please?"

Joshua blurted out a few words of prayer for God's help, and they held each other in silence.

Faith had been deliriously happy since her husband had become a believer. She was definitely not looking for her life to change. It took three full days of struggle, heartache and tears before she submitted to the frightening prospect of giving God complete control over her life, in obedience to what she believed was His word, and made her unconditional surrender.

The morning after, Joshua came dripping into the bedroom straight out of the shower. There was a triumphant light in his eyes as he waved his still-unused towel in the air and cried, "Do you remember how just a few weeks ago I said, 'I'm nearly thirty and I still don't know what life is about'? It suddenly hit me: I'm not EVEN thirty yet, and I know who I am - I belong to God - and I know where we're going - wherever He leads us! I'm so excited, aren't you? And to think, we have our whole life still in front of us..."

Faith giggled at the sight of her naked husband standing in two growing puddles of water. "That's certainly quite a contrast, Joshua. I'm thrilled. You're so Heavenly-minded, darling. Now just answer me one question: who's going to mop up after you?"

> **"I tell you the truth, unless you change and become like little children, you will never enter the kingdom of heaven."**
>
> *(Matthew 18:3)*

2

Prophetic Gifts
(November 1972 - February 1973)

"**Trust in the LORD with all your heart and lean not on your own understanding; in all your ways acknowledge Him, and He will make your paths straight.**"
(Proverbs 3:5-6)

"Are you planning to move?" asked Deborah, a twinkle in her eye as she ushered the couple into her sitting room. "You know, you don't belong 'way out there in the cow pasture. I want to bring you closer in, around NIH[7]."

Joshua and Faith sat down heavily and exchanged a bewildered look. A gentle but persistent inner nudging had led them to consult Deborah for a third time, but moving house was the last thing on their minds that afternoon in early November.

"This impression is very strong indeed," continued Deborah. "The house has a low stone wall of some kind, and I can see large birds to the right of the house." She arranged her chair and turned on a table lamp before sitting down opposite the couple. "When you find it, you'll just say, 'Ah, that's our house.'"

"Really?" gulped Faith. "How soon?" She reached uncertainly for her husband's hand.

"I feel you will be in your new home before the snow sticks to the ground, so it'll be very soon," Deborah answered cheerfully. "Now, let's begin..."

---

[7] *The National Institutes of Health (Bethesda, Maryland).*

After praying for God's protection and guidance, Deborah went on to tell the stunned pair that they would be involved in a project somehow connected with NIH; that they would have a third child; and that Joshua would one day be on an airplane and think, 'Mission Impossible'.

"But it will NOT be 'Mission Impossible', it will be 'Mission POSSIBLE', and 'Mission COMPLETED,'" she said with great emphasis and assurance.

"Both of you will one day be involved in a project," she went on. ***"A very great project, bigger than the government! You are standing together, smiling and holding hands, with a beautiful rainbow shining over your heads...***

"You are waiting on a shore and a row-boat comes to pick you up. You get into it - and your parents are doing the rowing! They take you out into deep water where an enormous ship is waiting. It has the number '7' on its side. A man is on the ship waiting to help you climb on board...

"Hmm... that's interesting," she added. "He looks like my husband![8]"

Afterwards as the couple was leaving, Deborah gave them a radiant smile. "You know," she confided, "the Spirit with you both is so intense and beautiful, so full of light. These sessions have been very special - unique! It's been a great privilege, thank you."

They climbed into the car and began the long drive home, too shaken to speak. Each tried to digest the 'news' that they were going to have a third child and become involved in mysterious projects and missions, in addition to moving house almost immediately.

"How could we possibly afford a house near NIH, even with you working, Faith?" exclaimed Joshua at last. "That's Bethesda-Chevy Chase, one of the highest-priced neighbourhoods in the Washington area. No way..."

He chewed his lip in silence. "I think we'd be taking a serious financial risk buying a house down there, like stepping into quicksand. And for what?" He frowned at his wife. "Is this really from God?"

"I don't know, darling. I'm just as perplexed as you are, and rather scared," she replied slowly. "But we were pretty sure that God was prompting us to visit Deborah today. And the two other times we consulted her we were convinced God was speaking to us through her..." Her voice trailed off.

---

[8] *Deborah's husband was a publisher.*

Joshua glanced over his shoulder, signalled a turn and took the exit to Montgomery Village. He noticed the cows grazing in fields on either side of the road and gave a dour laugh.

"Why SHOULD we leave the cow pasture? We only bought our house six months ago and we've barely settled in. Our life is good here. If we moved down near NIH I'd have to drive three times as far to work every day."

"It doesn't make sense, does it?" sighed Faith, staring into the distance. Her thoughts swung from the house to the prospect of having a third child - she was already in a state of near-exhaustion caring for two children. As they reached the end of the broad divided avenue and turned right through a maze of newly-laid-out streets, she admired the amenities everywhere: swimming, tennis, boating, bicycle paths, shopping centre. *"Isn't this the American Dream?"*

Meanwhile, Joshua was making a mental inventory of their finances. He had just cut up all their credit cards and had at last paid off their remaining student loan from graduate school. Aside from a modest mortgage payment on the townhouse, their only obligation was to Faith's parents who had advanced them the down payment for the house. For a couple still in their twenties, they were in excellent financial shape.

"Why give all this up?" they both wondered as the car came to a halt outside a pretty four-bedroom end unit. They went through the door and saw Jacqueline running around the sunny back garden playing tag with the babysitter, and Richard gurgling happily in his baby carrier.

Faith picked up her six-month-old and cuddled him. She turned towards her husband with a dark look. "To be honest, what really bothers me is that we might not even LIKE this house that God has apparently chosen for us..." She came back into the living room with Ricky and seemed to make a decision. "Joshua, can we agree that we'll only think of buying another house if we absolutely love it? I mean, one that we love so much that we'd buy it even without any birds or stones?"

"That must be a bare minimum, certainly," agreed Joshua with some reluctance. He gave three dollars to the sitter, who ran off.

"Okay, little one, up you come," he cried, and scooped his daughter over his head and onto his shoulders. Her legs kicked about wildly and one foot caught on his glasses, sending them flying.

Faith retrieved them with a laugh and placed them back on his face. "You know, honey, I was just thinking: God is a good Father, isn't He? He wouldn't do anything to harm us, would He?"

"Surely not... He loves us," Joshua responded, keeping a tight grip on Jacqui's restless feet. She pounded her fists on his head instead, trying to get him moving.

"Then why don't we just trust Him to take care of us?" She tilted her head to one side and smiled at the comical struggle between father and daughter. "After all," she added, "didn't we ask our Heavenly Father to direct our steps? Didn't we surrender our lives to Him?"

"Very good point... but I'm sorry, I have to lea-hea-hea-heave now," neighed Joshua as he galloped off with his insistent rider.

During the evening, the couple took turns reassuring each other and finally decided to call an estate agency in the morning, if only to satisfy their curiosity. Before they went to sleep, Joshua turned off the bedside lamp and sighed, "I just remembered: November and December are the worst months to try and sell a home... that is, if we do decide to move. Good night, sweetheart."

Stones and Birds

With the children in tow, the Alexanders spent several hours that Saturday and Sunday with a real estate agent, Jane, combing the area around NIH for a 'rustic kind of house'... Although they looked at several large and increasingly-expensive houses, not a single bird - black or white, large or small - was to be seen anywhere. Jane was disconcerted by their preoccupation with stone walls and trees ("It takes all kinds..."), but the Alexanders were in fact her first clients. She decided to do her best to help them.

Faith and Joshua, on the other hand, were all too aware of the irrational basis for their quest and felt quite embarrassed. The weekend was fruitless and tiring. They did not know whether to laugh or cry.

Three evenings later, after supper, Joshua was idly scanning the classified section of the *Washington Post* when he saw a box entitled, 'Chevy Chase Village'. The description of the house was so exceptional that he persuaded his wife to bundle the children into the car and go for a drive-by, even though it was already dark (a definite drawback for bird watching).

Fantastic Adventures In Trusting Him

The house was set high above a quiet, narrow street. Joshua manoeuvred the front wheels of the car around huge piles of dead leaves and then onto the curb so that the headlights shone upward, illuminating the building.

In front of them they saw a low stone wall and a steep pathway of irregular stone steps ascending to the front door. The house was old but charming, with steep gables and white siding in the Williamsburg Colonial style. The windows had freshly painted frames but were dark and bare. Evidently the house was not occupied.

Giant stacks of vines and scrub had been cleared to one side. Immediately to the right of the house and visible in the light of the car were several very tall old trees swaying in the strong autumn wind, stripped of all their leaves.

The family clambered out of the car, leaving the headlights on. Jacqueline jumped up onto the wall and ran nimbly along it. She waited for the others on the first step of the stone pathway.

Halfway up, Joshua let out an enormous cry of surprise. "Ho-o-o-o! Look at those nests, three enormous NESTS! Do you see them there, to the right of the roof?" He pointed excitedly and then ran up to the front door. On an impulse he tried it. "Hey, come on, it's open!"

The others ventured into the dark entrance hall after him and stepped into an elegant room that extended the entire length of the house. They all stopped, transfixed. The shafts of light coming up from the car were reflecting off the white-painted walls and a mirror set above a large marble fireplace. A magnificent hardwood floor, refinished to a glass-like sheen, ended under a graceful alcove. High above their heads stretched beautiful old wooden beams.

It was love at first sight. The couple felt as if they belonged there and had 'come home'. Even Jacqueline seemed to take possession of the property, squealing her approval as she ran through the exquisite sitting room. The family left after a few minutes, certain in their hearts that this was their house.

Seeing it with Jane the following afternoon by the light of day, certain deficiencies became evident. The kitchen had only one tiny drawer; the bedroom floors sloped at queasy angles; the basement had a dirt floor; and the plumbing and wiring were ancient. These drawbacks, however, did not affect the Alexanders' decision. Their hearts had already spoken.

Unexpectedly, the seller lowered his price to within their reach, yet he refused to allow any contingency opt-out or even any delay in the 60-day settlement period, in the event that their present home might not sell. The

Alexanders signed the contract with hearts full of faith in God, and instructed Jane to put their townhouse on the market.

Four Mortgages

Six weeks passed by to mid-December, but no one came to view the attractive, roomy townhouse. Obliged to purchase their new home by early January, the couple decided to accelerate the move so as to enjoy the Christmas holidays settling into Chevy Chase.

As the family waved goodbye to the movers, swirls of tiny snowflakes were blowing in the air - the first of winter. Faith and Joshua watched in fascination to see whether the flakes would settle, but they did not stick to the ground. The prophecy about their house had been fulfilled in every detail.

But the fulfilment was costly. The initial deposit had taken every penny of the couple's savings. The contract on their new house (which was very old) required them to take on two mortgages from the seller - a heavy commitment. In order to come up with the down payment they had to borrow a 'bridge loan' against the equity in their old house (which was very new). This loan, of course, was in addition to the original mortgage on the townhouse. Consequently, the Alexanders were committed to four mortgage payments each month until the townhouse could be sold.

Faith tried to find a job at NIH or at NIMH (the National Institute of Mental Health) or anywhere, but it was all 'NIX'. Soon the winter heating bills were rolling in for the poorly insulated dwelling, and still no one was interested in the Alexanders' empty townhouse in Montgomery Village. What had they done?

Joshua's worst fears were realised as month after month he found himself spiralling deeper into a financial abyss. He took the only avenue available to him. He applied to innumerable banks to borrow against credit lines and credit cards in order to avoid defaulting on the four mortgages. Intending to use them only as a short-term measure, he remained confident that God would provide His long-term solution.

These financial difficulties impelled the two of them to prayer. Uncertainly at first but with increasing persistence, they cried out to their Heavenly Father to confirm whether or not this reckless move had been His will. The voice of reason was deafeningly clear: they had surely made a catastrophic mistake.

As they prayed, they were both encouraged by an extraordinary inner peace which defied any kind of understanding, and which deepened and endured in spite of their deteriorating finances. The couple begged the Father to help them out of their financial crisis by selling the townhouse and providing them with additional income. Although their praying did not lead to any immediate, visible answer, it led to a deepening of their new relationship with a personal, invisible God, and to a strengthening of their faith. They realised that they didn't even mind that their trust in God was making them look like utter fools. They were too much in love with Him to care.

Learning to Listen

One evening after their customary time of prayer, Faith was unusually reflective. "Darling, I love our prayer times together, but I'm sensing there is so much more that God wants to tell us and show us, and that there's something that we can DO about it. I'm grateful for the inner peace and the little nudges from God every now and then, they are certainly reassuring, but my heart isn't satisfied. I'd like MORE. I remember what we talked about last September, that we'd like to be able to hear God's voice clearly and consistently, as Deborah does."

"That would be wonderful," Joshua replied, "but what can we do about it? How can we learn to hear His voice? We're trying to obey God as best we can... The problem is, how do we know what He wants us to do if we can't hear Him for ourselves? We shouldn't - and I think we mustn't - keep on consulting Deborah as our intermediary. I'm sure God would prefer us to communicate directly with Him, don't you?"

"The Bible says exactly that, Joshua. In fact, I recall that some of the Old Testament prophets were actually taught how to prophesy: Samuel was trained by Eli, and Elisha studied under Elijah. There must be a skill involved, which was passed from one prophet to another..."

"But of course!" he broke in. "We know a prophet - Deborah! She clearly has that skill. Couldn't we ask her to teach us?"

"Exactly what I was thinking! That way, whenever God has something to tell us we'll be able to hear His voice and do whatever He says...

"As a matter of fact, there's something about the way Deborah hears from God that reminds me of the Old Testament prophets," mused Faith. "She has such reverence for God – hardly surprising since she's the daughter of a rabbi.

Do you know what she told me? All she truly wants is to serve God by using her gifts to help people like us come into a relationship with Him as 'Father'."

Deborah, after praying about it, kindly offered to start them out with private lessons and then to put them into a prayer group later for 'prophetic training'.

At the introductory lesson she explained, "It all starts with a grateful heart, so you can enter God's presence with thanksgiving.

"Second, sit so that you are completely relaxed but at the same time stay mentally alert. Keep reminding yourself to unclench your jaw and relax your shoulders. Above all, don't try to force anything.

"Third, you must pray for God to protect you because the spirit world has darkness in it as well as light. Evil spirits are all too eager to get you off track and confuse you. But God has called you to be 'children of light' - His light surrounds you both with beautiful protection!

"You know, I saw that light the first moment I met each of you, and it is so precious. Walk in that light and He will show you His way and His truth.

"The spiritual realm has both positive and negative beings. We call the positive beings 'angels', while the negative spirits are evil demons that thrive on negativity and dwell in darkness. Make sure your heart attitude is always positive: 'pray the solution not the problem', and call on God's angels to scatter any darkness.

"Now," she continued with a smile, "you must understand that God usually speaks to us using our 'inner' senses. Think of yourself as having inner sight, inner hearing, inner smell, inner taste and even inner touch. The easiest one to work with is inner sight, but it's essential - this is the difficult part - it's essential to learn to distinguish the impressions given by God from the imaginations that come from within yourself. This part takes practice and experience, and of course faith.

"God often communicates with us using a special symbolic language that we can 'see', as well as using words that we can 'hear'. Because symbols convey a lot of meaning depending on their context, they are a very efficient way of communicating. The Bible is full of symbolism and parables."

Faith interrupted. "So you're saying this language is like some kind of shorthand?"

"Precisely. I'll teach you how to receive these symbolic messages, and then how to interpret them. Do you recall Jacob's ladder in the 28th chapter of

Genesis? In a dream he saw a ladder stretched between heaven and earth, and angels were going up and coming down on it. They were carrying messages. The word 'angel' in fact simply means 'messenger'."

The couple was nodding. "Of course," exclaimed Faith with enthusiasm. "So it is God's angels who carry our prayers and questions up to God, and who bring back His messages and answers - largely in the form of symbols?"

"That's exactly right. The messages are usually straightforward. For example, with your inner eye you might see a new-born baby. What do you think that might represent?"

"You mean, other than the obvious - having a new baby?" replied Joshua, remembering their previous consultation with Deborah.

"Don't take anything for granted or reject anything just because it's obvious," she admonished. "So what else?"

"A new idea or venture?" suggested Faith.

"Good, that's the ticket." Deborah nodded, smiling. "You need to examine everything very carefully. Ask questions inwardly. Be alert to any details and observe everything that might give you a clue as to any context or association. When you ask the right questions, you are given the right answers – and you'll just know it.

"After all," she continued brightly, "God is your Teacher. He'll give you precisely what you need, step by step, in order to develop this skill - because it is an acquired skill. All I can do is point you along the way and help you interpret the symbolism. The Father will do the rest.

"You'll feel a bit like a beginner starting on the piano. First you must learn how to read the notes, and then how to exercise your fingers to bring out the music. The rest is practice... and before you realise it," concluded Deborah, "you'll just open up your mouths and God will be speaking through you!"

"Joshua, I'm so excited," bubbled his wife as they were driving home. "Now we know that hearing from Heaven is not just possible but actually quite easy! We ALL have the tools - our inner senses. We just have to recognise that the tools are there and start using them. The one thing that's always held me back was not realising it was POSSIBLE for me to hear God speaking – but I have confidence now, and I'm sure I'll be able to hear Him. He's probably told me lots of things in the past that I've just shrugged off, thinking they were my own ideas."

"This heavenly shorthand thing, don't you think it's brilliant?"

"Yes - and it sounds quite simple to learn."

"Well, simple maybe, but as Einstein would have said, subtle," he quoted. "Now, my love, listen to me: I have an idea. Surely, if everyone is equipped to hear God's voice, it is because He created us that way. Doesn't it follow that God designed our human brain specifically so we could communicate with Him? Don't you think it might be possible to figure that out?"

"Well, why not? Here we are living almost next door to the National Library of Medicine: why don't I go over there and see what I can find out about how the brain works? What a fascinating study that would make," she declared with a glint in her eyes.

A Powerful Lesson

"The light shines in the darkness..."
(John 1:5a)

Within a few weeks the couple began attending Deborah's group sessions. Together with a handful of other students, they shared impressions received in prayer and learned to interpret them under Deborah's expert guidance.

One Wednesday evening Deborah turned to Faith and gave her an unexpected word of warning. "You know that God has always protected you from harm. But now I see that He's going to withdraw that protection - if only very briefly - because He wants to teach you something important."

Faith raised her eyebrows in some anxiety. "That's so strange. Can you explain?"

"Of course. I saw an open umbrella over your head, symbolising your protection. The umbrella was taken down and folded for an instant, and then it was opened over you again. But please, don't be worried about it. It surely must be necessary for your growth. It won't be more than a temporary condition or problem. You will learn the lesson, and then you'll understand."

A girl named Paula was visiting the class that evening. Afterwards there were comments from several others that Faith and Paula looked as if they could be sisters. Amused, they started to chat together, exchanging details about their lives. Paula confided that she was lonely and unfulfilled. She asked Faith if she could call her the next morning to set up a time to visit.

On the way home, Faith casually remarked, "I have a funny feeling about Paula. I think she might be jealous of me..."

"What an odd thing to say," replied Joshua, glancing at his wife. She had just slumped over in the seat, with her head leaning against the door.

"Darling, what's wrong with you?" he cried in alarm. "Speak to me!" He reached over and took her hand. It was completely limp, and her eyes were glazed over. "Please, say something!"

"Ve... ry... www... weak," she whispered.

Joshua drove on quickly, praying under his breath for Faith's restoration and looking over at her frequently to see if there was any improvement. There was none. Arriving home, he lifted her in his arms and carried her up into the house. Faith was almost incapable of movement.

As he brought her into the living room, the babysitter exclaimed, "Mrs Alexander, what's wrong? Your face is as white as the walls!"

Once upstairs Joshua sat on the bed next to his wife, appalled at her sudden and inexplicable collapse, yet confident that God would raise her up again. He prayed for some time before noticing that she had fallen asleep.

In the morning Faith was exactly the same. Joshua was beside himself with concern as he took care of the children's needs and then dressed himself. A final look at his immobile wife, just before nine o'clock, caused his faith to crumble. He decided to look in the phonebook for a doctor and left the room.

Faith had been like a zombie for almost 12 hours, with scarcely any thought, speech or movement. Alone in the bedroom, she heard an inner voice gently saying, **"Look at page 14 in the book behind your head."**

Her arm felt like a dead weight, but with great effort she managed to grasp a slim volume from the headboard. She turned to page 14 and her eyes fell on the sentence, 'Where there is no darkness, no darkness can remain.'

Faith stared at the words. *"What mumbo-jumbo!"* she thought, sighing with disappointment. *"What possible use is that? I don't even believe in the darkness. Are you saying there is darkness in me, Father?"*

"Yes, Faith. It's an evil spirit. Send it away!"

"But I feel so stupid. Is this really necessary?"

"Send it away..."

Half-audibly, she declared as firmly as she could, *"I command any darkness to go back to wherever it came from and NEVER bother me again!"*

The effect was instantaneous. Faith felt her strength return and she bounced out of bed just as Joshua came back in. He stopped and looked at her with amazement and relief. "What happened to you, Faith? You look normal again. Are you really okay?"

"Yes I am, Joshua, I feel totally fine. Thank God, He delivered me!"

"Delivered you? How?"

She explained briefly. "I could barely move or speak because of an evil spirit. Then when it left me, I was immediately well again. I must admit that I'd have a very tough time explaining this to my fellow psychologists; they'd call it 'an hysterical episode.'" She shrugged her shoulders. "I can't say that I'd blame them. If it hadn't actually happened to me I would never have believed it either."

Paula visited the class again the following week. When it was over and the others were leaving, she cornered Faith. "I'm so sorry I didn't call you last Thursday, but after I got up in the morning the strangest thing happened. Out of nowhere, seven huge ulcers seemed to hit me in the mouth. They were so painful! One moment I was fine and the next I couldn't even speak."

Faith recoiled in shock. "How awful, Paula. I'm so sorry. What time did this happen?" Anxiously Faith tried to recall exactly how she had prayed when she sent away the 'darkness'. Could she have been somehow responsible for Paula's affliction?

"As a matter of fact," answered the young woman with a frown, "it was just about nine o'clock. But I'm okay now - the sores finally went away today."

"Oh no!" thought Faith. *"That was the exact time when I prayed and got delivered!"* She muttered a few words of sympathy to Paula, and quickly left with her husband who was waiting by the door.

"Oh Joshua, this is horrifying! Paula got hit with terrible sores right after I sent the darkness - that evil spirit - back where it came from. I got well again, but she got ill! We have to make sense of this." They climbed into the car.

"Okay, okay, let's think. How did it all start?" Joshua started the engine, made a U-turn and drove towards home. "It was here in the car, exactly a week ago. You were talking about Paula, and then you collapsed."

"Yes, I remember now. I was saying that Paula might be jealous of me. But why would that make me collapse? It's so weird."

"Darling, you were judging her. You must have opened yourself up to an evil spirit – the spirit of jealousy, literally. Then, when God told you to send it away, you sent it back where it had come from. Evidently, that was Paula."

"I guess I should have sent the spirit to where it wouldn't bother anybody, instead of just 'back'... Yes, that makes a strange kind of sense. When I collapsed it felt exactly as if someone or something was holding me down. I was being pressed down by a force much stronger than myself. It was really dreadful."

"No wonder you were so weak, oppressed by a demon!"

"Darling, I guess I've been TOTALLY wrong about evil spirits. Whenever I've read about Satan and evil spirits in the Bible, I've always thought they were a kind of allegory or something. At church I'd be laughing to myself during baptisms when people were asked, 'Do you renounce Satan and all his works?' I dismissed it all as superstitious nonsense. But now, after this experience, I must confess that I DO believe in - and renounce! - Satan and all his works. It certainly is no laughing matter. How sophisticated I thought I was with all my 'modern' psychological knowledge."

Joshua was shocked by this admission. "But Deborah has been warning us for months about evil spirits and urging us always to pray for God's protection from them. Weren't you listening?"

"Yes, but evil spirits just didn't seem real to me till now. Obviously, I've been dead wrong: demons and devils are as real and personal as God's angels - as real as God Himself."

"Quite right," replied Joshua. "And it's clear to me that we have to be a lot more careful about the things we think and say."

"Good point! Apparently words and ideas are powerful. They seem to have a life of their own. Our mind must be like a battleground where thoughts are weapons, either for God or for Satan. Jesus said we mustn't judge or we will be judged - and I was judged for judging Paula.

"So let's keep our thoughts centred on God and His truth, and not give the devil any power over us. Otherwise the darkness will get in through our careless thoughts and words, and we'll suffer the consequences as I did. I think I understand it at last."

"You know, Faith, I find it amazing that you could have sent the demon away like that," Joshua mused. "It would only have obeyed you if God Himself had given your words divine authority. That means He was in control all along... Sweetheart, I just thought of something!" he said, looking at his wife with compassion.

"What?"

"Do you remember the warning Deborah gave you last week, that God would lift His protection so you'd learn something important? Isn't that exactly what happened?" He smiled.

"Wow, what a lesson! It makes me realise what powerful protection God has always surrounded us with. Thank you, Heavenly Father! But then I think of poor Paula... No wonder she's been so oppressed and unhappy with that demon dragging her down."

"Hmm. We must never take Father's protection for granted. It's a strange thing, but my faith has really been strengthened by what happened, especially knowing that God is such a strong shield against the power of the evil one. Isn't He wonderful?"

Faith rejoiced with her husband. "What a gift to live under His protection!"

"...The Lord is faithful, and He will strengthen and protect you from the evil one."

(2 Thessalonians 3:3)

3

Crystal Clarity
(March - May 1973)

"Today, if you hear His voice, do not harden your hearts."
(Psalm 95:7)

One Sunday morning in early spring, Joshua came downstairs in his pyjamas to find his wife squatting by the bookcase. His baby son was crawling around under the grand piano and his three-year-old daughter was doing heart-stopping pirouettes on the edge of the coffee table.

"It's here, it's HERE!" proclaimed Faith on seeing her husband. She held up an open atlas.

"What's here?" He planted Jacqui's feet firmly onto the floor.

"*'Alacrán',*" she grinned delightedly, and handed him the large volume. "*'Alacrán'* is IN here... I can hardly believe it."

"What on earth are you on about?" asked Joshua. He squinted at the tiny dot where her finger was pointing and made out the name *'Alacrán'*. It was a minuscule island off the coast of Mexico. He frowned and gave his wife a suspicious sideways glance. "Do you have a fever, or am I on *Candid Camera?*"

"If you're going to be difficult I won't tell you," she retorted, picking up Ricky on her way to the breakfast room where she settled him in his high chair. She busied herself in the adjacent kitchen.

Joshua sat down uncertainly at the table and poured a tall glass of juice. He was frowning.

"So?" he asked after several swallows. "Faith, would you please explain what's going on?"

"You're ready to listen, are you?" she teased, obviously happy about something. She helped Jacqui butter some toast and then looked her husband straight in the eye. "You'll probably find this a teeny bit hard to believe..."

"I've no doubt. Go ahead, I'm sitting down." He tried to keep a straight face.

"Okay then. I guess it was about five o'clock this morning when I climbed back into bed after changing Richard's nappy. I tried to get back to sleep but I became aware of a picture, an outline in my mind like something drawn on a screen. After a while I realised it was the shape of the Yucatán peninsula in Mexico." She paused for effect.

"The Yucatán... peninsula? Isn't that what you were just looking at in the atlas? That's very weird. Were you dreaming or was it your imagination?" he asked with eyebrows raised.

"Well, I knew I wasn't dreaming. And it might have been my imagination except for one thing: 'Alacrán'." She beamed at her husband in triumph.

He put down his glass and gaped at her. "Are you telling me that you were given the name of that tiny island?"

"Yes! My eye was drawn to the north coast of the outline, and I heard this name, something Spanish-sounding like *'Alicán'* or *'Arayán'*. I couldn't quite make it out. Obviously it was *'Alacrán'*. That's close enough, don't you think?"

Her husband ran a hand through his tousled brown hair. "I'm stunned. What else did you hear?"

"Well, before I was given Alacrán I heard some other things. I guess Alacrán was to confirm that they weren't my imagination - you know how Deborah tells us to always ask for confirmation so we can sift out our own imaginings. Only I didn't have to ask..."

"But what did you hear?" he persisted.

"I'm getting there. I heard the words, *'undercover work'*..."

Joshua interrupted, guffawing. "Undercover work, in Yucatán? You mean secret agent stuff? This is rich. You're joking, surely?"

"No I'm not, that's what I heard," she protested. "I don't know what it means, except that I had the impression that you'd find some... uh... crystals there."

"Me? Find crystals? Now why didn't I think of that?" He slapped the table loudly a few times and howled, "Why not find Montezuma's gold while I'm at it? At least that would help pay off our bills." Tears of laughter began rolling down his cheeks.

The children were never ones to miss an opportunity to add to the general hoopla around them. Jacqueline and Richard began banging cutlery, whooping and kicking their feet up under the tabletop.

Faith stared at the others in surprise before finally breaking into uncertain laughter herself.

The family at last quietened down. Joshua stroked his short beard with a mischievous look and suddenly stood up and headed for the door. "I'm going upstairs to pack my bag," he announced with an exaggerated flourish.

Faith's heart sank at this unexpected development. *"Could he be serious?"* she wondered, panicking at what she might have set in motion. She picked up Richard and hurried through the house after her husband, Jacqui giggling at her heels. "I'm sorry, honey, I'm sorry," she called after him. "I should never have said anything. I just didn't think. I was so excited to find that name in the atlas. Here we are completely broke and we still haven't sold the other house. You can't be serious about going to Yucatán. How could we afford it? It's madness..."

Joshua turned at their bedroom door and smiled at her consternation. "It's okay, darling, don't worry. I know we're broke. And God knows we're broke. (God knows, we're broke!) But I'm beginning to realise that He isn't interested in money. What really interests our Father is that we trust in Him whatever our circumstances. And maybe, just maybe, He really does want us to go to Yucatán."

"But Joshua, be reasonable, please. Can't we just forget about the whole thing?" she implored. "I was so stunned to find Alacrán on the map. I couldn't help myself. I should have kept my big mouth shut." She was on the verge of tears.

He led her into the bedroom and they sat down on the bed. "Calm down, darling, please calm down. What if Father has purposely brought about our difficult situation? Not so much to make us broke, but to teach us to depend on

Him and obey Him in spite of our circumstances. Our finances are not the main issue. What matters is whether or not God has spoken."

His wife quickly recovered herself. "You're so right, that is the issue - but He'll have to make it very clear. And if He wants us to go to Yucatán, He'd better sell the townhouse before we leave. Also, He'll have to provide someone really special to take care of the children while we're gone."

"We certainly have a lot to pray about."

Stepping Out

A few days later Faith was rocking Ricky to sleep when, quite unexpectedly, she heard a quiet inner voice say ***"Felipe Rodríguez"*** with a perfect Spanish inflection.

She then 'saw' four vivid scenes with her mind's eye: a man with a moustache; a blue car with a sloping back like a VW; a little 'plaza' with traffic circling around a statue; and finally, some brilliant yellow blossoms hanging from tree branches.

These and many other specific details were given - and some even confirmed - during the next two weeks. The Alexanders became convinced that God was calling them to step out in faith and GO.

When a close friend offered to look after the children they decided to book their tickets (by credit card of course), even though the other house had not yet sold. Joshua made a written record of everything they had been 'given' regarding Yucatán. On the day before they were to leave he mailed copies to himself and to a friend in dated, sealed and not-to-be-opened envelopes, to serve as documentary evidence in case it all turned out to be real, and not some convoluted daydream.

Just in Time

That evening, April 25th, the Alexanders were upstairs packing for their Mexican adventure. The doorbell rang and Joshua went downstairs to answer it. He was surprised to see their estate agent.

"Hello, Jane, how nice to see you. Come in. Please sit down and make yourself comfortable. Do you have some news about the house, perhaps?"

She gave him a wide smile. "I sure do, Dr Alexander. It's been a long haul, but look here!" She pulled a legal-sized document from her briefcase.

"What? A contract? Tonight?"

"That's right. All it needs are your two signatures and the sale will be in the bag. There are no contingencies and I think you'll be very happy with the price you're being offered."

"Wait a second, please, Jane. Faith! Come down quickly!" he called over his shoulder before responding to the news. "I'm truly stunned. Did you know this was coming up?"

"Not at all - the whole transaction only took place this afternoon. A couple came in and asked to see your house, then decided to buy it on the spot. I'm as amazed as you are."

Jane showed him the contract. It was for practically the full asking price – and was the only contract to have been offered on the townhouse in six months on the market.

The Alexanders signed the longed-for document, and Jane left with it.

Overwhelmed with emotion, the couple were silent for a long time.

"Well, God did it after all," rejoiced Joshua, "and at the very last moment. Darling, you wanted Him to confirm this trip to Yucatán by selling the house before we left, and He's come through. This walking by faith is unbelievable, isn't it?"

"Yes it is! And what's amazing is that no one had to do anything to make the sale happen – except for God. That's our Daddy!" She snuggled up to her husband. "He couldn't have chosen a better, more touching moment to show us His faithfulness, could He? It was well worth waiting for."

Searching for Felipe

The Alexanders flew into Mérida, the capital of Yucatán, at the height of the burning season. Stepping out of the cool airplane into suffocating heat and smoke was like walking into a brick wall. They would have turned around and flown straight home again but they had already rented a beach-house near Progreso, and the agent was waiting at the airport to take them to the property.

As soon as they were installed in the villa they opened up the back doors and stepped right onto a sandy beach. The fresh breeze off the choppy waters of the Gulf of Mexico revived them. They changed and took a dip in the sea (Faith staying rather close to shore).

Crystal Clarity

That evening, Joshua was swaying in a string hammock in the gentle breeze. He sighed with pleasure. "How perfect to be right on the beach - and for a whole week. This seems much more like a holiday than an assignment to me. God is so good to us."

"Hmm, yes. Far better than being holed up in Mérida right now. I think the smoke and heat would have killed me off there," added Faith as she sipped a tropical fruit drink. "But remember, we're here thanks to 'Alacrán'."

"'Alacrán'," Joshua repeated softly. "Yes, I guess that's why it was given, since we know now that it's nothing but a reef. There's no point in looking for crystals on a reef."

"Right, we'll cross it off our list," she quipped. "Now then, 'Holmes', where do we go from here? What's the plan?"

"It's elementary, my dearest 'Watson'. We find Felipe Rodríguez, he leads us to the crystals and that's it." Joshua made a sudden face at his wife like Harpo Marx's 'Gookie' and they both broke into helpless laughter. This behaviour was becoming standard operating procedure.

The 'undercover work' began early the next morning. The couple rented a jeep-like *Safari* and returned to Mérida. They drove around slowly and aimlessly, becoming ensnared in heavy traffic. They found themselves circling a small plaza with a statue in the middle.

"You know, Joshua, this 'plazita' is very much like the one I saw... and look over there!" she pointed excitedly. "Look at those trees with the yellow blossoms: they are EXACTLY what I saw. Let's stop and take a closer look, please?"

They parked under the trees. The beautiful blossoms hung over their heads like a canopy of pure bright gold. Faith waylaid a passer-by and asked him in Spanish about the trees.

"Ah, sí, this is the famous 'Llúvia de Oro' ['Golden Shower'] tree which blooms only at this time of year," he responded with pride. "You are fortunate to have come now. They are at their peak and will only last a week longer..."

Leaving the Safari parked there, the couple went searching for a Mérida phone book. It took nearly an hour before they found one, in a pharmacy. Checking the hundreds of Rodríguez listings, they were relieved to find only one under 'Rodríguez, Felipe', and two others under 'Rodríguez, F.' After writing down the three addresses and buying a Mérida street map they made their way back to the car.

Two of the addresses were nearby, but Faith was not at all impressed with the appearance of either house and rejected them as possibilities. They continued on to the third address, that of 'Rodríguez, Felipe'. Joshua struggled through the dense traffic and smoky heat, driving right across to the other side of Mérida.

Parking opposite the house, Joshua switched off the engine and sat back exhausted. His wife was squinting in the bright sunlight to try and make out what lay in front of them: a blue VW in the driveway, and a cascade of 'Llúvia de Oro' blossoms hanging gracefully to the side of the house. They sat motionless under the shade of the car's canvas top, staring at the scene.

"I never thought this would actually happen, Joshua," admitted Faith at last in a shaky voice. "This is exactly what I saw. This house is definitely IT, but now I'm suddenly so nervous. Maybe we could come back later?" She turned to him with imploring eyes. "What on earth are we doing here, anyway? What possessed us to come on this crazy trip?"

"Well, don't look at me," he countered.

They sat in silence for a few more excruciating minutes, then Joshua announced, "This is ridiculous. We've got to find out if this is your Felipe. We've travelled thousands of miles and now we seem to be sitting right in front of his house - so let's GO." He climbed out of the vehicle and walked around to the other side. His jaw was set as he took his wife's arm and helped her out.

"That's easy for you to say," she complained, "but I'm the one who'll have to do the talking."

A middle-aged man in a white undershirt answered the door and greeted them. "Bueno' dias?"

"Buenos dias," responded the couple. Faith continued in hesitant Spanish. "Our name is Alexander. We have come from the United States." The man smiled and gestured for them to enter his house.

With some surprise they followed him into the living room and sat down. She resumed, "We were given the name of 'Felipe Rodríguez' as being a person who would help us find some... uh... crystals." She swallowed hard.

"Sí, I am Felipe Rodríguez," he replied in Spanish, "but I'm sorry, I know nothing about any crystals." He shook his head slowly. The Alexanders exchanged an agonised look. There was a long embarrassed silence.

Faith had a sudden thought. "Señor, do you know anyone ELSE called Felipe Rodríguez who could lead us to some crystals?"

Their host frowned with intense concentration before breaking into a broad smile. "Ah sí, mi HIJO, Felipe Rodríguez HHUNIOR," he announced proudly. He was referring to his son, Felipe Junior. "He knows everything about the Mayan ruins, so he might know about crystals too. He often takes American tourists all over Yucatán, to the pyramids, the islands, everywhere - and he speaks very good English."

Then his face fell. "But he is away until Tuesday, in Cozumel! And he told me that on Tuesday evening he will go away again, to stay with his friend Jorge, near Progreso."

"Near Progreso?" the couple chimed in together.

"Sí, in a remote little resort, a tiny village. You certainly won't know it. It's called Chicxulub."

"Chicxulub!" they laughed. "But that's exactly where WE are staying!"

Joshua wrote out a message asking Felipe to meet them at their rented beach-house on Tuesday evening and left it with Felipe Senior. He and Faith went on their way in a daze, marvelling at the fact that *Felipe Rodríguez was real.*

"Tell me, darling, what on earth do people do on vacation when they don't have a mystery to solve?" Faith chuckled. Then she added under her breath, "Hmm, I wonder if Felipe will have a moustache?"

The Crystals

"God said, 'I will be with you. And this will be the sign to you.'"
(Exodus 3:12)

Felipe and Jorge were charming 21-year-old students. They were happy to accept the ham sandwiches and beer, and chatted in English with the Alexanders. Very casually Joshua asked Felipe if he might know the whereabouts of any crystals.

Felipe reflected for some time in silence. Then he answered hesitantly, "I do know of some crystals, but it's a kind of Mayan legend. I recall something about a huge cavern not far from the pyramids of Uxmal, and in it there are these seven immense 'bolas de cristal' - crystal spheres - hidden deep underground.

"Yes, now I remember!" he exclaimed. "Only three Mayans, called the 'Guardians of the Cave', have ever seen these 'bolas'. You see, a couple of years ago a university friend of mine invited me to visit his tiny village and I met these 'Guardians' - and that's how I know about the crystals. In fact, hardly anyone in the whole of Mexico knows about them - but I do," he beamed.

The Alexanders looked at each other in shock.

Felipe sipped on his beer and asked, "By the way, how did you get my name?"

"Well, you may find this difficult to believe," ventured Faith, clearing her throat. "I was praying a few weeks ago and I was given your name by… God. God gave me your name."

All colour drained from the young man's face. He crossed himself without a word.

"I'm sorry, I didn't mean to upset you. There's no reason to be afraid," she tried to assure him. Then she laughed. "It's funny, though. I was sure you'd have a moustache, Felipe."

Felipe's hand shot to his upper lip. "But I did!" he choked. "I shaved it off just two days ago." They all sat up and stared at one another.

Jorge broke the silence. "What amazes me," he confessed, "is that you're staying here, right across the street from my house in this tiny village of Chicxulub, so far from everywhere - it just can't be a coincidence. Meeting you like this has really strengthened my faith in God."

"Mine too," mouthed Felipe, who was holding his head, his eyes still wide with astonishment. "In fact, I would never have been able to see you otherwise. Un milagro - it's a miracle."

"We think so too," smiled Joshua. "Now Felipe, would you be willing to help us find these crystals?"

"Normally, I would not even consider taking foreigners to that village," replied their new friend, "but because God has led you to me by name, I can only say 'yes'. I will be back on Thursday evening, so the earliest we could get to the village would be Friday morning - will you still be here then?"

"Oh, we'll be here! Friday was to be our last day in Yucatán, but we can arrange to stay a day or two longer if we need to."

So they made their plans: the couple would pick up Felipe Thursday evening and travel to Uxmal for the night, making a start before dawn on Friday. Felipe would then locate the 'Guardians of the Cave' to show them the way to the crystals.

As promised, Felipe found the Mayan Guardians and persuaded two of them to take Joshua down into the caves for a modest fee. Joshua was upset not to have Felipe come along, but Felipe just smiled and shrugged.

Joshua looked like a giant next to the diminutive Mayans with their smiling round nut-brown faces and unpronounceable names. He decided to name them "Pepe" and "Coco". After they had rounded up two primitive torches, a bucket of kerosene fuel and a long coil of rope, Pepe and Coco beckoned Joshua to follow. Looking very relaxed, he went off expecting an undemanding stroll through a series of large underground caverns (as described by Felipe). A camera case was slung over his shoulder, also containing a compass, flashlight and some sandwiches. Felipe and Faith waved him goodbye and decided to remain in the village until he returned.

Joshua surfaced a couple of hours later. He had the blackest look on his face that Faith had ever seen. He refused to talk about the experience. Aching and exhausted, he was almost unrecognisable from the thick dried mud encrusting his arms, legs and torso. Grim-faced, he climbed into the back seat of the Safari and asked Felipe to drive them back to the hotel.

Gradually recovering under a hot shower, Joshua asked his wife to scrape the mud off his back. The mud had penetrated his shirt and had dried onto his skin like stucco, hard and unyielding. She joined him in the shower.

He eventually began his harrowing tale. "You cannot imagine what a nightmare it was," he moaned. "It started out okay, though I was a bit worried about how to communicate with the Mayans. They spoke only a few words of Spanish between them, not many more than I do.

"We descended through a couple of large caverns. Then Pepe and Coco soaked their torches in the oily fuel and lit them. The fumes were noxious and began to turn my stomach. And yes, that piece of watermelon I stupidly ate this morning was doing its work as well." He grimaced.

"Oh Joshua, no! I thought you were over 'Montezuma's Revenge'?" lamented Faith as she continued to peel mud off his skin with her fingernails.

"Unfortunately not... and things went from bad to worse. Instead of a leisurely walk, we were rock-climbing virtually in the dark. Everything was wet and slimy. We had to go along narrow slippery ledges and down sheer drop-offs (using Coco's rope). None of this was any problem for the two Mayans. They were barefoot and incredibly nimble, but it was tough going for me because I was too big to crawl along on all fours like them. Instead I had to slide on my back down chutes, around precipices, under stalactites. And all the while I had this terrible stabbing pain in my stomach. Ugh!"

They stepped out of the shower and dried themselves. "How ghastly," she muttered. "Why did you keep going?"

"I don't really know. I suppose partly because it was my 'mission', partly out of pride, and partly because little Coco was telling me all the time that it wasn't much further: 'Pocos minutos, pocos minutos!' At one point I despaired of seeing daylight ever again - and coming back to you - when I slipped on a ledge and nearly fell down into what looked like a bottomless pit. You know, if I'd broken my leg down there I don't think anyone could have carried me out."

"Thank God you're safely back here! Just hearing about it makes me feel sick. You've had such an awful time, I'm so sorry." She found her husband a clean change of clothes and they both got dressed.

"By now I was getting really scared, AND miserable from the pain, AND shaking from the exertion. Our progress was agonisingly slow. Then just as I thought I would absolutely have to give up, we entered a very small, dry and level cave. It looked like a dead end. Pepe pointed to a large rock in one corner. I took out my flashlight and forced myself to take a look. All I wanted was to get out of there as soon as possible - and alive. I'd lost interest in anything else.

"But the rock was in fact a huge mass of crystal, though it wasn't one of the seven 'bolas' that Felipe told us about. It was something quite different, according to Coco. I took a photo of it and - with the Guardians' permission, of course - broke off a tiny little corner piece and put it in my camera-case. It's over there…"

Faith stuffed her husband's ruined clothing into a plastic bag and went over to examine his prize. It was as big as her fist, but otherwise not remarkable - a chunk of transparent, colourless crystallites.

Joshua continued his story while she finished packing. "Next, Coco called me over to a large flat stone. He carefully slid it to one side and exposed a small hole in the ground. It was scarcely wider than my shoulders! He asked me if I wanted to keep on going to see the 'bolas de cristal'.

"I shone my flashlight down the hole. The tunnel was long and narrow and very steep. I was appalled. I looked over at Coco and shrugged. He waved his hands and managed to communicate to me that the journey would now be 'difícil' [difficult]. The way I figured it, I'd barely survived what Coco had described as 'nada fácil' [not easy], so 'difícil' was definitely OUT. I got the message. Shaking my head, I held my stomach and looked sick. The two Mayans just nodded, smiling at me with totally pitying looks. So we all turned back.

"I was incredibly relieved and grateful. Everything in me was screaming to get out of there. Strangely enough, the closer we came to ground level and freedom the better my stomach felt. I had been praying the whole time that Father would protect me. Now it occurred to me that perhaps He had kept me safe by allowing my stomach to hurt so much - at least until we turned around. Otherwise I might have been pigheaded enough to tackle the difficult part of the journey down to the 'bolas', and I might never have returned.

"What I've really been wondering is this: why did I ever agree to go down there in the first place? It's more disgusting than you could ever imagine."

Faith closed the suitcase and straightened up. "Oh Joshua, I'm so sorry. Thank God you're alive and back here with me." She took him in her arms and gave him a long embrace.

A Heavenly Perspective

Later that day on the flight home (which they nearly missed), the couple pondered their adventure with despair at how little they had accomplished. The journey seemed to have been a farce, and their pride was hurting. After having imagined great and exciting discoveries to God's credit, they had only managed to bring back a nondescript lump of calcite crystals.

After a couple of hours of doubting and questioning, Joshua ventured to say, "Faith, perhaps we should try and see things from a different point of view - you know, try and get God's perspective? I've been thinking of all the items we were given in prayer before we left home that were clearly verified in Yucatán, but I've actually lost count. There were SO many confirmations! I'm really glad I wrote them down before we left. And do you know what? If we hadn't trusted Father to come on this crazy trip, we would never have found out that everything He told us was true!"

She perked up. "So you're saying that He took us on this adventure simply to prove that we've learned to hear His Voice? You genius, why didn't I think of that? You're right, that's what it was all about." She laughed quietly. They relaxed into a peaceful sleep.

Jacqueline and Richard were thrilled with the Mexican gifts and insisted on swinging in their new hammock. Bedtime came hours later than usual for the two joyful, overexcited children. Eventually their exhausted parents sat down to pray and to thank God for His faithful care and protection.

To her surprise, Faith sensed words coming gently but distinctly into her mind and she spoke them aloud as effortlessly as if she were taking dictation:

"I led you to Yucatán and showed you by the confirmation of much physical evidence that you CAN hear Me clearly. From now on, I will be teaching you spiritual truths that you will not always be able to confirm directly. When you feel that you are out of your depth, just remember Felipe Rodríguez!"

"Faith, you did it! You PROPHESIED. Well done! And it was such a helpful word. *Thank you, Father.*"

He stood up and embraced his wife. "How could we ever forget Felipe? It was such an amazing thing to have found him. As he said himself, 'un milagro'."

"Joshua, isn't it incredible that God would send us to Yucatán when we were flat broke, just to strengthen our faith? I'm so grateful He did, though. Having a strong faith is worth everything. We may be poor, but somehow I feel tremendously rich."

He agreed happily. "Aren't God's ways extraordinary? It seems that the more we place our trust in Him and follow what He says, the more He gives us of Himself - and the more we can understand His ways."

> **"The people went... to celebrate with great joy, because they now understood the words that had been made known to them."**
>
> *(Nehemiah 8:12)*

4

Silver Linings
(December 1974 - April 1975)

**"When you walk through the fire, you will not be burned;
the flames will not set you ablaze."**
(Isaiah 43:2b)

It was a frosty morning in mid-December, exactly two years after the Alexanders had moved into their house. Faith had just dropped Jacqueline and Richard off at a friend's birthday party. She came upstairs to the bedroom and found her husband sitting at the desk, surrounded by bills, bank statements and chequebooks, with his head in his hands.

"Is there anything I can do, honey? Can I help you with all this?" She put her arms around him.

"It's no good, Faith, our situation is impossible," he groaned. He looked helpless and defeated.

"**'With God nothing is impossible'** - you know better than to use the 'I'-word, Joshua." She pulled over a chair and sat down next to him.

He sighed deeply. "You're right, you're right. But unless God does something to rescue us 'pronto' we'll never get out of this financial mess. I've tried everything, but no bank will loan us any more money on my signature, and we're mortgaged up to the hilt. We've come to the end of the line, Faith. There's no more credit left and I can't possibly cover all the payments and bills at the end of this month on my paycheque alone. And next month will be even worse."

"But I thought things would be okay after we sold the townhouse 18 months ago?" replied Faith nervously.

"I thought so too, but when the proceeds didn't cover all the short-term loans, I had to keep borrowing more and more each month just to keep up. It's like an avalanche that started quite small but has now become huge. It's all because of the compounding interest."

"You mean we've been borrowing just to pay the interest?"

"Yes, and interest on the interest! If I miss any monthly payments, the banks and credit cards will shut off our credit lines (what's left of them) and the whole thing will unravel. The whole mountain of debt will fall on us." Joshua lifted his wife's hand and kissed it.

"I knew things were bad, but you make it sound so melodramatic," she responded as lightly as she could.

"I've prayed and prayed but God hasn't given the answer. What I'm trying to tell you is..." he paused.

"...that we'll lose the house?" she finished, her eyes wide.

"It's possible, darling. In fact, more than possible..." He gave her a sad, weary smile. "I'm so sorry."

"It doesn't really matter, Joshua. You've done everything you could. And remember, we're only in this financial mess because we were obedient to what we thought God was telling us. We are still convinced it was Him, aren't we?" (He nodded.) "So God will keep us in this house for just as long as He wants." Faith spoke with renewed assurance.

"You always look on the bright side, sweetheart. Thank you."

"It's good to count our blessings, isn't it? These two years have been so rich! Being in this house has made lots of things possible, especially having baby Andrew. The separate bedroom and bathroom were perfect for our succession of housekeepers. You know I couldn't possibly have taken care of our third child without their help, Joshua - I was so dreadfully weak. But I guess we'll have to let this girl go since I've finished my work at the library."

He nodded gratefully, and added, "Andy came at a perfect time for our family, didn't he? What a gift! Remember how both he and this house were prophesied together, along with the 'NIH Project'?"

"Yes, all those prophecies have come true. With the National Medical Library practically on our doorstep it was so easy for me to get over there. Do you realise I've been going in almost every day for the past 18 months? It's been a fascinating job, even though it was unpaid. Perhaps someday, someone will be interested in our ideas, even though they refuse to take us seriously right now."

Joshua shook his head sadly. "It's inconceivable to me that we can't get research funds to test out our theory. Our fellow so-called scientists are so inflexible about new ideas, especially when they come from people working outside their own field.

"I must admit that a research grant was my last hope financially. It's all so confusing, Faith. Our theory about how the brain works came to us through prayer, and God was guiding you so skilfully in your library research. He gave us all these clarifying ideas – so why did He let the whole thing die? It doesn't make sense. And why did God even bother to give the prophecy about NIH in the first place? I'm really discouraged."

"I know, Joshua. I am too. God's ways are so peculiar, but I'm convinced that nothing is impossible for Him - not even our finances!" Her clear eyes gazed steadily into his.

"I hope you're right..."

There was a quiet knock on the door. Joshua stood up and went to open it.

Patty, their latest housekeeper, was standing at the top of the stairs motionless, looking down at the floor. She started to speak slowly, almost in a whisper. "Umm, excuse me... can you tell me - how do you put out an oil fire?"

Joshua searched the girl's expressionless face in perplexity. Glancing over her shoulder he looked down the stairs. There was an ominous orange glow reflecting off the white walls near the bottom of the stairwell where it curved out into the living room. With an anguished cry he pushed past the girl and launched himself into the air, almost flying down the steps.

"Where's Andy?" cried Faith in sudden fright, realising Patty was empty-handed. Not receiving any reply, she hurried downstairs after her husband. She ran with increasing alarm through the long living room. The walls were flickering with bright orange light and she could now hear a roaring and crackling noise. No Andrew... She turned the corner into the breakfast room, its walls were even more vividly orange. Still no Andrew!

The door to the tiny kitchen was open and she stopped involuntarily at the sight of blindingly bright orange flames leaping up to the ceiling. A large frying pan full of oil was burning on the electric stove and the element under the pan was bright red. Joshua was already there and he beckoned urgently to his wife, bending down to the floor. Not three feet from the stove sat nine-month-old Andy, mesmerised by the brilliance and roaring of the flames. Patty had abandoned him there in her confusion.

"Quick, darling, get Andy out of here and close the door!" Joshua handed her the baby. "I'll try and deal with this..."

"But shouldn't we call the Fire Department?" she implored, clasping Andrew tightly in her arms.

"Please give me a moment and I'll let you know. The flames are already burning the ceiling. There must be something I can do to keep the house from catching fire," he persisted.

Faith swung the door closed and backed well away, trembling. The fearsome roaring of the fire was still audible through the closed door.

There was some muffled clattering and banging, followed by footsteps. Suddenly a crackling sound like rapid automatic gunfire detonated in the kitchen to the accompaniment of yelling, and then came loud splashing noises for what seemed an eternity. Finally, total silence. Faith let out her breath and gingerly approached the kitchen door even as it swung slowly open.

Her husband stood in the doorway with great clouds of black smoke swirling about him, but there was no trace of fire. His clothing was mottled with soot, as was his face. He had a shocked, dazed expression and took an uncertain step towards his wife and baby son. (Patty, who had crept into the breakfast room after them to see what was going to happen, slunk away to her own room.)

"Joshua!" stammered Faith, "are you all right? Are you burned? How did you put out the flames?" She went to embrace him. Through the smoke behind him, by the faintest glimmer still coming from a ceiling light, her formerly white kitchen appeared coal-black. It was quite unrecognisable. She closed the door quickly and took his arm, leading him to a chair.

"I'm okay, I'm okay," he muttered, "but I can't believe how stupid I am. This is going to be hard to live down." He shook his head and gave a short ironic laugh as he sat down unsteadily and put his head in his hands.

"Why? What do you mean? The fire's out, and you're not burned - or are you?"

"It's out, but I did everything wrong. If God hadn't protected me, I'm sure I would have been very seriously burned." He paused for a few moments, examining the back of his right hand. "Actually I do have a slight burn here on one finger... and I guess up here on my forehead... But that's all. Amazing." He shrugged and gave another hollow laugh.

"Wait a moment, I'll try and find you some ice." Faith placed their nine-month-old down on the floor and gingerly stepped back into the tiny kitchen. Holding her breath and covering her eyes against the smoke, she pulled open the narrow back door that was between the stove and the sink. Then she struggled with the handle of the outer storm door until it yielded, and pushed the door wide open to let in some fresh air. After taking a few deep breaths, she adjusted the overhead catch to keep the storm door from banging shut again.

Faith groped around blindly in the ancient refrigerator-freezer until she found some ice and quickly returned to the breakfast room. Closing the door to the kitchen she puffed, "I'm airing it out... Here's the ice. Joshua, what on earth made everything burn up like that? The kitchen looks like the inside of an incinerator."

He groaned. "It isn't a pretty sight, is it? Well, here's what happened. First I turned off the electric element. (Patty had left it on the highest setting, believe it or not.) Then I looked for something to cover the frying pan and stop the burning, but there wasn't anything big enough.

"I tried to get around the stove to open up the doors to the back garden but couldn't squeeze past the flames. So I took hold of the frying pan and placed it on the edge of the sink, but there STILL wasn't room to safely open the doors. Again I looked for something to cover the pan, or some stuff to throw on the oil to smother it, but couldn't find anything.

"By now the flames were starting to burn the ceiling again and I had to do something at once. I guess I lost my head. I turned on the cold water, pulled the spray hose out of the sink and did what you should NEVER do: I sprayed water onto the oil!

"It was like being inside a huge fireworks display... no, more like a blast furnace." The ice cube Joshua was holding to the burn on his forehead was now melting, causing black streaks to run down his face.

"Joshua, how frightening! I heard all those strange noises through the door and I was so torn. We really should have called 911 for the Fire Department."

"You're right, and I'm sorry. But more to the point, we should have had a fire extinguisher in our kitchen."

"That's for sure. But I still don't understand how you escaped being badly burned?" She wiped the soot off his face with a tissue.

"That was truly a miracle, Faith, because when I sprayed water onto the burning oil the mixture actually exploded. I was less than three feet away from it. It was terrifying! I cried out to God to help me…

"When the burning oil and boiling water erupted like a volcano, flames shot out in every direction in the kitchen and set everything on fire that was flammable. But NONE of the burning oil came onto me!" he marvelled, shaking his head. Faith gasped.

"God protected me," he continued. "An angel must have shielded me from the fire because I was virtually untouched. It was quite incredible being in there, in that bubble of safety. The kitchen was like an inferno, with flames on the walls, ceiling, floor – everywhere! I kept spraying and praying. After managing to put out the oil fire I sprayed water over the whole kitchen, even up onto the ceiling, until I couldn't see any more flames. God is so merciful! He never fails us - even when I'm a total jackass."

Strangely enough, the fire was God's direct answer to the Alexanders' prayer for financial help - the black clouds literally had a silver lining. The insurance company settled their claim within days based on two professional work estimates, and the couple set about doing most of the work themselves over the Christmas holidays. As a result they had a considerable amount of cash left over.

During the same week Joshua was stunned to receive another credit card in the mail with a $2,000 credit line (entirely unsolicited) thanks to his outstanding credit history [!]

This last-minute reprieve meant that the Alexanders could keep their creditors at bay for another half year. Their hearts overflowed with gratitude and they were stirred with a keen sense of expectancy as they 'prayed in' the New Year.

A Lenten Exercise

"I pray that you may be active in sharing your faith, so that you will have a full understanding of every good thing we have in Christ."

(Philemon 1:6)

One evening in January 1975, a man telephoned. "Hello? Is this Faith? Oh good! I'm calling about your offer. My name is Father Reed, the youth pastor at Christ Episcopalian Church..."

"What offer?" she wondered, her forehead wrinkling with concentration.

After some moments it all came back. Nine months earlier they had been praying about where to have Andrew baptised and she had heard the name **'Father Jones'**. The next day she had found a notice in the local paper for an Easter Saturday baptismal service at Christ Church, to be celebrated by one Father Jones. Rather than the usual gift of money after the baptism, the Alexanders had been moved to offer their services to the church's youth group (having assumed there was one) to 'lead meditative prayer and help with hearing the Lord's voice'.

"Oh, you must work with Father Jones," ventured Faith brightly.

"That's right, yes. We were hoping you'd be interested in leading our young people in a course of meditative prayer during Lent, for seven Sunday evenings. Would you be available? I believe it's just what the kids need..."

The Anglican priest visited the Alexanders a few days later to get acquainted and discuss the details. The young cleric was kind and enthusiastic. He explained that he was merely being obedient to the voice of his Master, having no qualms about the couple because they had been 'okayed from above'. It was a courageous step of faith on his part, because they were completely unknown to anyone in his parish, including himself.

Joshua and Faith, however, were rather awed and apprehensive about their new assignment. After the priest's visit they asked each other, "What were we thinking of when we wrote that card? Did God nudge us into making the offer? We'd better dig out a Bible and see what we can find in it to help us..."

Faith dusted off her old black King James Bible after years of neglect and she and Joshua began to read through the New Testament together.

It was a delightful, surprising feast. The couple found they were not merely reading words but understanding the Spirit behind the words. They were excited to read about the gifts of the Holy Spirit[9], and noted how extensively they were on display throughout the New Testament. Obviously, these manifestations had been commonplace among the early Christians. Could they still be found in 20th-century churches? What about in Christ Church itself?

Gradually it dawned on Joshua and Faith that they had personally experienced a number of these gifts themselves, without knowing that they were 'scriptural'- words of knowledge, wisdom and prophecy; the discerning of spirits, gifts of healing; and in particular the gift of faith.

They were riveted by the Apostle Peter's statement[10] about **"the Holy Ghost, whom God hath given to them that obey Him."** The Alexanders reflected on the past two years and more, how their Father in Heaven had wooed them and pursued them to be obedient in both large and small things, and how He had nurtured a passionate desire to do His will in both of their hearts. The Holy Ghost had certainly been with them, working many wonders.

"It's a good thing the God of the Bible is no respecter of persons[11]," they laughed. "Otherwise He'd have had nothing to do with the likes of us!"

As they studied the New Testament, the Alexanders realised how pivotal Christ's prayer-life was to His daily communication with God the Father and to the releasing of power for His ministry. **"I do nothing of Myself**[12]**; I speak that which I have seen with My Father**[13]**; he that is of God heareth God's words.**[14]**"** The Father had given them a taste of this kind of intimate relationship with Him, together with an awareness of His kingdom. After praying they realised it was precisely what God wanted to pass on to the young people.

At the first session, Joshua read to the youth group from a copy of the Episcopalian *Authorised Services* (1973): "'Therefore with angels and archangels and with all the company of Heaven, we laud and magnify Thy glorious Name!'" He and Faith asked the nearly 20 teenagers what this acclamation might mean, and began to share with them about the unseen spiritual world.

---

[9] *I Corinthians 12*
[10] *Acts 5:32 (KJV)*
[11] *Acts 10:34 (KJV)*
[12] *John 8:28 (KJV)*
[13] *John 8:38 (KJV)*
[14] *John 8:47 (KJV)*

Faith quoted from the Creed: "We believe in one God, ...Maker ...of all that is seen and unseen." She read, "Give Thy heavenly grace, ...that with meek heart and due reverence [Thy people] may hear and receive Thy holy word." They were off and running. The youngsters were fascinated to hear the good news that God actually can speak, and desires to speak, to His children.

After this opening, the kids were eager to begin meditative prayer and receive God's 'holy words'. The silence in the room was quite exceptional as the teenagers meditated on the person of Christ Jesus and waited intently for His voice to speak to their hearts. Afterwards nearly every boy and girl in the group shared impressions, feelings and questions.

The presence of God's Spirit had become more and more palpable during the meeting. Many had heard the Lord speak to them for the first time in their life, or had seen Him with new 'spiritual eyes'. The Alexanders were astounded how quickly these young believers had yielded to the Holy Spirit, and Father Reed was beside himself with delight. He confided that many of the kids had never opened their mouth in the group meetings until that evening.

The group grew larger and more enthusiastic week by week. Eager to know God better, they were all learning to pray and were growing in wisdom through the Holy Spirit. As Lent drew to a close, several of the youngsters came privately to Faith and Joshua to confess that their hearts had undergone a real transformation. They were glowing with a new love for God. Some of them even declared that the seven weeks had been the most meaningful of their whole life. It had been a great privilege for the two of them to see the dramatic changes in the teenagers' lives, and to experience the strong, almost intoxicating presence of the Holy Spirit for those seven Sundays.

God was surely with them.

"If any of you lacks wisdom, he should ask God, who gives generously to all without finding fault, and it will be given to him."

(James 1:5)

5

Roman Holiday
(May - July 1975)

"From a far-off land [I summon] a man to fulfill My purpose."
(Isaiah 46:11b)

The spring air was fragrant and warm. A fountain splashed gently by the stone bench in the garden of Casa Santa Maria, the North American Bishops' College in Rome, Italy. Faith and Joshua were seated on either side of their new friend, a Roman Catholic priest.

"Can you imagine how we felt, Father Pete? Being given a 'mission' to write a letter to the Pope and to deliver it to him in Rome?" chuckled Joshua. "Who are we to write some super-spiritual letter, anyway? We're not even Catholics! Besides, we're almost flat broke and we needed someone to care for our three little children. It was quite absurd."

The tall American priest rubbed his hands together, his eyes sparkling. It was evident that he relished this kind of story.

Faith explained: "When God told us in prayer to write the letter, He said that its focus should be about listening to His voice, and that its purpose was to urge the Pope to issue an encyclical on the power of prayer. It was all so bizarre! We asked our Heavenly Father to confirm His leading with a clear sign."

Joshua resumed: "Faith asked me if I might possibly be sent to Germany again on company business to oversee a research contract there. I said,

'Impossible, the work's almost finished and it has gone extremely smoothly. In any case, my company just imposed a complete freeze on any more business travel.'

"But Pete, I'm learning! ...learning not to use the 'I'-word, 'impossible', whenever God is involved."

"Amen," added the priest with a delighted smile.

"Well, the next morning was a Monday. As I stepped into my office the phone was ringing." [He imitated a German accent:] "'Doktor Alexander? I don't know kvite how to say zis, but I'm very much zorry... er... afraid, zat all ze final zamples of ze vork haff been rrruined! Ve can't undershtand vhy zis has happened, but it means zat ve haff a big prrroblem. Till ve find ze zolution, ve cannot make ze rrrepresentative zamples und finish ze contract. Ve are zo zorry.'

"I told him I'd call him back and went upstairs to share this setback with the Lab Director. He said I should fly to Germany and help solve the problem. When I asked, 'What about the travel freeze?' he simply said, 'I'm overriding it.' That's how my ticket was provided most of the way to Rome, and only 12 hours after being given the assignment."

"Wow, that was some sign," exclaimed Father Pete.

"I was in shock. On the phone again, Heinz (my German contact), asked me to give his team a couple of weeks to try to solve the problem. He suggested that if they couldn't solve it by then, I should please fly overnight to Germany on April 29th. I had to agree to this, though I was unhappy about the delay - we thought God wanted us to arrive in Rome on May 1st. I was being asked to start my work in Germany on April 30th, the day before.

"I couldn't do anything about it. Perhaps we'd heard the date wrong... Meanwhile I prayed that God wouldn't LET them solve the problem, because otherwise the trip (and my paid ticket) would have to be cancelled."

Faith interrupted, laughing. "But we arrived in Italy right on schedule, just as God had said."

"How did He manage that?"

"Verrry... interrresting," mimicked Joshua. "When we flew into Frankfurt two mornings ago, Heinz was waiting for us at the airport, grinning ear to ear. He was bursting to tell me the news: the problem with the samples had been solved the previous evening while we were on the plane! There was nothing left for me to do."

"Superb," laughed the priest. "Only God has such perfect last-minute timing."

"That's so true. Then, to cap it all, Heinz told me with great embarrassment that his factory had just voted to close for the next 12 days to bridge two long holiday weekends, May Day and Ascension Day. He apologised on and on for bringing me over at the 'wrong' time! (Of course, this was God's plan all along.)

"'Never mind,' I told him, 'I'll take some holidays and be back here on the 12th,' and that was that! We arrived here on May 1st, having done absolutely nothing to make it happen."

"Hallelujah! Thank you, Jesus!" Father Peter stretched his long arms around their shoulders and hugged them, saying, "That's my God all right!

"But let's get back to your 'Epistle to the Romans', if you'll forgive the pun," he continued. "I skimmed through it earlier and thought it was really very potent. How did you go about writing it?" The priest leaned back, his long fingers now holding onto one knee. He was perching precariously near the edge of the bench.

"All yours, Faith." Joshua motioned to her, grinning.

"The letter only took a week to write, though at first it was rather slow going. As it began to take shape we got more and more enthusiastic. One of us would write while the other searched the Scriptures, praying about what to include. We went through the whole of the New Testament at least three times, just for a letter of five pages."

She took a deep breath before continuing. "Father Pete, what was wonderful was recognising so many things in the Bible that God had already been teaching us. Many of the Scriptures we had heard before, of course, but now we were recognising the Spirit behind them..." (The priest nodded and smiled broadly.)

"It was magical," added Joshua. "When the letter was done we were astonished that we could have written it down, but we obviously didn't do it by ourselves. Even now we find something new each time we read it."

"That doesn't surprise me at all. I was talking to Father Paul at lunch (he's a doctoral student in spiritual theology), and found out that he'd read your letter. He told me it expresses the cutting edge of Catholic thinking in his subject today and then some! I was really struck by that."

"Isn't that amazing?" Joshua shook his head. "We had no idea."

"Now the question is, how can you get the letter into the hands of the Pope? What did my friend the Director offer in the way of advice?"

"To be honest," admitted Joshua without expression, "he tried to explain as kindly as he could that it would be impossible to get the letter to the Pope. He used the 'I'-word, Pete. And when Faith chimed in with her usual, **'But with God, all things are possible,'** he corrected her - he actually corrected her - saying, 'Maybe so, but NOT in the Vatican.' He was serious!"

The priest shook with silent laughter, trying in vain to control himself. "I'm SO glad I met you guys here today, this is so rich." He wiped his eyes.

Joshua smiled in acknowledgement. "It's mutual, Peter."

"So then, what can I do for you?" asked the priest with an earnest tone, spreading out his hands. "I'm free for ten days until the Convention starts."

"What Convention is that?"

Father Pete looked at Faith with astonishment and countered, "You don't know? It's the worldwide Catholic Charismatic Convention. The Pope himself will open the proceedings on the evening of the 11th, Pentecost Sunday."

"The 11th? That's too bad - we have to fly back to Germany that day," exclaimed Joshua. "What do you mean by 'Charismatic', anyway?"

Peter peered at him closely to see whether he was joking and countered, "I thought you WERE Charismatics, or Pentecostals. You really don't know?"

The couple looked puzzled. "Know what? Are we missing something here?"

"No, I don't think so, it's only a matter of terminology. *Charismata* is the Greek word meaning 'gifts' - as in the Gifts of the Holy Spirit."

"Oh yes, I remember that," said Joshua. "That's in one of Paul's letters to Corinth, isn't it?"

"Yes, in the first one, chapter 12. The Catholic Charismatic Movement started in 1967 when a small group of believers were praying to be filled with the Holy Spirit. After much prayer, they suddenly broke out speaking in tongues and prophesying, just like the early Christians in the Book of Acts, chapter 2."

"Speaking in tongues?" asked Faith. "You mean other languages?"

"Yes, and in particular a Heavenly spiritual language - a language that the Holy Spirit gives to believers to help us pray and hear from God. You don't know about that either?"

Joshua had a sceptical frown. "We did read about 'tongues' in the Bible but thought it was a miraculous ability to speak in someone else's human language. We don't use a Heavenly language. We had no idea about that."

"Then how do you pray?"

"In English, or in silence," replied Faith. "We just wait on God to speak to us or show us whatever He wants. Isn't that all right?"

Peter laughed. "Of course it is. If it's good enough for the Lord it should be good enough for me or for anyone else. Why should everybody be the same and pray the same way?"

The priest smoothed back his dark hair and then added, choosing his words with care, "It's quite clear to me that you belong to God if you can hear His voice. The Bible says so in the 8th chapter of John: **'He who belongs to God hears what God says.'** Actually, you seem to hear the Lord at least as well as anyone I know. Besides, the gifts of the Holy Spirit are His to distribute just as He wishes.

"So let me ask again: how I can be of help to you dear people? My parish sent me here as a gift to attend the Convention, but they insisted I come two weeks early to make it a holiday. I was a student here in Rome several years ago, you see. So I'm completely at your service."

The priest's loving acceptance of the Alexanders as a brother and sister in the Spirit, as well as his eagerness to help, deeply touched them. In an odd way his attitude reminded Faith of Saint Peter's acceptance of the Roman centurion Cornelius in the Book of Acts [chapter 10]. It seemed to both Faith and Joshua that God had specially prepared the three of them for each other.

"Please pray for us, Father Pete," responded Faith after a pause. "That's the most helpful thing. To tell you the truth, we don't know exactly why we're here. We have a sneaking suspicion that the letter was just a ruse to get us to come. But with God's grace we'll be at the right place at the right time, and He will accomplish whatever purpose He has in bringing us here."

"Amen," chimed in the others.

Coming to the Altar

"Since we live by the Spirit, let us keep in step with the Spirit."
(Galatians 5:25)

The next few days were delightful. The couple walked all over the city in the May sunshine and enjoyed wonderful lunches. The odd thing was how often they kept bumping into their new friends, Father Pete and Father Paul, and how easily they were persuaded by them to attend one prayer meeting after another.

On one occasion, at an ecumenical service in English near St Peter's Basilica, Faith and Joshua discovered that they alone were the entire congregation. (The regular attendees all had a scholastic conflict.)

The American clergyman gave a homily about being open to the Holy Spirit's promptings, which he likened to showers of rain. While he was preaching it began to rain very heavily.

Rather than go outside after the service and get wet, the couple stayed behind to talk with the priest. To their surprise, he had been expecting them. He even knew about their letter, which he asked to see. He read it through carefully and was quiet for some time. Then he looked up and suggested that they adjourn to a café.

A light rain was still falling. Halfway across a busy street the priest suddenly stopped, a distracted expression on his tanned face. "You must go into St Peter's right NOW!" he declared. The couple looked at him, wondering if they had heard correctly. The Roman traffic howled around them.

"Yes, go now! I was told the Pope might be in there giving some people a special audience (they were crowded out this morning). It's your chance to give him the letter - GO!"

Startled, the couple thanked him and ran across the road to relative safety. They felt propelled onward as they hurried, arm in arm, down the wide avenue of the *Conciliazone* to the steps of the great basilica. They climbed and climbed, and finally stepped through a huge door into darkness.

The building was deserted except for a dozen or so black-robed priests milling around the distant altar, and some officials noisily rearranging barriers and benches. No Pope.

"Let's pray," breathed Joshua in an undertone, pulling Faith aside into the shadows. *"Dear Father, we don't have a clue why we've been sent here, but please guide us to someone who'll understand about Your letter and who will get it into the Pope's hands. Thank You. Amen."*

He smiled at his wife and whispered, "This is fun! Just follow me and don't look any of the guards in the eye. Convince them that we're supposed to be here. Actually, I believe we are..."

With determination he pushed through a heavy barrier and started walking with quiet authority down the middle of the immense nave. Faith followed with a quaking heart. It seemed like forever until they rounded the altar steps at the end and sat down behind the altar area on some chairs, as if by appointment.

The cluster of priests gathered up at the high altar appeared to be rehearsing some important occasion and took no notice of them. Out of the corner of their eyes the pair could see some of the guards squinting in their direction and before long one swarthy fellow came over to investigate them. Joshua was smartly dressed in a dark suit and tie, and had a briefcase on his lap. He stayed in his seat and explained in rather fractured Italian that they were there to meet one of the priests at the altar. He used expansive gestures to emphasise his (hypothetical) point.

The guard backed away with reluctance and evident suspicion.

Some moments later, the tall young priest who had been directing the rehearsal came down the altar steps and approached them with a welcoming smile. He looked as if he might have stepped out of a Botticelli painting, with his handsome Italian features. To the Alexanders he looked like an angel.

"May I help you?" he graciously inquired in exquisite Italian.

Joshua explained their 'mission' as briefly as he could. Searching for the right Italian words, he declared that they had written a letter by the Holy Spirit's impartation and now needed to deliver it to the Pope. The young priest nodded and smiled warmly. He seemed to understand their dilemma after just a few moments, in spite of Joshua's struggle with the language.

The guard reappeared with a growl but the priest waved him away without a word.

The priest then exclaimed (in Italian), "I know EXACTLY how to help you with your mission." His eyes sparkled. "Tomorrow morning, before the Holy Father celebrates Ascension Day Mass here, I shall meet with his personal private secretary. If you would allow me, I will tell him about you and give him your letter to pass on to his Holiness the Pope. Would that be all right?"

Delighted, Joshua nodded and passed over a copy of the letter. The priest received it into his hands as if it were some precious rare manuscript.

"You can rest assured that it will certainly get into the hands of the Holy Father. Just leave it to me." He bowed deeply, and in parting he added, "Renato di Gesù, at your service."

A Question of Trust

The next morning the couple returned to St Peter's. They scanned the enormous Ascension Day crowds for some glimpse of their 'angel', Renato. After searching for only 15 minutes, they caught sight of him talking to two cardinals in full regalia. The crowd jostling around them suddenly and unaccountably thinned out. At that very moment Renato looked straight at them. He immediately recognised the Alexanders and signalled discreetly that the job was done, smiling broadly. Then, just as abruptly, another wave of humanity pushed between them and they lost contact. A few minutes later Joshua and Faith went tripping out of the cathedral even as thousands more people crowded in for the special day's Mass.

"Well, with God everything IS possible," proclaimed Faith, "EVEN in the Vatican."

They celebrated over lunch, a marathon affair in a tiny, out-of-the-way *trattoria*. They took their habitual (and by now needful) siesta but overslept disgracefully for the four-o'clock prayer meeting to which they had been invited by Father Paul.

Paul was unperturbed to see the couple arrive just as everyone else was leaving. He greeted them very warmly, joined by Peter who, inevitably, was also there.

The two priests were thunderstruck to learn that the letter had definitely found its way into the Pope's hands. "That certainly is a Grade-A miracle!" exclaimed Father Paul. "Please, come and walk with us across the Janiculum Hill - the view is so tremendous - and tell us all about it. By the way, we're just going to celebrate Mass at a little convent across town. Won't you join us?"

Paul was an excellent guide and pointed out many of the Roman landmarks, ancient and modern. The day was clear and warm and everywhere there were children running happily and eating ice cream on their Ascension

Day school holiday. The dark brooding evergreen trees of the Janiculum Park towered over their heads like sentinels watching over the city. Jumbled red rooftops and stone chimneys and towers, festooned with antennas and clotheslines, spread out in every direction from the foot of the ancient Roman hill. The view was unforgettable.

Then they were crammed into a taxi, laughing uproariously as they crossed the city at breakneck speed to reach the convent in time. It was extraordinary to Joshua and Faith how delightful it could be to spend most of their free time in prayer meetings and worship services.

Only a very few people were present in the convent chapel. Father Peter had been asked to say Mass in the intimate little building, and when it came time for the homily the priest pulled up a chair and sat down facing the Alexanders.

He seemed to be preaching to them alone. "If Jesus were to say to you, **'Come, follow Me!'** would you hesitate? Could you bring yourself to reply, 'Yes, Lord,' and not look back? How many of us can follow Him without making our excuses? 'First, let me go and bury my father,' or 'First, let me go back and say goodbye to my family…'

"We are so quick to formulate our objections, to make our excuses, to justify ourselves, and we are so slow to trust God and obey. We all want to be perfect and enter the Kingdom of Heaven here and now. But how many of us would honestly rejoice if Jesus were to say, **'Come, sell everything you have, give to the poor and follow Me'**? Do we trust Him that much?

"How many of us have treasure in Heaven? **'For where your treasure is, there your heart will be also…'** Yet it is only by following the Lord Jesus that we will find that treasure and so inherit eternal life…"

The priest's words burned deeply into the Alexanders' hearts.

The Spanish Steps

They were invited the next day to attend yet another prayer meeting. This one was made up almost entirely of the 'core' group of people who were hosting and planning the International Charismatic Convention. They worshipped with songs and thanksgiving. Many prayers were offered up for the success of the Conference - some ten thousand people were expected to come from all over the world. The Holy Spirit was at work touching hearts and bringing prophecies and praise to God. There was reverent, expectant silence as well as enthusiastic singing and testimony. *"This is the way to have a prayer meeting!"* thought Joshua and Faith.

When the meeting wound up, one of the leaders made a beeline for the newcomers and introduced himself as Philip. "Tell me, Joshua, that marvellous reading you gave us - where was it from?"

"Reading? Oh, you mean the prophecy? Well, that was from the Holy Spirit, I hope," he replied, grinning.

"Are you joking? My heavens, I've never heard a prophecy with so much meat in it before. Thank you so much, it was tremendous..."

"That's kind of you Philip, but it wasn't mine. Just thank God."

"Yes I know, I know, but if we only had more prophecies like that in our meetings, especially the big Sunday meetings, then more people would be encouraged and built up in their faith."

Someone suggested it was time to search out some supper, and the Alexanders were caught up in a large group wandering down dark and narrow cobbled streets in the warm evening air. One *trattoria* was tried after another until, at last, they found one that could accommodate them all. With great upheaval and noise the waiters rearranged all the other diners in the restaurant in order to make one continuous long table for the group. The process of taking the orders and eventually serving the food seemed to take an eternity (typical of life in the Eternal City).

Philip had plenty of time to ply them with questions about their spiritual experiences. He was particularly interested in how the angels and the Holy Spirit had protected, directed and taught the Alexanders. They also discussed the Charismatic Movement.

Joshua was frank in stressing the need for silent waiting on the Lord: "Otherwise, a prophecy may end prematurely because of other people's noisy encouragement distracting the 'prophet'."

As the meal wound down, Philip disappeared for a few minutes. He returned with Stephen, the leader of the group, who bore the lion's share of the burden for the Convention. Faith sensed the strong presence of God with this young English priest.

Philip introduced them. "I've been trying to convince Stephen to find some time to spend with you people and hear what you have to say." To Stephen he said as persuasively as he could, "I think it would be really helpful, brother."

"Gosh, Phil, if only I had a little time I'd really love to. But on top of the work preparing for the Convention, I'm being loaded down with assignments from my professors right now. I just can't!" He looked intently at the couple and seemed to relent. "How long are you staying?"

"Only till Sunday morning," they said in unison.

Stephen frowned unhappily. "Well, I'll tell you what, maybe we can get together tomorrow? I'll try and phone you around four o'clock at your hotel. I'm sorry I can't be more definite. Will you mind hanging around for my call?"

"Not at all, we have nothing planned. Here's the hotel card and our room number." Joshua handed it over, smiling as he said, "If it's God's will that we get together, nothing will keep us apart!" They shook hands and Stephen was gone.

Philip shook his head with concern. "He's so busy, so very busy. But you've GOT to get together, I just know it!"

It was nine o'clock the next evening when Joshua finally turned to his wife. "Honey, let's go out and take a walk. Stephen isn't going to call now: it's five hours after he said he might – that's long even for Rome. How about salvaging the evening with a walk across the river, maybe to the Spanish Steps?"

"That's funny, I was going to suggest the same thing! You don't think it's too far?"

"Half an hour, maybe? We have to walk off all our pasta from lunch anyway, and perhaps we'll have some more when we get there. Anyhow, let's go. I have a strong sense that the Lord wants us over at the Spanish Steps."

"I do too - maybe we'll meet someone there or something…"

The evening was breezy but warm. The walk took far longer than it should have because Joshua kept taking short cuts (using his miniature street map) overriding Faith's objections.

"But the map shows it THIS way…"

"If you'd only listen to me, darling," she pleaded. "This is the direction: please take your nose out of the map for a moment and look!"

"Never mind the direction. Believe me, this is the best way. This is Rome!" laughed her intractable husband.

The couple went down tiny alleys and through arcades, getting lost over and over again. Continually retracing their steps, they spent over an hour of this kind of amused frustration before finding themselves at last in the popular but now deserted Piazza di Spagna.

Roman Holiday

They entered from the opposite end from where they would have come if Faith had had her way. As they walked uncertainly into the piazza, they approached a tiny alley opening from their left. A figure of a man came abruptly out of the darkness and would have collided with Joshua had they not both quickly side-stepped, apologising with "Scusi!" All three of them stopped and squinted at each other.

"Joshua? Faith? This is a divine appointment if ever there was one," rejoiced Stephen, hugging the couple who stood there speechless. "This is extraordinary! I've been wandering all over this area for a good 20 minutes looking for a telephone because I've got to make a call. I finally headed up here to the Spanish Steps because I remembered a little restaurant with a phone that actually works. But what are you doing here, on the opposite side of the river from your hotel?"

Joshua finally found his voice, and the otherwise empty square echoed with their laughter. The three of them hung onto each other as if afraid of being separated again. Stephen found the pizzeria and made his phone call. They sat down at a table together.

Each of them wondered, *"Why has the Lord gone to such lengths to arrange this meeting?"* If there had been a thick fog they would have bumped right into each other: they had been on a divinely navigated collision course.

The Alexanders took turns going over the same ground as they had with Philip the previous evening. In particular they shared their impressions of the previous Sunday's Charismatic meeting in Rome. Stephen sat and listened in silence with frequent nods of agreement.

After they were finished, Stephen gazed at each of them with eyes that were moist with emotion. His fair hair and reddish beard framed a face radiant with the joy of the Lord.

"Oh, how can I ever thank you enough for sharing this so honestly with me? You see, I've had exactly the same thoughts myself, but I've never been completely certain whether they were from God (and so needed to be acted on), or merely from myself. I've prayed and prayed for guidance, and now, at last, I have certainty - it WAS the Holy Spirit telling me! To think, He brought you all the way from Washington DC to confirm it, and just in time, before the Convention! It is all so incredible and beautiful. God is SO good. Thank you, Lord Jesus!" They worshipped together there in the little restaurant.

Faith was reminded of the previous Friday when they had been praying after lunch at the Casa Maria with Peter, Paul and several others. Peter had shared a word of knowledge from the Holy Spirit: "I believe God has brought you two to Rome because He has a word to give somebody through you."

"Stephen," she now asked, "isn't there a Scripture somewhere about God bringing people from the ends of the earth?"

Stephen pulled out his pocket Bible, found Isaiah chapter 41, and read from verses 9 and 10: "**'I took you from the ends of the earth... I have chosen you and have not rejected you. So do not fear, for I am with you; do not be dismayed, for I am your God.'**"

The couple parted from Stephen with embraces and tears. The next day they flew out of Rome, exhilarated at how their Heavenly assignment had been accomplished without any effort on their part, requiring only simple obedience to the moving of the Holy Spirit.

Once in Germany, however, Joshua experienced a strong sense of anticlimax that he found most upsetting. His technical work seemed insignificant, even trite, after the extraordinary spiritual 'highs' enjoyed in Rome.

Together on Monday evening, the couple thanked God for His grace in guiding their steps. During a time of silent prayer, Faith was irresistibly drawn back to the words of Father Peter's homily. Afterwards she asked her husband if he still remembered them.

He nodded and looked at her intently. "Of course, my love. How could I ever forget what he said?"

"Well, what about it?" she pressed. "What IF God were to ask us to... sell out?" She held her breath.

There was a pause. "I'd be thrilled," he said quietly.

This was not the response she had expected. "Thrilled? How come?"

He smiled. "Because it would mean that God wants to take care of us Himself. I feel there's so much more that He wants to teach us. Just think, if we were placed in the position of having to depend on Him alone, wouldn't He open up all His riches to us, His whole treasure house? That's very tempting."

"You're insatiable, Joshua. You're not your practical self."

"I know, darling, and I may never be again! Anyway, I've been thinking about my work, about our life in Washington, about how ill you get in that awful climate. What are we doing there? I mean, really doing? And what's the point of my work? Who am I really helping?" He gave a long, helpless shrug. "I have to admit, I'm no longer attached to my job, the house or anything. Just to God."

Home, Sweet Home?

"We know also that the Son of God has come and has given us understanding, so that we may know Him who is true."

(1 John 5:20)

The Alexanders returned to Washington on May 16th to find the capital in the grip of an early heat wave accompanied by deadly oppressive humidity. However, thanks to their friends' loving care and air-conditioned house, the children were in excellent shape. Jacqueline and Richard could not stop talking about the fun they'd had, and Andy cooed his agreement as he stroked his mother's face.

Then came the moment of truth: a frightening pile of bills and bank statements was waiting just inside the front door. The cost of their trip (even with one ticket paid) had been the final nail in the Alexanders' financial coffin. All of their credit cards had bumped up against their limits. With a sick feeling, Joshua had to acknowledge that 'the jig was up'.

Coming home from his first day back at work, he barely recognised his wife. She was at a point of physical and emotional collapse from the humidity and heat, and from the constant struggle to keep up with three perpetual-motion machines aged 5, 3 and 1. Several more hours passed before the children would go to sleep and Faith could come downstairs, leaning heavily on her husband's arm. The two of them retreated into their favourite little alcove for some refreshing prayer.

Before they knew it, the Holy Spirit was speaking independently to each of them, saying, *"Leave Maryland... Head west..."* Opening their eyes, they exchanged notes. Was this from God or just wishful thinking? Did it mean yet another journey, or a real move? They returned to silent listening.

After some time Faith strongly sensed Father Pete's words from Ascension Day yet again, and she obediently spoke aloud this prophecy: *"Would you really sell everything and follow Me? Listen to Me carefully: I want to lead you as your Shepherd and take complete charge of your life. Can you place your life in My Hands, and trust Me with every detail?"*

Fantastic Adventures In Trusting Him

Joshua was overjoyed and called out, *"Yes, Lord, we do trust You! Just tell us where and when to go. Thank You so much."*

"Dearest Faith, I haven't a doubt in my mind, have you?" he asked, raising his arms victoriously. "This is from God. Come on, let's dance." He jumped up and pulled her out of the chair.

Her strength suddenly restored, she waltzed around the living room in Joshua's arms. They laughed and cried like two prisoners unexpectedly released. "We are so incredibly blessed," she said at last. "I feel like I'm being brought back to life again."

"Sweetheart, isn't this wonderful? God has offered to be our Shepherd and to take care of us... It's like manna from Heaven. How could we even consider staying on here in Chevy Chase after a divine invitation like that?"

"Impossible!" She threw back her head and laughed.

God's plan was simplicity itself. The Alexanders began to generate cash from selling off all their belongings [other than clothing, toys, books, memorabilia and a few sticks of furniture], and their overwhelming financial crisis seemed to melt away. Eventually their house was sold for 50 percent more than they had paid for it only two and a half years earlier, and they relished the prospect of paying off all their debts after the close of sale in late summer.

What an outstanding financial investment God's 'house near NIH' had turned out to be! More impressive, however, was the outstanding faith investment that God had made in their hearts, which He had cultivated so carefully in the pressure cooker of their circumstances.

"If you call out for insight and cry aloud for understanding, and if you look for it as for silver and search for it as for hidden treasure, then you will understand the fear of the LORD and find the knowledge of God."
(Proverbs 2:3-5)

6

The Treasure House
(August - November 1975)

> "Everyone who listens to the Father and learns
> from Him comes to Me."
> *(John 6:45)*

The undulating ribbon of Interstate Highway 90 seemed to lead directly to the sun as it sank behind the dark Wisconsin hills in a majestic display of colour. Clouds scattered across the sky after a summer storm were glowing with every conceivable hue from flaming orange to dark crimson.

Tall stands of pine trees came marching over the horizon as the family sped westward in their ancient but faithful blue-and-chrome Buick, with a full U-Haul trailer behind it and its roof rack loaded with luggage. Costing only $175, the car had chugged along without complaint through the most intense heat wave to hit the eastern seaboard in years.

Jacqueline, Richard and Andrew squealed with surprise and looked up from their toys in the 'backety-back' as the station wagon surged abruptly over the crest of a hill. Cool air fanned their cheeks as they climbed higher into the hill country, reviving the family after three days of travelling without air-conditioning in temperatures well over 100 degrees Fahrenheit. Then Faith cried out, "Look!" and pointed at the highway sign ahead, 'Eau Claire, 65 miles'. The family was nearing their God-given destination at last. It was August 5th 1975.

Their new home had been unveiled through daily prayer yielding occasional tantalising clues: *"Go west, into the pine-trees, but NOT west of the Rockies... to Water Clear and Half Moon Lake... 'dans le jardin'"* [French for 'in the garden'].

Faith had also received a vivid impression of a canoeist on a white-water river, and Joshua one of a tall factory chimney.

"We must keep on trusting God," Faith had declared. "At the right time He'll give us the key to the puzzle and we'll find our 'Water Clear'. I'm sure that if you wait until we've found it before giving notice at work, your timing will be perfect. *'Remember Felipe Rodríguez!'"*

During the long Independence Day holiday weekend, while tracing routes westward in a big road atlas, Faith had unexpectedly stumbled on 'Eau Claire' [French for 'Water Clear']. All the lights had flashed 'yes' in her spirit and a subsequent visit to the local library to check the *US Gazetteer* had completely solved the riddle. 'Situated around Half Moon Lake and at the conjunction of the Eau Claire and Chippewa Rivers, Eau Claire is a canoeist's paradise.'

Joshua had given notice to quit his job the next day. It was his declaration of dependence on God.

On arrival in Eau Claire the family rented a holiday cottage and started to search for their home. In prayer during the previous two months, God had provided the couple with extraordinary detail about the house He had chosen for them. They were looking for a white ranch-style house with walkout basement, beautiful garden, double lot, with the number 1819, located near a river.

They scoured newspapers and called rental agencies but found nothing for rent with this description. The alternative, buying a home, was very unsettling but now seemed inevitable. They stepped into a real estate agency.

"I'm sure we can find you something suitable. What are your requirements?" asked the agent.

"Would you mind if we just looked through your multiple-listings book by ourselves, please?" chirped Faith. Mr 'Red' Fox raised his bushy ginger eyebrows in surprise but politely obliged. He installed the family in his office, providing toys for the children and a thick listings book for each parent.

Some minutes later Faith stabbed her finger on a page and crowed with delight. Joshua came over to read the description, which was exact in every detail. Then he checked the street address: 1819! They went at once to see the house, which was perfect for the family, and Mr Fox drew up a sales contract contingent on their being granted a suitable mortgage.

"Trust Me..."

Seated in one of Eau Claire's banks, the Alexanders struggled to keep their squirming children quiet. The loan officer slowly repeated, "I'm sorry, I'm really sorry." He stared at them through rimless glasses without a trace of sorrow. "As I told you, we can't make any exceptions. The Board has made a firm rule: no employment, no mortgage. At least one of you must have gainful employment." The man folded his hands and leaned back in his ample chair.

Joshua tried again. "But sir, one of us could go out and find a job, have you approve the mortgage, and quit the job the next day. You wouldn't foreclose on the mortgage, would you?"

"No, young man, we wouldn't," the banker answered tartly.

"So then, listen to my offer: I'll put aside a year's worth of mortgage payments - even two years if you like - into an escrow account. That will show our good faith," he said earnestly, spreading out his hands.

"I understand what you're saying. I see your point. But... we have to go by the RULES. It's just the way we do business in this town. We are, uh, perhaps more conservative here than in the east, where you come from." He allowed himself a little smirk.

The family left the bank in disgust. It was the fourth bank to have rejected them in two days for the same reason. There was a fifth bank in Eau Claire, but Joshua and Faith could not face another humiliation. Why bother with it, since mortgages were granted solely on the basis of actual income?

Back at the real estate office Mr Fox phoned the seller and tried to persuade him to rent his house, but without success. "What are you going to do?" he asked them with concern in his voice.

Faith decided to share the truth of their dilemma. "Mr Fox, we are in Eau Claire because God led us here and this is the house He described to us in prayer before we left Maryland - even down to the street number. We can't rent it and we can't find a mortgage to buy it. What else can we do?"

Red Fox's eyebrows bobbed up and down with the effort of digesting this information. "I find this amazing," he muttered at last. "I'm a deacon of our church, but I've never heard of anyone hearing so specifically from God. I don't know what to say."

"Isn't there another possibility?" persisted Joshua, but half-heartedly.

Red made an effort to concentrate. "Well, you can of course legitimately drop out of the contract," he offered, "but that wouldn't solve your problem if what you're saying about the Lord's guidance is correct. That leaves only one other option: to pay cash for the house and own it outright." He gave them an uncertain smile. The family thanked him for his help and left.

Joshua turned to his wife as they headed back to the lake cottage and groaned. "Why did God choose Eau Claire for us anyway? And why did He pinpoint that particular house, knowing what was in store for us?"

"Oh Father, help us," pleaded Faith. *"How can we buy this house? You saw what happened at the banks. Won't You please change Your mind?"*

"How does this make sense, Father?" added Joshua. *"If the proceeds from Chevy Chase go into buying this house instead of paying off our banks and credit cards, it will be like using credit cards to buy the house! Isn't that absurd, Father? What will happen to us then?"*

That evening they waited on God for His decision. His voice came softly but distinctly to Faith's heart: ***"My dear children, Whose money is it? Whose debts are they? Who gave you the house in Chevy Chase? Who released you and led you here? Who directed you to this house? Trust Me and buy the house. Buy it for cash."***

He said almost the same thing to Joshua: ***"The gold is Mine and the silver is Mine... and your debts are Mine. The day will come when I shall remove them completely. Meanwhile, take the money from your other house and put it into this one, pay cash. Put all your trust in Me - not in a bank, not in a mortgage, but only in Me."***

The two of them gulped as they shared these words with each other. Faith tried one more time, praying, *"Father, do please forgive us, but if we buy this house for cash, don't You realise what it will mean? We won't be able to pay off our debts, and we'll have to live on credit indefinitely. We won't even have a paycheque coming in."* Her voice trailed off in tears.

"Trust Me and buy the house." God had spoken; the matter was settled.

On closing day, Joshua presented Mr Fox with a cashier's cheque for $28,000 (almost the entire proceeds of their recent house sale in Maryland). This 'selling everything and following' had turned out to be very different from what he had imagined, but at the same time he was surprised and grateful that God had taken full responsibility for removing their mountain of debt.

The Promise of Work

Once they were settled into number 1819, the Alexanders took comfort from the fact that God's Spirit had chosen it for them. They enjoyed the view across the Eau Claire River and were reassured to see a factory chimney a few blocks away, as prophesied. It was a relief to be in their own place after a month of quasi-camping, and the children were overjoyed to play on a swing-set again in the warm September sunshine.

The couple started to look for work in the continuing hope of a mortgage (and salary) but every place firmly showed them the door. Even bottle-washing was unavailable due to the sky-high local unemployment rate. *"What are we doing in Eau Claire?"* they wondered, and not for the last time.

Soon every possible avenue had been exhausted, and they perceived that if and when their Heavenly Father wanted to give one of them work, He would open the doors, just as surely as He was now closing them.

While reading the Gospel of Luke, their hearts were touched by the words in chapter 12, verses 32 and 34: **"Do not be afraid, little flock, for your Father has been pleased to give you the kingdom... For where your treasure is, there your heart will be also."**

"What can this 'gift of the kingdom' be?" they wondered, and asked the Father to reveal it to them.

Meanwhile, with nothing else to do, Joshua ripped out the ugly, slipshod paneling around the basement until he had laid bare the cinderblock walls. As he surveyed the empty shell, he thought, *"Why not remodel this basement into four rooms?"* - ignoring the fact that he knew little or nothing about how to do it. So he went out and bought some materials and tools and set to work.

His progress was snail-paced and was punctuated by frequent crises. One day he called his wife downstairs to vent his feelings. Shaking his head in disgust and wiping caked sawdust and sweat from his glasses, he wailed, "Will I ever learn, Faith? Whenever I forget to pray I make a stupid mistake - EVERY time. But when I do pray, the cuts are perfect, the corners are square and it all fits properly. You know, I believe I'm being helped by Someone Who's an expert at carpentry. The trouble is He will only help me when I ask

Him to! I don't know whether to laugh or cry... and now look at this terrible mess," he moaned.

"I'm sorry, darling," responded Faith from the safety of the stairs but with scant sympathy, having endured two weeks of non-stop noise, mess and general aggravation. "I'll pray for you."

"Hah! I'll just have to remember to pray ALL the time... but in case I don't," he growled ominously in her direction, "you'll all do well to keep your distance." He lashed out at a piece of two-by-four that went flying. He quickly turned away to hide the pain on his face.

In spite of his black mood, Faith came bouncing back down the stairs again only a few minutes later, laughing. "Guess what?" she called across the sea of waste materials.

"I can't guess, just tell me!" muttered Joshua the handyman, squinting at a twisted tape measure. He straightened up and smiled weakly in apology. "Come on then, tell me before you burst."

"I was praying for you (yes, really) when I thought I heard the Lord say, *'Your work is on page B4 of the newspaper.'* And the very next moment a newspaper hit the front door, thud! So I looked on page B4 and what do you think I found?" She paused melodramatically.

He shook his head and laughed at his wife. "What?"

"Just listen to this: 'SEMINAR ON THE HOLY SPIRIT.' Isn't that great? It starts on Monday and goes the whole week, morning and evening, at a church not far from us. What do you think of that?"

Joshua waded over, blinking sawdust out of his eyes. "'Prayer and Share'? That sounds funny... but good," he grinned. "We certainly have a few things to share about the Holy Spirit, don't we?"

The Treasure Beyond Belief

"I am the Good Shepherd; I know My sheep and My sheep know Me
- just as the Father knows Me and I know the Father."
(John 10:14, 15)

The pastor and people of the Pentecostal church welcomed the young family of five and seemed genuinely pleased to meet them. The man leading the meetings was Brother Svenson, a loveable Swede from Minnesota with a rare sense of humour and great teaching ability. To the Alexanders' surprise (but apparently to no one else's) he focused almost exclusively on the Person of Jesus Christ. He only touched on the Holy Spirit when referring to His gifts and His fruit (already familiar ground to the Alexanders). But the couple had never seen people so excited about Jesus Christ and showing Him such devotion, except perhaps Father Pete in Rome.

Christ was presented as central to everything to do with the things of the Spirit. He was masterfully portrayed as the Vine, whose branches [Christian believers] were to bear the nine-fold fruit of the Holy Spirit: love, joy, peace, patience, kindness, goodness, faithfulness, gentleness and self-control [as listed in Galatians chapter 5, verse 20].

Furthermore, Christ Jesus was proclaimed to be the source of the greatest gift, the Holy Spirit Himself, according to the testimony of John the Baptist: **"I baptise you with water, but He will baptise you with the Holy Spirit."** [Mark 1:8.]

The days of inspirational teaching and worship ended on Sunday evening with altar calls and many people receiving prayer to be baptised with the Holy Spirit. Up to this moment, Faith and Joshua had been keeping the difficult issue of exactly who and what Jesus claimed to be 'on the shelf', in keeping with an earlier promise to the Father to only believe what He revealed to them by His Spirit. (They had heard so many conflicting and confusing teachings throughout their lives that they had decided to trust only what their Father taught them.)

By now, however, they were burning to ask their Heavenly Father about Jesus of Nazareth. Was He REALLY God's only Son, risen from the dead, ascended above all the angels, the King of kings and the Lord of lords, the Saviour of the world? Was he really *GOD?* They had to know at last, once and for all.

The children went to sleep without any fuss that Sunday night and their mother and father were grateful for the exceptional, awesome feeling of peace in the house. They tidied up the living room and sat down to commune with God with a tremendous sense of anticipation.

Within seconds Faith sensed a special radiance around her. She opened her eyes for an instant but the room lighting was normal. In her spirit she could still discern the same radiance.

With her eyes closed again, the radiance became brighter and even brighter until her inner eyes were dazzled. She was seeing a vision of heavenly light that transcended anything in her experience. Slowly the figure of a Man resolved out of the brightness. He was radiating the beautiful, glorious light and was holding His hands out towards her. She knew in her heart that this was the Lord Jesus, perhaps as He might have appeared on the Mount of Transfiguration.

Then He spoke. The voice was loving and gentle, and she recognised it at once. It was the beloved inner voice she had heard so often speaking to her in prayer, guiding, teaching, consoling, reproving, and convincing her to trust and obey God. Hot tears of joy flowed down her face as she listened to what He had to say:

"How I have longed for this day, to reveal Myself to you both. For I AM Jesus, your Shepherd. I have been your Shepherd from the very beginning of your spiritual journey. I was the One who spoke to you through Deborah three years ago... I was the One who revealed the Father to you... and I was the One who filled you with the Holy Spirit.

"You are My sheep - because My sheep hear and know My voice! You did not know Me by name, but you knew My voice and followed Me by faith.

"Yes, My beloved, I AM the only Son of the true and living God. I AM your Saviour who went to the Cross for you and rose from the grave with a resurrection body. I AM the promised Messiah of God. All that is written about Me in the Scriptures is true - learn from them.

"I have so much to teach you. There are many false teachings that you have ignorantly accepted in the past. You must sift them out and discard them, always praying for the Spirit of discernment.

"I have taken you on a long journey indeed. I implanted and nurtured faith in you by leading you to Yucatán, to Rome, and now here to Eau Claire. I brought you by this roundabout way, using Deborah and others, so that you would learn how to hear My voice. There are so many who call themselves by My name who do not listen to Me, and there are so many more who do not even believe that I CAN speak to them.

"Your walk with Me has been most Biblical. As I revealed the Father to Abraham, I revealed the Father to you. As I poured out My Spirit upon the elders of Israel in the wilderness, so I poured out My Spirit upon you. And as I showed Myself to My disciples after My resurrection, so I am showing

Myself to you as the Risen Christ, the only Begotten Son of the Most High God. I am showing you My glory, the glory My Father gave Me, so you may know My name and believe in Me. I AM the way, I AM the truth and I AM the life. No one comes to the Father except through ME!

"I have loved you always, since before you were born. It was I who brought you two together and I who filled your hearts with such love for each other. It was I who sent My angels to protect you, time after time. They continually camp around you to keep you safe from the evil one.

"I have jealously kept you for Myself, and I call you now to be My apostles. I will never leave you or forsake you..."

The Lord finished speaking and His figure disappeared, but the radiance remained in and around Faith's spirit. When at last she opened her eyes, the room still seemed suffused with the same glorious radiance of His Presence. She looked over at Joshua just as he opened his eyes. They both wiped tears from their faces.

"Faith, dearest, did He appear to you too? The Lord, the Lord Jesus?" he whispered. He took her trembling hands in his.

She nodded in wonderment and asked, "What did He tell you?"

"Amazing things! Wonderful things! He explained everything that's happened to us; that He's been our Shepherd all along; that He's the LORD... And He called us His apostles! Think of that, Faith. I had such a strong sense of His Presence that I could almost see Him. His light is so beautiful... but when I heard Him say that He died for us on the Cross and that He rose from the dead..." [Joshua was weeping] "then... then I was convinced. JESUS REALLY IS GOD."

At last the couple knew their Shepherd by name: Jesus. He was so powerfully present with them in that house that they found themselves talking and communing with Him almost continuously for the next ten days and more. They laughed and cried with Him as Bible verses and many personal experiences came to their memory. Their hearts were so filled with joy that they fell in love with Him all over again, because Jesus had revealed Himself to them as the true and living God. He was the Treasure of all treasures. The King had given them THE GIFT OF THE KINGDOM. Joshua and Faith now belonged to Him completely.

The Grace of God

"There is no fear in love, but perfect love drives out fear..."
(I John 4:18)

The accident occurred just before Thanksgiving. The Alexanders had gone to Minneapolis to attend a special counseling session for all of Faith's family at her eldest brother's request. The children stayed behind at their day-care centre (it was the only time the couple had left town without them.) At about three o'clock in the afternoon Faith was suddenly and unaccountably filled with foreboding. Standing up, she apologised and left abruptly. Joshua, who had been sitting outside the meeting room for most of the day, was also feeling anxious and wanting to leave.

They arrived back in Eau Claire two hours later to learn that Andrew, now 20 months old, was in the hospital. On the way over to see him the couple prayed and committed their son into the Lord's hands. Mary (Andy's favourite teacher) saw them coming and hurried over. She was pale and agitated, and explained that he was not swallowing properly. She described how he had crawled up unnoticed behind one of the staff who was cleaning out a toilet, and he had picked up a discarded empty bottle of *Mister Plumber* (a sulphuric acid mixture). The girl had turned round to see Andy with the bottle up to his mouth. Everyone assumed that the bottle had been empty, but just in case Mary had brought him to the Emergency Room.

The physician on duty had just pumped Andy's stomach, and now decided to lecture the Alexanders sternly on proper poison control. He ended his tirade by declaring there was nothing else he could do, but added, "Perhaps you should get in touch with your paediatrician."

They took Andy home, stopping on the way to see their other two children who had been picked up earlier by a friend. Richard and Jacqueline were invited to stay overnight there and the couple gratefully agreed.

Though their baby was not in any obvious pain, whatever went into his mouth promptly came out again. He was drooling continuously and could not swallow. Faith remembered the doctor's suggestion and decided to call her paediatrician sister who was still in Minneapolis.

Normally imperturbable, Elaine responded urgently. "This is terribly serious. You must take him to the hospital again, a different one if possible, and at once! Find an ENT [ear, nose and throat] specialist and a local

The Treasure House

paediatrician, and GO! You see, Andy's oesophagus is very small and delicate, and the tissues could swell up and cause him to suffocate. Tomorrow is too late! You must get help TONIGHT. Pumping his stomach was not at all the best treatment - the tube might have damaged his oesophagus further…"

"But Elaine, what can they do for him? What would you do?"

"If it were up to me I'd check his oesophagus and give him sulpha antibiotics and a steroid to control the swelling. Get help now. Hurry! A few more hours and it may be too late."

Despite the deadly seriousness of the situation, an extraordinary calm filled the couple's hearts. After finding a list of ENT specialists in the Yellow Pages, they prayed over the names, and Faith dialled the number of the specialist that the Lord was highlighting to them both. The doctor himself answered, and listened attentively as she described the problem and her sister's recommendations. He offered to contact a paediatrician colleague himself, and advised them to bring Andy without delay to the other Eau Claire hospital.

When the Alexanders arrived with their toddler just ten minutes later they were astonished to find the doctors already waiting for them. The two specialists carefully reviewed the details and proceeded to emphasise the seriousness and possibly fatal result of Andy's condition. As the couple nodded in agreement, the physicians looked at them with some disbelief. Thinking they had been misunderstood they each repeated the warning: "ANDREW COULD DIE."

"We understand," said Joshua, "but we believe that God is the One in control. He might take Andy home to Himself or He might heal him - either way, the situation is in His hands."

The Lord was filling them with a gift of supernatural faith. It was His special gift to carry them through this crisis and teach them about His ways.

The doctors disappeared into an examination room with Andrew, who wailed in protest at being separated from his parents again.

Nurses were going to and fro. One of them came up to the couple and confided, "You're so fortunate to have those two doctors, especially that wonderful ENT man. How is it that he's still working? He retired two weeks ago. Yours must be a very special case for him to have accepted it!" She smiled reassuringly and was gone.

Eventually the physicians returned. "We're finding this problem rather perplexing, I'm afraid," the ENT doctor admitted. "We've examined Andy very carefully. There are no acid burns visible inside his mouth or on his lips. Had he been brought here earlier, we'd have suggested a general anaesthetic to check his oesophagus properly. We still don't know the cause of his drooling. It may merely be an after-effect of having his stomach pumped."

"It's really difficult to know how to proceed," added the paediatrician. "It's so late now, and your poor little boy has been through such a lot already - and we've no idea if we would find anything using oesophagoscopy. However, there is a very SLIGHT chance that he may have 'chugged' some drops of acid without burning any part of his lips, tongue or upper throat. In that case, his oesophagus is most likely to have been burned and his condition is extremely serious.

"We see two options. The first is to take your son home and put him to bed and hope for the best. The second is to authorise us to put him under general anaesthesia and examine his oesophagus for burns. Each option presents some risk."

As the Alexanders listened, common sense was telling them to go home to bed. Surely Andy would be okay, and they were all exhausted. Was it right to put their baby through a potentially risky examination? They looked at each other and knew it was time to pray.

"If you'll please excuse us for a few moments, we need to ask our Heavenly Father what to do," Joshua responded. He took his wife's hand and they crossed the hall to a quiet corner. They stood there together with eyes closed, listening. After quieting their minds, each one heard an inner voice clearly saying the same words: *"Do it, do it, DO IT!"* The decision had been made for them in seconds.

While signing the consent form Joshua declared, "Please proceed at once. The Lord was perfectly clear: He wants you to do the examination. And thank you so much. We appreciate your help more than we can say. God be with you."

The next two hours passed slowly but without anxiety. The couple marvelled at the peace that was filling their hearts, recalling how (on a recent occasion at the lake cottage) they had been thrown into panic when Andy had bitten into a tube of glue. They had run up and down looking for an emetic to make him throw up, and there had been screaming, swearing and general pandemonium over something relatively trivial by comparison. But that had been 'BC' (before Christ). Now the two of them were witnessing and experiencing the keeping power of the unshakeable peace of the Lord.

The clock showed well past midnight. The halls were as silent as their hearts. Finally there came the sound of the doctors' footsteps.

"It's SUCH a good thing you agreed to the esophagoscopy procedure. It's hard to believe, but Andy's oesophagus has been severely burned. We're really sorry," the paediatrician reported.

"What are his chances?" Faith asked in a low voice.

"We won't be able to say for sure until tomorrow or even the day after. Perhaps you'd like to stay here overnight with your son, Mrs Alexander. There's an empty bed next to his crib and you are very welcome to use it."

Eventually the nurses and doctors left the hospital room. Joshua reluctantly parted from his wife and son, giving Faith a tight embrace and Andy one last, lingering kiss. He wondered if he would ever see his baby boy alive again, but as he drove home he felt strongly encouraged by the Holy Spirit.

He fell right into bed and slept soundly. Waking up refreshed just as the sun was about to rise, he began to praise the Lord. He had complete heart-assurance that Andy had been divinely healed!

He hurried to the hospital and found Faith cross-legged inside the tiny crib holding their baby son and grinning from ear to ear. At the sight of his Daddy, Andy jumped up out of her arms (leg splint and all) to hug him. His joy and energy seemed boundless and he let them both know that all he wanted to do was play.

"Look at this," Faith pointed to an empty dish of jelly. "He ate it all just now, without any drooling. Isn't that great? The nurse was so thrilled. She's coming back any moment to take off his leg splint."

"I knew it!" cried Joshua, kissing and hugging his little boy. "I knew Jesus had healed you, you little monkey."

"Here, give me a hand." Faith grabbed his free arm, slowly stood up and then manoeuvred herself out of the crib.

"How did you ever manage to squeeze yourself into that tiny space? Did you spend the whole night in there?" he asked with astonishment.

"Yes, actually I did. But the Lord made it easy."

"How do you mean?"

"Well, a beautiful thing happened. After you left I just stood by the side of the crib looking down at little Andy. He was gradually coming out of the anaesthetic and looked forlorn and uncomfortable. He was fussing without actually crying, and the IV and leg splint were obviously bothering him. I looked at the empty bed next to his crib but it was cold and uninviting. I decided that if Andy was dying I had to be with him. So I kicked one leg and then the other up and over the crib rails. It was no mean feat, I can tell you. My ballet training finally came in handy."

He smiled with admiration. "So what happened?"

"I managed to pick him up along with all the paraphernalia and took him in my arms. He relaxed at once and fell into a peaceful sleep, with his face resting on my heart. I was so grateful to help him get comfortable at last.

"For a long time I just looked into his sweet little face. After a while my thoughts went back to Deborah's prophecy that the Lord had a third child for us, and that he would be the 'dessert' of our family. How true! In his short little life he's brought so much joy and laughter to all of us - always smiling, never complaining. And then I thought about how much fun the three kids always have together, how they really delight to be in each other's company. I thanked God that Andy has been such a blessing to us, and for the precious gift of his life.

"It was then that I realised the Lord was waiting for me to surrender Andy to Him. My heart immediately broke and I dissolved into tears. Finally I prayed: *'Dear Lord Jesus, I know our children don't belong to us - they belong to You. You gave us little Andy. You can take him back if You want him to be with You. Your will be done.'*

"As I finished praying, the reality of Andy dying gripped me with a horrible icy fear. I began to panic. I was so scared. My heart was beating wildly and I cried out in desperation, *'Lord Jesus, help me. Please save me from my fears. I need You!'*

"As soon as I cried out for help, the Lord was with me instantly. His peace came over me again like a warm, protective blanket, and my fears melted away.

Then He spoke to me. Oh Joshua, it was so wonderful: ***'My dear child, is there any reason for you to fear death? Dying in Me is like being born. Just as everyone must leave a mother's womb in order to live on earth, so everyone must die to the body in order to live with Me in Heaven. I have overcome death and the grave! You have nothing to fear because you belong to Me and I have given you everlasting life. Heaven is a beautiful place and if Andrew were to die right now he would leave your arms and come straight into Mine...'***

"While the Lord was speaking to my heart, I began to see beautiful scenes of colourful gardens and happy children playing in them. He actually gave me a glimpse of Heaven! It was more beautiful than I could ever describe. And it was so peaceful and joyful, Joshua. What a lovely homecoming we'll have one day in Heaven when we get there!

"I was totally reassured of God's amazing love for Andy, for me and for our entire family. The Lord's presence stayed here with me, filling me with complete peace. The night passed very quickly. I was in His embrace, just as surely as Andy was in mine."

As she finished telling the story the nurse came in to take off the baby's leg splint. Andy was delighted to be free again and was soon playing boisterously with toys on the playroom floor.

Word had soon flashed around the hospital that the little boy who had swallowed poison was up and around, kicking up a ruckus in the nursery. Doctors, nurses, administrators and general well wishers began parading through the playroom to witness the miracle baby for themselves. The joy of the Lord filled the hospital.

Andy's doctors were astounded at his remarkable and total recovery and acknowledged that he was healed, discharging him later that morning.

Joshua and Faith found themselves alone in the room as they dressed their wriggling youngster before leaving the hospital. Faith confided to her husband that two miracles had taken place that night. Not only had Andy's life been saved, but the Lord had also used his illness to deliver her from a crippling, lifelong fear of death through this stunning vision of Heaven.

"Now I know for sure that I'm really a Christian," declared Faith with authority. She wrestled one of Andy's rubbery little arms into a sleeve.

Joshua looked at her with a smile. "Why do you say that?"

"Because I have no more fear of death!" Tears of joy and gratitude splashed down her cheeks as their eyes met. "The terror that has tormented me all my life is gone. I've been delivered! God's grace is so amazing... We've sung about it so often, but now I really KNOW it."

"I guess He used little Andy as a kind of sacrificial lamb to heal you," marvelled Joshua. Stealing Andrew out of her arms he tossed his giggling miracle-baby high up in the air and caught him at the last moment to a huge whoop of delight.

As the Alexanders stepped through the revolving doors of the hospital, their hearts were bursting with thanksgiving for all that the Lord had done in less than 24 hours. They suddenly remembered: it was Thanksgiving Day.

> **"You may suffer grief in all kinds of trials... so that your faith - of greater worth than gold, which perishes even though refined by fire - may be proved genuine... For you are receiving the goal of your faith, the salvation of your souls."**
>
> *(I Peter 1:6,7,9)*

7

The Good Shepherd
(December 1975 - May 1976)

> "The LORD is faithful to all His promises and loving toward all He has made... The eyes of all look to You, and You give them their food at the proper time. You open Your hand and satisfy the desires of every living thing."
> *(Psalm 145:13b, 15-16)*

Now that the Carpenter of Nazareth had been invited to take up permanent residence in the Alexanders' hearts, Joshua's work in the basement proceeded smoothly and rapidly. Before long his children were invited downstairs to inspect the big sunny playroom where they would spend most of the coming winter.

The couple's spiritual mountain peaks made a stark contrast to the ever-deepening valley of their finances. While their home at number 1819 was worth tens of thousands, this equity was locked up in the cinderblocks and roof tiles. In order to buy bread and keep servicing their many debts, Joshua had to borrow ever more heavily against the few remaining lines of credit.

The end of 1975 approached to the old familiar tune of paying one bank by squeezing a little from each of the others, a repeat performance of the previous Christmas. Joshua knew that their situation was hopeless unless the Lord intervened once again.

But how could He intervene and through whom? The pair had been commanded by God not to breathe a word to anyone about their financial situation. All possibilities of employment had been investigated: nobody seemed to want their services but the Lord Himself. The Alexanders were obliged to trust in God and depend on Him only, without any kind of safety net.

The proverbial Christmas goose was getting fat, but this little family had no expectation of tasting it. Nevertheless Jacqui, Rick and Andy were confidently looking forward to the gifts and merrymaking. Their helpless parents begged the Lord to grant the children their hearts' desires.

On December 22nd, the family refrigerator and pantry were bare, without any earthly prospect of being filled. The doorbell rang to reveal two well-dressed men who announced, "Merry Christmas! Here are some provisions for the holidays." The family stared open-mouthed as the men handed them two huge boxes of tinned food, and then presented Faith with a voucher for a giant turkey or ham (plus all the Christmas trimmings).

"Thank you, thank you! You have no idea what this means to us. Who ARE you?" asked Faith and Joshua in unison.

"We're from First American Bank of Eau Claire. Have a Merry Christmas now..."

"Yes, to you too, but... but... how did you get our name and address?" Faith asked, stupefied.

The men looked at each other and shrugged. "Someone must have put you on our list." They turned and went to their car.

"Thank you, and Merry Christmas!" the family called after them.

Faith thoughtfully examined the tin cans. "Honey, did I ever tell you that as a junior in high school I was in charge of the 'canned-goods drive'? We had over a thousand tins of food in our attic at home and every month I'd take about a hundred tins over to the family our Leaders Club had adopted. I had no idea what a precious gift just one little tin can of food can be. Hmmm. I wonder who could have told the bank about us? It's quite incredible to see God's hand feeding us, isn't it?"

There was more: three large plastic bags appeared mysteriously on the doorstep on Christmas Eve, each bearing the name of one of the children and bursting with gifts. At the last moment other packages - many more than expected - arrived by mail from relatives and friends like a sudden flood. On Christmas morning the children howled with delight at all their fine gifts, while Faith and Joshua rejoiced to celebrate their first Christmas knowing Jesus as their Risen Lord.

The Way of Escape

"God is not a man, that He should lie, nor a son of man, that He should change His mind. Does He speak and then not act? Does He promise and then not fulfill?"
(Numbers 25:19)

The Alexanders knew that their God would keep His word to provide them with a financial solution. In the last hour of the year, He spoke to the couple as they were praying for His blessing on the New Year.

Faith repeated the words as she heard them: *"My children, you have now lived in Eau Claire for almost five months. In fact, you have been here for exactly half the time you will be here altogether. You will be leaving after five more months - by the end of May.*

"Your work now is to start writing down your spiritual journey. Only when you have completed this work will you be released. But I will be with you to help you.

"Go to 'Calder' of First American Bank. When you tell Mr Calder that you're leaving Eau Claire soon, he will arrange a mortgage on that basis... Trust Me! This is for My glory, that you may know that I am your Provider in everything."

Joshua gazed appreciatively at his wife as she ended this prophecy, because he had been given the very same name, *'Calder'*, but without having any idea of the context. They worshipped and praised the Lord for this word of confirmation and for His promise of rescue, again remembering *Felipe Rodríguez*.

Joshua stood up, went over to the desk and began to work through a stack of bills. "That should take care of everything," he announced at length, looking up with relief. "I've just written out cheques for everything that's due. They have to be sent out within the next four days or our finances will collapse."

He held up the sealed envelopes and prayed, *"Lord Jesus, we commit these cheques into Your hands, and we thank You that the loan will be granted just as You promised, and in time to cover these payments."*

"Amen!" responded Faith with her whole heart. Then she recalled with a start, "Sweetheart, do you realise that First American was the ONE bank we didn't try for a mortgage when we got here? Isn't that ironic? The Spirit must have kept us from going in there. Otherwise we might have obtained a mortgage and we would never have become so dependent on God or seen His lovely, amazing provision..." She glanced at her watch. "Joshua my love - Happy New Year!"

Two mornings later on the first working day of the New Year, the thermometer was registering -24F (-31C). Joshua bundled himself up and, full of faith in God's word, ventured into the bitter cold to find and meet the promised 'Mr Calder'.

Once inside the bank building, he loosened some of his many layers of clothing and stepped up to a teller. "Do you have a Mr Calder working here?"

"Mr Calder is the president of the bank, sir. His office is just up the stairs. Over there, please," she pointed. Joshua was duly ushered straight into a large office. He admired the wood-panelled walls and plush carpeting as he approached a large mahogany desk.

"Mr Calder," he began, introducing himself and shaking hands. "You don't know me at all, but my wife and I were greatly blessed by your bank's wonderful generosity just before Christmas. The turkey and tinned goods were a literal Godsend and made our holiday special beyond words. Thank you so very much."

"You're welcome. It was our pleasure." Mr Calder, a large, kind-faced man who smiled easily, motioned for him to sit down. He seemed to have the whole day to chat with his visitor.

Joshua came to the point. "I don't know how else to say this, except that when we were praying over the holidays, the Lord specifically gave us your name, Mr Calder. He told us that you could help us get a loan on our house."

The bank president was not in the least bit taken aback by this statement, but warmly replied, "Dr Alexander, I'm really glad to hear you say that! I'm a praying man myself, and I'm delighted that the Lord would send you to me. So now, tell me about your house."

Joshua described the house and location. "We originally paid cash for the house, but now we need money urgently," he explained. "Since the Lord has told us that He'll be moving us on again in late May, would it be possible to borrow against our equity? We'll be putting it up for sale anyway..."

"Yes, of course it's possible, and I actually remember that house, we held the original paper on it. You should have come here sooner - we'd have gladly financed the house for you. But never mind all that, how much money do you need?"

"To tell you the truth, I haven't even thought about that," he answered, somewhat abashed.

"Well, would ten thousand dollars be enough?" (Joshua nodded, staring.) "Shall we make the maturity date the end of August? That will give you some leeway. And don't worry about making any payments because there's nothing due on this kind of loan until the house is sold, and then it will be paid off automatically on the day the sale closes."

"Thank you Mr Calder, that's tremendous. Would there be any way to process the loan in the next couple of days?"

"No problem at all, assuming the documents are in order and you list the house right away with a real estate agency. In fact, here's what I'll do: I'll process the loan MYSELF to make sure you get the money in good time. Don't worry, I'll take care of everything."

Mr Calder was true to his word - and so was God. Every payment was covered and there would be plenty to live on until the family was scheduled to leave Eau Claire. The Alexanders had been rescued at the very end of their rope, yet again.

The Gates of Death

"For the LORD your God is... a jealous God."
(Deuteronomy 4:24)

As January progressed, Joshua developed a cough that got deeper and uglier. His usually healthy complexion deteriorated to a pasty grey. By early February he lay weak and helpless in bed, so weak that every movement was an effort and every breath a stab of pain.

Although Faith and many others prayed repeatedly for his healing, he grew steadily worse. When she and Joshua asked God about admitting him to a hospital, they received a resounding *"no"* despite the bleakness of his condition, which appeared to be double pneumonia. (Having no health insurance was of course also a factor.)

One afternoon Faith became convinced her husband was dying. She left him for a few minutes to be alone with the Lord in the kitchen. She collapsed in a heap onto her knees and began to pray in anguish.

"Lord, why don't You heal Joshua? I don't understand. We keep praying yet he keeps getting worse. What's WRONG?"

"I want to heal you."

"ME?" she protested. *"There's nothing wrong with me - I'm fine."*

"No, you're not. Look at your heart," insisted the gentle voice.

Faith turned her sight inward and discerned a white screen with her sin spelled out in red flashing letters. Confronted with the truth, she felt her cheeks flush with a fire of conviction. Her face was down to the floor as she bowed herself before the Lord.

"Oh, Lord, please forgive me! I've been jealous of You, haven't I?"

"Yes, My daughter."

It was inescapable, Faith was jealous of her husband's whole-hearted love for Jesus. In the past she had always been Number One in his heart, but now she was definitely Number Two. Over the past few months she had become increasingly vexed as Joshua lavished more attention and love on the Lord than on her. Faith had once prayed fervently that the Lord would reveal Himself to Joshua, and now that He had, she was jealous.

Distraught by her sin and panicked by her situation, Faith recognised she was in terrible trouble. Sin had undermined and almost destroyed her relationship with the Lord, and her husband was at death's door. She was about to become a widow with three children under 6 years old.

"I'm so sorry, Lord Jesus," she sobbed. *"Please, please forgive me of this awful sin of jealousy. Help me change, Lord. But please, don't leave me!"*

With a deep moan of pain and regret she now released her husband: *"Lord Jesus, You know how I love Joshua. I'll miss him terribly if You take him away, but I know he belongs to You and not to me. Your will be done..."* She wept in helpless misery.

Unusual sounds coming from the next room broke in on her tearful misery. She stood up and stumbled over to investigate.

She blinked her eyes in disbelief, Joshua was standing on his feet, his arms raised above his head, and he was singing. His face was a healthy colour and he was full of joy.

"What's going on here?" she gasped, her face still wet with tears. She slowly approached him. "I thought you were DYING!"

"I was... but the Lord just healed me this moment. Lord Jesus, thank You, thank You! Hallelujah!" he worshipped, laughing. He stretched out his arms to her and gathered her into a strong embrace.

Through the laughter and sobbing she tried to find words. "I was just praying in the kitchen... Oh Joshua, I have been jealous, jealous of all the praise you shower on the Lord instead of on me. It's all my fault you were ill. I am so sorry..."

He wiped the tears off her face with his pyjama sleeve and tried to quiet her. "Just a minute, honey. Jesus had a lot to say to me too."

"He did? Tell me! What happened in here? I was so sure I was going to lose you..."

"Well, as you know I was lying in bed, in a really bad state. I was so weak that I couldn't even make my little finger move. Getting up from the bed was out of the question. I wondered what would become of me, and for the first time I seriously considered the reality of death, that I was going to die. I moved my eyes around the room and noticed that things seemed to be getting much dimmer. I couldn't breathe properly and hardly any air was getting into my lungs. Everything around me seemed to slow down to a stop, and I became very aware of the presence of Jesus right next to me.

"Faith, I heard Him. I actually HEARD His voice speaking to me audibly, as clearly as I can hear you. His voice was so lovely... He was close by, just by my ear.

"He said, *'My son, can you praise Me for not having healed you?'*

"I was utterly shocked by His question. I couldn't respond for a while. Then I said to Him (silently, of course, in my spirit), *'Yes I can, Lord... I DO praise You. I praise You and thank You for... NOT healing me! And Lord, I'm sorry. I didn't realise how much I was taking Your gift of healing for granted. Forgive me, please. I know that if You'd wanted to, You would have healed me, but You chose NOT to heal me. You are Sovereign, and I praise You. I praise You for WHO You are...'*

"'*Well then,*' broke in the voice of Jesus, '*if you can praise Me, then SING!*'

"You know, sweetheart, I found that really comical. After a moment I replied, *'Lord, I can't even breathe, let alone sing. You know that taking even a small breath makes me cough my lungs out. How can I possibly sing?'*

"I felt helpless. You know how pitiful my singing is at the best of times.

"'*Sing!*' He repeated, ignoring my protest.

"'*Well, Lord, if You insist...*'

"'*I do insist. Sing: "The Joy of the Lord is My Strength!*"'

"'*Oh Lord!*' *I said in my spirit, even more amused, 'You know that's the most difficult song You could have chosen for me. Okay, I'll sing, but only because You say so. I'll just seize up and choke, and then I'll be with You in just a couple more minutes...' Darling, I was convinced it was the end, but there was no resisting Him! He is the King...*

"So I obeyed. I opened my mouth and began to croak, 'The jo-oy of the Lo-o-o-ord is my strength,' when I sensed an intense POWER hovering over me. An instant later this divine power entered my body, and flowed through me. I felt it surge from my head right down to my toes! That's when I jumped up out of bed, because I felt strong and well again. And I was still singing, and not choking. Then in you came. Isn't that totally magnificent?" His face was shining. Truly the joy of the Lord WAS his strength.

"Utterly awesome and amazing. But Joshua, do you realise? God was healing me of my jealousy and you of your presumption at the same time! Then He took care of your illness too. You look so well! Your colour is completely normal now - it's wonderful. Are you totally healed?"

"Well, let's see. I can breathe okay, though I'm still a bit congested..." (He coughed up some phlegm.) "But I can speak, and sing, and I'm not choking or in pain. Best of all, I feel really fine."

Holding hands, the two gazed lovingly at each other, their hearts overflowing. By God's grace, Joshua had been brought back from the grave to vibrant physical health, and both he and Faith had been restored to spiritual health. They had experienced for the first time the purifying fire of God's loving correction in their lives.

"You'd better take care of yourself now... and I promise not to be a jealous wife ever again. That's a lesson I don't care to repeat. Once is enough."

"They... drew near the gates of death. Then they cried to the LORD in their trouble, and He saved them from their distress. He sent forth His word and healed them; He rescued them from the grave. Let them give thanks to the LORD for His unfailing love and His wonderful deeds for men."

(Psalm 107:18-21)

The Plum Tree

They learned of their next destination in a surprisingly casual way. Grace, a close friend and fellow-believer, had come over to celebrate Faith's 33rd birthday in early 1976. She enjoyed cake and coffee with the Alexanders and chatted happily with them. Then they all settled into their customary worship and praise, followed by a time of silently waiting on the Lord.

Afterwards Grace turned to Joshua with a quizzical look. "I got the most unusual impression for you." She gave a little laugh. "I saw you in a house, but the only thing noticeable about it was the beautiful plum tree in the front garden." She enunciated slowly and carefully, wondering what her words might signify.

After blank looks all around, Joshua cleared his throat and looked directly at Grace. "Was it a Santa Rosa plum?" he asked, and sat back in surprise at his own words. He almost missed her reply.

"Yes, that's it. How silly of me to forget, it WAS a Santa Rosa plum tree. How did you know?" she bubbled over.

"I didn't know. The words just came out of my mouth. In fact, I'd forgotten that a Santa Rosa plum even existed."

"But what could it mean?" persisted Grace.

Faith sprang up and ran over to the bookcase, trilling, "That's it! That's where we're moving to when we leave here: Santa Rosa. And here's the atlas..." She placed it provocatively on the table. "Where shall we look?"

"It sounds like some place in California, doesn't it?" hazarded Grace. She felt great surprise at being involved in God's process of directing her friends' life. Seconds later Faith was pointing to a location 50 miles north of San Francisco, abounding in vineyards, orchards and redwood groves - a mouth-watering prospect.

God is Never Late

"Let us hold unswervingly to the hope we profess, for He who promised is faithful."
(Hebrews 10:23)

Wisconsin's winter was exceptionally cold that year and stretched on well into what should have been spring. As a result the Alexanders stayed indoors, keeping at their God-given task of writing until they had completely recorded the previous three and a half years of following their Shepherd.

On Friday May 21st, Faith was vacuuming the kitchen and chatting with the Lord. *"Well, Lord Jesus, we've finished it, though I guess we could have done a lot better. It's Your move now, Lord. You did promise to release us when we finished our work, remember? And You said we'd be out of here by the end of May...*

"But can You really sell this house and move us out of Eau Claire in just ten days? Not one soul has been to view the house since we listed it more than four months ago."

An unpleasant voice broke in on her and suddenly attacked her: *"You dreamer! You know it's not possible to sell a house that quickly in Eau Claire. You'll be lucky to get out of here by September, you utter fool."* A verse came strongly to her mind, however: **"Is anything too hard for the Lord?"** (Genesis 18:14.)

She determined to trust the Lord to make His move, and found faith rising strongly in her heart again. She rebuked the spirit of doubt and derision, then prayed, *"Oh Lord Jesus, I know You're in charge. Forgive my doubts. You can do anything! I'm trusting You to bring us a buyer for the house TODAY."*

Faith turned off the vacuum cleaner and leaned on it for a moment, enjoying the sight of their attractive little home. She wanted to remember every nook and cranny of this precious place where their Good Shepherd had revealed His name and person to them - their Treasure House. Gazing out of the window, she smiled with pleasure to see the lovely garden now blossoming in pinks and whites and yellows. She prayed, *"Maybe one day our hearts will look as beautiful to You as that garden does to me, Lord Jesus. I do hope so."*

Joshua walked in whistling, having stored the fresh manuscript safely in a box downstairs. "Well, when is the Lord sending us our buyer, today or tomorrow? Won't it be fun to see how He keeps His promise, darling?"

God's Spirit was infusing both of their hearts with His gift of faith.

An hour later Faith was clearing away the family lunch dishes when Red Fox (their real estate agent) called with the news that he wanted to bring over a couple right away. She rounded up the children, glad that she had been obedient to clean and tidy the house that morning, and they all made themselves scarce.

The Good Shepherd

On returning home they found a note from Mr Fox: "Thanks, expect us back at 7pm."

Again they left the house, finding another note on their return: "Please call my office first thing tomorrow."

By 9am the next morning, the Alexanders had signed a sales contract at the full asking price with one contingency, they had to give up possession of the house by June 1st.

Red's eyebrows and moustache were doing a dance together as he confessed, "Never, in all my years in Eau Claire, have I brokered a sale like this, closing in ten days. It's unreal! And you... you'll be on your way EXACTLY when you said you would. Last year I found it very hard to believe it when you said you could hear God's voice, but I believe it now! You really do hear the Lord speaking, don't you?"

A Heart-Changing Prayer

"I think we should fly!"

"But we need a car out there – and ours is so reliable, we should keep it. We need to drive to Santa Rosa," countered Joshua. "Besides, think of all the luggage we'd have to take by plane."

"I can't face days and days of driving with a trailer behind us, going over the Rockies and through the desert." Faith was adamant.

The argument went on for hours, without any peace. Finally the pair came to their senses and went to the Lord in prayer.

"Lord Jesus, if I'm wrong, would you please change my heart? And if Joshua is wrong... then please change HIS heart! We have to have peace about this..." prayed Faith. They spent a few minutes in silence.

"Sweetheart, I'm sorry. You are absolutely right. Let's take the plane!" They hugged each other with relief.

Just then the phone rang. It was Grace "Dear ones, I was praying for you and got a picture from the Lord that I don't understand at all. It was of a statue called *Winged Victory...*"

Faith was astonished at how quickly the Lord had resolved the issue and brought their hearts into complete peace and harmony, and had even provided this delightful confirmation of His will. From that time on, whenever she and Joshua had a significant argument and remembered to pray this 'heart-changing prayer', the Lord always responded. He never failed to bring them into agreement.

Moved by the Holy Spirit

Two days before their flight to San Francisco, the Alexanders were holding a garage sale. A woman walked in. She didn't buy anything, but fixed a firm yet friendly eye on Joshua, who was sitting there alone waiting for customers to buy the surplus items inevitably accumulated over 10 months. "You people are moving to Santa Rosa, aren't you?" she asked in a confident tone.

Startled, he stood up. "Yes, how did you know?"

"Quite simple. We have a mutual friend, Lois, who has been babysitting for you. She told me some of your testimony and mentioned that God was sending you to Santa Rosa. I got very excited because I have a dear friend who lives there. I've come here to ask you a favour. Would you please look her up? She's originally from Eau Claire and she was here visiting me only last week. I know she'd be very touched to hear about your walk of faith. Here's her name and address."

"Sure we'll call her, but who are YOU?" called Joshua as she started to walk away. The woman laughed and wrote down her name. He carefully tucked the square of paper into his wallet. "It'll be very good to have someone to contact in Santa Rosa…"

The final afternoon before they were to leave, Faith and Joshua were wondering what to do with several pieces of furniture that had not been sold. They watched as a pickup truck backed into their driveway. Out hopped Father Meinen, a frequent visitor to the weekly prayer meetings at number 1819.

"Hi there," said their friend with a wide grin as he stepped through the open door into the living room. "Do you mind if I look over the furniture you haven't yet sold?" The pair looked at each other with astonishment and laughed delightedly as they took him around the half-empty house on a 'grand tour'.

"Why," exclaimed the priest, "I can use EVERY one of these things. I'll buy the lot. It's a good thing they haven't been sold." He pressed a large amount of cash into Joshua's hand with a great smile and an unmistakable twinkle in his eyes. This was a true love gift.

After his truck was loaded up, Father Meinen put his arms around Joshua and Faith and gave them a farewell embrace. He prayed for their whole family, and with tears brimming in his eyes, he added, "You know, I've been realising that you dear people are just like the first-century Apostles - you simply go wherever the Holy Spirit moves you. God bless you both for your faith and obedience."

"...Be encouraged in heart and united in love, so that [you] may know the mystery of God, namely Christ, in whom are hidden all the treasures of wisdom and knowledge."

(Colossians 2:2-3)

8

Golden Prospects
(May 1976 - June 1977)

"Do not worry... Seek first His kingdom and His righteousness, and all these things will be given to you as well."
(Matthew 6:31a, 33)

Its red-tiled roofs gleaming in the sunshine, Santa Rosa was jammed with visitors enjoying the brilliant spring flowers. The fact that it was Memorial Day weekend had never occurred to the Alexanders and they arrived without room reservations. After two hours of trying every hotel and motel in town, the couple realised with mounting anxiety that their new hometown had 'no vacancy'.

"Sweetheart, I'm really sorry. I should have foreseen this," groaned Joshua as he parked the rental car and shut off the engine. "At least we had the sense to leave the children with Aunt Emily in Berkeley - I only hope she can manage. Wasn't it great to see Rick and Jacqui fly into her arms again?" He leaned back in the driver's seat and closed his eyes.

"I'm almost done in," came the faint response. "I have to get to bed soon and sleep." Faith rested her head against her husband's shoulder. "I don't think I've ever been this exhausted... What time is it anyway?"

He peered at the dash clock through the gathering darkness and closed his eyes again. "Just after eight."

"But what's that in Eau Claire time? Ten o'clock? How long have we been going today?" she murmured.

"Must be 18 hours," he sighed. "We've got to pray…" But Faith was too dejected and tired even to think.

Some time passed. Joshua roused himself and pulled out his wallet. "Darling, do you remember this?"

Faith slowly opened one eye to see her husband dangling a little square of white paper over his nose. He was crossing his eyes. She forced a smile. "No I don't, what is it?"

"It's where we're going to spend the night. I'm going to call the number now…"

"You're what? Who ARE they?" She tried to understand.

"I told you about the woman at the garage sale who gave me her friends' phone number here."

"You MUSTN'T," huffed Faith. "Joshua, don't you dare call them. We're supposed to be a blessing to them, not a curse."

He looked at her with compassion and kissed her forehead. "My poor darling, you're so tired. I'm really sorry." He prayed some more while she dozed. Then he opened his door and stated quietly but firmly, "I'm making that call now."

He returned crestfallen. "No answer. They must be out - Saturday night. I was so sure I should call them."

"You and your wild ideas," she sighed. "Now what?"

He started the car again. "Let's try some nearby towns. Otherwise, we can always check into a jail somewhere, or better still, a mental hospital…" His wife grunted at his feeble attempt at humour.

Every hotel and motel they tried was full. Joshua tried the Santa Rosa number from time to time, but without success. He finally pulled up in the centre of a sleepy little town, baffled and exhausted. Faith opened her eyes and discovered it was already night. She peered through the car window. Across the street was a Catholic Church, and next to it a huge rectory.

"Joshua, I'll drop dead if we don't find a room soon," she moaned. "Couldn't we try that rectory over there? Surely they can help us find something. I just can't face spending the night in this little car, doubled up like a pretzel."

They got out and crossed the street slowly, rehearsing what to say. Joshua checked his wristwatch before ringing the bell, it was nearly 10pm. An outside light came on. The door creaked open but only as far as a safety chain allowed it, revealing a round red face framed by untidy long white hair and a clerical collar. Small pale eyes squinted out at them.

"Excuse us, Father, may we come in? We need some help."

After a pause, the chain came off and the door slowly opened.

"I'm MONSIGNOR Murphy," crackled the priest with a strong Irish accent and some evident bitterness. "I'm de only one here t'night, so make it short. Come into de office." He led the way. The heavy front door closed by itself.

Murphy, at first merely hostile, became increasingly choleric as Joshua explained that they had been led to Santa Rosa by the Lord, that they had left their children with relatives and that they had come on ahead to look for a place to live. Having found no accommodation for the night, they were hoping the Monsignor might possibly help them.

With rising voice and trembling nicotine-stained fingers, the priest soundly rebuked them for irresponsible behaviour. Then he let loose a tirade: "Of course dere's no room - what did you t'ink? This is Memaahrial Day weekend - haven't you heard o' reservations? It was stoopid of you to've come out here at all."

Murphy took a cigarette out and lit it. "An' I'll have ye know I am a very busy man," he continued, spluttering. "D'ye realise, I've buried over one hondred and forrty people, just since Janooary? And here I am, de only one left in de rectory t'night. Everyone else is away off havin' a good time, so don't you be comin' to ME fer any charity!"

The couple sat appalled, unable to think of an appropriate response. At last Joshua cleared his throat and asked with what courtesy he could muster, "Do you know anyone who might take us in for the night? After all, aren't Christians supposed to help one another?"

Murphy rose from his seat and his bloated face turned from red to a pale white. "Are ye seriously suggestin' that I should call a parishioner at ten o'clock of a Saturday night? Absolutely NOT."

Joshua sighed and stood up also, pointing to the telephone. "Would you please let me make a call to Santa Rosa? I'll be happy to pay you for it. We were given a number before we came out here, and I'd like to try it again."

The Irishman blew out a huge cloud of smoke and shook his head in disgust. "Nobody, but NOBODY, would take in a stranger at dis hour..." He turned his face away and coughed hoarsely. "Call if ye like," he threw back at last, "but it's a blessed waste o' time."

Sitting down again, Joshua dialled his contact and this time somebody answered. After explaining why and from where he was calling, he held the phone for a long time. Then he spoke shortly, jotted down some directions and hung up with a triumphant expression.

"Well, Monsignor, we've been invited to spend the night at the home of complete strangers. The Lord certainly looks after those who trust in Him, doesn't He? Here are two dollars for the use of your phone... May the Lord Jesus Christ be with you." Joshua took his wife's hand and they exited past the clergyman. Murphy seemed to be in a state of shock.

The couple felt revived as they skipped down the steps and across the street to the car, arms around each other, with Joshua loudly proclaiming, "Let de dead burry deir dead - all one hondred and forrty of dem."

Brotherly Love

David and Christine welcomed the exhausted travellers with open hearts. They sat the couple down at a table to eat and drink, and waited on them to make them feel at home. All of them instantly warmed to one another and before long they were sitting in the family room having an intense discussion about what it means to belong to Jesus Christ and to follow His voice. There followed a deluge of questions about the Lord and about the Alexanders' experiences in Eau Claire.

A little past one o'clock in the morning, Christine sat up straight, struck by a recollection. With a slight tremor in her voice she confessed, "When I visited my friend in Eau Claire a couple of weeks ago, she told me a lot about belonging to the Lord, but I wasn't really interested in listening to her."

She shook her head and laughed. "She then told me that the Lord would send someone to me within two weeks who would tell me about Himself and how to follow Him by the Holy Spirit. I just realised it was a prophecy, because here you are doing just that! It's weird, really weird... but I do believe every word you've been telling us," she marvelled.

Dave nodded his agreement, then asked, "Why on earth didn't you call us when you first got in? We've been home all evening."

Joshua was perplexed. "But we did - we kept calling you from eight o'clock onwards but there was no answer. We finally got through when we called from the rectory."

"How strange... Oh yes, we were outside barbecuing and must not have heard the phone. But that was really a good thing, since the main reason we decided to invite you in, total strangers that you were, was because you were calling from a rectory! We're Catholics, you see.

"I have to confess something, Joshua. I called Monsignor Murphy after you left, just to make sure that you'd really been there. Boy, did he sound worked up. Why was he so upset?"

Joshua told the story quite colourfully and soon had them all in helpless laughter.

They ended the long day with prayer together, thanking God for having displayed such amazing love. As an afterthought, Faith asked their generous hosts for a Bible and prayed aloud that God would speak to them through it. She opened up the enormous family Bible at random, her eyes being drawn to her right thumb. It was resting under the 35th verse of Matthew's Gospel, chapter 25.

A shiver passed up her spine as she read: **"'For I was hungry and you gave Me something to eat, I was thirsty and you gave Me something to drink, I WAS A STRANGER AND YOU INVITED ME IN.'"**

She swallowed hard and paused for some moments to control her emotions, then continued with the 40th verse: **"'And whatever you did for one of the least of these brothers of Mine, you did for Me.'"**

The little group, complete strangers only three hours earlier, hugged one another in acknowledgment of what God had done and said. With tears in their eyes, Dave and Chris invited their new friends to stay with them as long as they needed, offering them help in finding a home and buying a car.

When Faith and Joshua were shown into the guest bedroom, they had to smile. The pillows and sheets exactly matched their own bed linens. It was the Master's touch to make them feel completely at home.

Dry Bones

"The law from Your mouth is more precious to me than thousands of pieces of silver and gold."
(Psalm 119:72)

Faith turned to her husband and muttered, "Joshua, have you heard anything from the Lord lately?"

He blew out a breath and shook his head forlornly. "Nope."

"I just don't understand it. We've been in Santa Rosa for weeks and we still have no idea what we're doing here. We've been ill... you cut your hands so badly walking into that glass door... and we're not even hearing the Lord's voice. It's dreadful," she complained.

"That's the worst of all," he agreed. "What have we done wrong, anyway? Why doesn't Jesus speak to us any more?"

"If only I knew. Is it Santa Rosa or is it US? In Eau Claire we heard Him so clearly - we even saw Him! He was with us continually. Now it's as if He's vanished. I can't stand it! Is He mad at us or WHAT?" she demanded with mounting frustration. "And now this heat-wave, on top of everything else." [Daytime temperatures had been well over 100 degrees all week.]

Joshua frowned. "All in all, this so-called paradise is becoming more and more like the 'other place' every day."

Faith was not listening, however. She had reached back into the bookcase for their new Bible and was reading it very intently.

"Maybe our predicament is the usual condition of most believers," wondered Joshua. With a sinking feeling, he realised there was nothing they could do about this 'blackout' from Heaven if God did not CHOOSE to speak to them. They had always presumed that anyone could hear from the Lord 'on demand' if he or she only had the faith.

"Dear Father," he prayed, *"We've been so wrong about this. I'm so sorry. The truth is, it's only by Your GRACE that we or anyone else can hear Your voice. And we certainly can't earn and don't deserve Your grace... Lord, please have mercy on us!"*

He felt greatly convicted. Tears came to his eyes as he recognised the pride lurking in their hearts: pride in their ability to hear the Lord whenever HE chose to speak, and pride in the strong faith that HE had given them. Joshua felt ashamed and bowed his head in his hands. *"Forgive us, please, Father, and start speaking to us again..."*

Faith broke the silence. "Sweetheart, do you know what I've been reading? Where the Bible just opened up to?"

"Let me guess: **'Judas went away and hanged himself**[15]**,'** and **'Go and do likewise**[16]**'**?" He grimaced.

"Not quite," she laughed, "but you're warm. Look here, in Ezekiel chapter 37." She handed him the open Bible.

Joshua read about a valley filled with very dry bones, and came to the Lord's question, **"Son of man, can these bones live?"** followed by Ezekiel's reply, **"O Sovereign Lord, You alone know."**

He looked up at her in surprise. "But that's exactly what I was sensing - that unless the Lord speaks, we can't possibly hear His voice and we're as good as dead - as useless as those dry bones. I do feel really dry inside, so dry in my spirit. Don't you?"

She nodded and came and sat by him on the floor. They read on together.

"Then He said to me, 'Prophesy to these bones and say to them, "Dry bones, hear the word of the LORD! This is what the Sovereign Lord says to these bones: I will make breath enter you, and you will come to life. I will attach tendons to you and make flesh come upon you and cover you with skin; I will put breath in you, and you will come to life. Then you will know that I am the Lord."'"

"So it's only by God's Breath, by His SPIRIT, that we can ever come back to life," she commented.

"God is really speaking to us through this passage," rejoiced her husband. "It's wonderful. Did you just open up the Bible anywhere, at random?"

"Yes, and it fell open to this page. But first I prayed that He would speak to us, just as He did at Chris and Dave's house. Look, the passage even says, **'Hear the word of the LORD!'**"

"That's our answer, then. We'll ask God to guide us and teach us - and speak to us - by His WRITTEN Word."

---

[15] *Matthew 27:5*
[16] *Luke 10:37*

On the Mountain of the Lord...

One sizzling day in August, the couple were driving homeward over the steep mountain roads between Napa Valley and Sonoma when the engine overheated. Joshua pulled over exactly at the crest of the mountain pass. After lifting up the car's bonnet, he sat down with Faith under a shady tree to wait for the radiator to cool down and stop steaming. Grapes were ripening on the vines, birds were singing and the combined scents of pine needles and wild flowers wafted all about them.

"Perhaps He'll talk to us today, up here on the mountain!" they said in unison, and laughed.

To be honest, they hardly expected to hear anything after two months of Heavenly silence, yet here came their Beloved's voice, as clear as ever. *"It's time for you to move again,"* each of them heard in their hearts. *"Go south, down the California coast - to San Diego."*

God Himself made the way for them. Their landlady allowed them to break their lease without a murmur, and their stuff was packed and shipped in no time at all. Only four days later the Alexanders were installed in a new home in San Diego (an all-time record for them). They had certainly been ready to leave the valley of dry bones.

...It Will Be Provided!

"I delight greatly in the LORD; my soul rejoices in my God. For He has clothed me with garments of salvation and arrayed me in a robe of righteousness."

(Isaiah 61:10a)

A couple of weeks after this lightning move, Faith was distressed to find that their daughter had outgrown all her good clothes. She asked the Lord in prayer if she should go shopping and spend their scarce 'plastic' money on some dresses for Jacqueline, who was about to start second grade.

"No," He replied, *"I have a better idea. Trust Me!"*

On the first Sunday morning in September, the Alexanders attended an open-air worship service at a park in a nearby town. Afterwards a woman announced, "There are boxes of things here donated by members of the fellowship for anyone who feels led of the Lord to take them. Please come and help yourselves." The family of five held back until everyone else had had their pick and dispersed.

The same woman beckoned to them and welcomed them warmly. She studied Jacqueline and then gave Faith a broad smile. "Sister, these are for you from the hand of the Lord. Please take them ALL." Several pretty dresses in different colours and styles lay there, looking as if they had never been worn. They fitted Jacqueline perfectly, and next morning she started school with a closet full of new dresses.

The whole family loved San Diego: its climate, parks, seashore and above all *Sea World* where they frequently spent their afternoons using an annual family pass (costing a mere $34).

Joshua and Faith, still unemployed, became very active in Bible studies and prayer meetings almost every morning while the children were in school. Everything else they attempted, however, came to absolutely nothing.

One of these Bible studies was led by Father Daniel, a Catholic priest who had made friends with the couple. Before long the meetings were overcrowded with churchgoers who were seriously interested in following the Lord as His disciples. Moreover, at the end of Sunday services Father Dan was now calling people up to the altar to receive Jesus Christ as their personal Lord and Saviour and to be filled with the Holy Spirit. This priest's passionate appeals brought many hundreds in his parish to a rich, intimate relationship with the Lord Jesus.

In early spring of 1977 the Alexanders attended a one-day 'Revival' meeting in La Jolla, under the leadership of a Franciscan priest who was a very gifted Bible teacher. The hall was filled to capacity.

Father James began by reading several Scriptures[17] regarding the terrible fate - unending torment - awaiting those who refuse God's invitation to be saved through trusting in His Son, Christ Jesus. The priest explained that the day of God's wrath was coming very soon and that whoever was not spiritually prepared for that Day would suffer endless pain and loss.

Unexpectedly he put on a recording of the first part of the *Dies Irae* ('The Day of Wrath') from Verdi's *Requiem Mass,* and sat down.

Four titanic chords crashed out of the speakers around the hall, followed by a raging fortissimo of winds, trumpets and strings and a chorus wailing, **"Day of Wrath, Day of Wrath!"**

---

[17] *2 Thessalonians 1:7-10, 2 Peter 3:10, and Revelation 14:19-20, 20:11-15*

Again came the four chords of doom, this time separated by the pounding of a bass drum, and again came the trumpets and the anguished soprano chorus.

Joshua's eyes widened and his scalp and neck prickled with fear. His whole body began to quake as he felt terror coming over him. The music, which was unfamiliar to him, surged onward. It seemed to Joshua that he was now suspended over a huge open abyss, and that he could actually hear the roaring of flames and the howling and screaming of condemned souls.

"Is this a glimpse of Hell?" he shuddered inwardly as he ground his teeth with anguish.

The music quietened. Voices intoned**, "Day of Wrath, Day of Wrath,"** with menacing runs on the woodwinds, followed by the eerie, unmistakable sound of approaching footsteps in the music.

"What great trembling when the Judge comes - He whose sentence shall be binding!" hissed the chorus.

A single trumpet sounded out, and a second one, and then many others summoning every soul to judgment before the Great Throne. The trumpets grew louder and louder to a piercing, almost unbearable climax.

There was sudden and complete silence. Joshua sat frozen with horror, overwhelmed by the conviction of his sinfulness.

Father James stood up and re-read the words[18], **"If anyone's name was not found written in the Book of Life, he was thrown into the lake of fire."** He paused.

"I have this simple question to ask each of you," he continued at last. "Is YOUR name written in that Book? Only through Jesus can your sins be forgiven and your name entered in the Book. Then you will be safe on that Day.

"Please understand this; Jesus died on the Cross in your place, taking your sins on Himself - ALL of them, past, present and future! The Lamb of God shed His precious, sinless Blood for YOU. Although Jesus died and went into the grave, He rose again from the dead to prove that He is Christ the Lord, our Divine Saviour. So now turn away from your sins and repent - CHANGE! Then you will be able to freely receive His forgiveness and enjoy His wonderful gift of eternal life.

---

[18] *Revelation 20:15*

"There is no other way: '**Salvation is found in no one else, for there is no other name under heaven given to men by which we must be saved.**'[19] It is all by grace, through faith in Him."

Hearing these words sent Joshua into a flood of grateful tears. He realised at last what his Lord had done for him on the Cross, dying the most painful, agonising death to save him from the unspeakable torment of eternity in the Lake of Fire.

At that moment the Cross became a glorious reality for Joshua. He recognised that it was truly the focal point of God's love for the human race. A Heavenly transaction took place in his heart as he embraced the truth that the just penalty of having to die an everlasting death for his sins had been atoned for and erased by Jesus. In place of death, God had mercifully granted Joshua everlasting life.

Absolute Surrender

"Offer your bodies as living sacrifices... Do not conform any longer to the pattern of this world, but be transformed by the renewing of your mind. Then you will be able to test and approve what God's will is - His good, pleasing and perfect will."
(Romans 12:1-2)

"Would you ever go back to the kind of job you had before in Maryland?" asked Fritz. He and his wife Joanne had just finished supper *chez Alexander* (beef-hearts, as usual).

Joshua melodramatically looked up to Heaven. "Father, surely You wouldn't put me back in that work again, would You?" Warm-hearted laughter erupted around the room.

"Seriously, Fritz, it would be really hard. Not only have I been away from engineering work so long, but I also love being at home with Faith, praying and studying the Bible together, and of course having lots of time to spend with the children. But still - if Father told me clearly to go back into technical work - I certainly would."

As Joshua said these last words, he felt a subtle shift in his heart. *"Lord, are You giving me the desire to be an engineer again?"* he wondered.

---

[19] *Acts 4:12*

Faith was unable to sleep that night. She tried to 'cast all her anxiety' upon the Lord[20] but instead alarming images came into her mind of what might soon happen if God did not come to their rescue.

"Lord Jesus, I don't see how even You can save us this time. Our lease expires at the end of May, in only six weeks - and then we'll have no place to live. We have practically no credit left or assets to sell, as You know.

"How much longer are we to live like paupers, Lord?" she questioned silently. *"Why is our life so different from everyone else's? Our life is so unsettled - why are we always moving?"*

Into her mind came a vivid image of herself and the three children trudging after Joshua on a dusty highway, all of them in rags and with bare feet, without food, shelter or even destination. It was a terrifying prospect. She lay there in the darkness rigid with anxiety, her heart pounding.

As if from a great distance she caught the faint whisper of the Shepherd's voice: **"Suppose it IS My perfect will for you to be homeless and to wander barefoot in rags on the highway? Can you accept that?"**

Her heart nearly stopped. Had she heard Him correctly? Could He be serious? Violent protests came into her mind: *"No, no, no!"* She did NOT want to be homeless or wander barefoot in rags. She struggled to silence and hide her rebellious thoughts from the Lord. She tossed around in bed and wept bitter tears. If it WERE God's perfect will, how could she say anything but *"Yes"*? What choice did she have? Everything in her, however, was shouting, *"No!"*

"My dear daughter, can you offer Me your life as a living sacrifice?"

"Oh Lord, this is so hard for me. Help me! Please make me more willing - I am willing to be willing - but only You can change my heart. I need Your grace to say 'yes' to this..."

The Holy Spirit moved in as a refining fire, causing the ugly dross of her worldly objections to come up to the surface where He could dispose of them, one by one. He demolished all of her arguments - that it wasn't fair, that it wasn't loving, that it wasn't right - with one undeniable truth: that her life did not belong to her because God had saved it at least seven times in the past.

Faith surrendered at last, praying, *"Yes, Lord, if this is Your perfect will, I agree to it."*

---

[20] *"Cast all your anxiety upon Him because He cares for you."* (1 Peter 5:7)

She felt empty and shattered as if her soul had been burned up, leaving only a heap of ashes. Exhausted by the ordeal yet still unable to sleep, she lay on the bed staring into the semi-darkness.

There was a sound of bare feet pattering along the hall. She listened, motionless. A tiny warm body climbed into bed and snuggled up next to her, and she heard a whisper in her ear: *"Jesus ...loves ...you, ...Mommy!"*

A few seconds later, little Andrew left as abruptly as he had come, having spoken the first complete sentence of his life.

It was like the visit of an angel, bearing Faith a precious message from the heart of God. Reassured of His immense love, Faith fell into a deep sleep until morning.

Housecleaning

"I was awake a lot last night too," responded Joshua at daybreak after his wife had described her extraordinary struggle and Andy's amazing words. "God began to deal with me about all those books and articles we've been carrying around ever since we left Chevy Chase. He asked me, *'Why are you holding on to them?'* Of course I couldn't think of any good reason, so now I'm going to throw everything out that doesn't glorify the Lord Jesus." He put on some clothes and headed out to the garage.

Opening up one box after another, he sifted out 'truth' from 'half-truths' (lies). When the children woke up they trooped in to see what the commotion was about. They giggled at the huge mess their father was making in the garage (and how happy he was making the mess).

"I've had doubts about this stuff for a long time. It feels SO GOOD to be rid of it all," he declared, dumping armloads of spiritual 'junk' into the trash can.

A little later during the clamour of breakfast, Faith was surprised to hear the Lord speaking quietly to her heart: *"Joshua's new job is in the morning paper. Go and buy it."*

After dropping the children off at their various schools, the couple bought a copy of the daily newspaper. As they were driving up the hill back to their house, Faith took out the classified section and opened it. Her eyes went directly to a large box advertisement: 'RECRUITERS IN SAN DIEGO THIS WEEK'. The ad was for a large company seeking engineers in many areas of technical specialisation, and it listed a phone number for the San Diego Hilton Hotel (five minutes from their door).

"Joshua, here it is!" declared Faith. "I'm sure of it - all the bells are ringing." She offered the paper to her surprised husband.

He parked the car and switched off the ignition. Looking closely at the list of specialised engineers, his face fell. "Faith, it doesn't mention anything I'm qualified for…" He paused. "But my heart is telling me - no, urging me - that this is my job. Look - today's the last day to call up for an interview. Let's go inside and pray."

A Heavenly *'Yes!'* was given, and Joshua called the Hilton.

After some discussion he shrugged and hung up the phone. "The recruiter said he didn't think they needed anyone with my speciality, though he asked me about my background (just to be polite, I think), and offered to pass on the information. He wasn't a bit encouraging. We may both be wrong about this."

After lunch the couple were praying silently. Eventually Joshua asked, *"Just so we can know it's really You, Father, would You please give us some kind of a sign that this job is Your will? Thank You in Jesus' Name. Amen."*

The very instant Faith added her *"Amen,"* the phone rang. She quickly went to answer it and passed the receiver to her husband, barely containing her excitement. It was the company representative calling.

Joshua's smile broadened as he heard, "I have some good news for you, Dr Alexander. Seattle really surprised me, they just called me back to say they're VERY interested in your qualifications. Our interviewer is flying in on Friday and would like to meet with you at two o'clock, here in the Hilton Hotel. Can you make it?"

"Sure, that'll be fine." Joshua gave his address for an application form, and hung up with a smile.

Then he frowned. "I'll have to work on my résumé now – what can I say about these two years without work, Faith? And what if the recruiter asks me a lot of technical questions?"

His face cleared. "I guess the Holy Spirit will take care of those hurdles, if this is my job."

Walking by Faith

'Now faith is being sure of what we hope for and certain of what we do not see.'
(Hebrews 11:1)

The company interviewer had a craggy face with a kind expression. As he read carefully through the application form, Joshua was reminding the Lord to please take care of the two years of unemployment and the technical questions.

"Well, Dr Alexander, I see you've taken a two-year sabbatical, and at your own expense. That's outstanding! It's exactly what I've been recommending to our technical managers for years. I believe you're just the kind of executive material our company is looking for. I'm sure we have a place for you." He sat back and smiled.

Joshua was stunned. Having experienced one rejection after another for two years, he hardly knew how to respond to this unexpected development. He pulled himself together. Taking the initiative, he asked questions about the company and about the life in the Pacific Northwest. After this opening there were of course no technical questions. The years of wandering had by some divine magic been transferred from the 'minus' to the 'plus' column. Joshua left the interview amazed at how the Lord had gone ahead of him and taken care of his 'adversaries'.

Monday morning brought devastating news, however. The interviewer phoned to say that the federal government had just cancelled a military contract affecting hundreds of engineers. The company was having to absorb them into other programs and had imposed an indefinite freeze on hiring any more engineers.

The recruiter apologised profusely and begged Joshua to keep his company in mind before accepting any other offer. He asked him to call after two more weeks in case the situation improved. "Dr Alexander, I want you to know that you are JUST the man we need here."

Joshua's renewed interest in engineering made him eager to find work in his field but he found himself in a quandary. Whenever he thought of looking through the classified ads, God seemed to slap his wrist with displeasure. Having made his application to the company of God's choice, Joshua was not being permitted to approach any other. All he could do now was 'watch and pray'.

The couple waited patiently on the Lord, giving themselves to prayer for several hours a day. One morning they were praying as usual side by side, cross-legged on the sitting room floor. Joshua had an unusually powerful sense of God's presence. He perceived the Father's arms reaching around the two of them, and he actually felt a physical touch on his shoulder.

His heart nearly burst as the Father said, *"Do not fear! It is My will that you work up in Seattle. I want you to be part of My flock there. Only trust Me, and exercise your faith in Me."*

Relief overwhelmed his wife when Joshua shared this encounter. The words activated faith in both their hearts, a supernatural, unshakeable faith given by the Holy Spirit.

A month went by without any outward sign of encouragement and the Alexanders' life was rapidly approaching a *dénouement*. Their credit lines were almost exhausted and their house had already been rented out to another family as of June 1st – in less than two weeks. Where were they to go? What were they to do? The Lord was telling them nothing. They prayed almost continuously to maintain their faith and peace.

On May 20th (a Friday), Joshua petitioned God: *"Dear Heavenly Father, You promised never to forsake us and never to abandon us, and You made us promise to tell nobody but YOU about our needs. Now, please, would You supply them?*

"You know we need $150 by Monday in order to cover this month's cheques. (And next month... well, Lord, I guess next month You'll allow me to earn a paycheque!) But meanwhile, we thank You so much that You've already arranged to provide us the money, and that it will bring You glory through Your Son, our Lord Jesus Christ. We look forward to seeing how You'll do it, Father!"

Joshua walked down to the local grocery store next morning. When he returned he announced with great fanfare, "Hear ye, hear ye! I want everyone to hear this. I just wrote out a cheque for groceries that left 3 cents in our account. Those 3 cents, together with the 11 cents we have left in cash, make up our entire fortune: FOURTEEN CENTS. Also, hear this! We have zero credit left. In other words, dear family, we're completely broke...

"So," he continued, smiling at one shocked face after the other, "we have no choice but to lean totally on the Lord for our needs. He is mighty, and He is faithful! I want to remind you all that exactly a year ago today the Lord sold our house in Eau Claire, just as He'd promised. Dear family, expect some wonderful miracles from our faithful Father in Heaven.

"In fact, here's one little miracle that happened as I was coming back up the hill. I found an unopened package of liverwurst lying in the middle of the road. I couldn't find anyone to claim it, so here, let's enjoy it." He roared with delight.

Faith laughed with him, but she secretly thought her husband had finally gone off his rocker. The children laughed because their parents were laughing. And God was (probably) laughing because He already knew what He was going to do.

The telephone rang before they had finished putting away the scant handful of grocery items.

It was Rob, their most sceptical friend from the church. "Joshua, I have no idea what your financial situation is, and in asking around it seems nobody else does either. But a thought has been going through my mind lately that things must be very tight for you, even though it's none of my business.

"Anyhow, this morning I was writing out cheques for my monthly bills as usual. When I was done, I found $100 left over in our bank account. I went through it all again and again. I have no idea where it came from - we NEVER have anything left at the end of the month.

"I think - no, I KNOW - that the Lord wants you to have this extra money. He's been after me all morning to call you, like someone kicking me in the pants. So there, that's it. Can you use some money right now?"

"Can we use some money? Rob, we've been praying that the Lord would supply our need - and here you are, the specific answer to our prayer," answered Joshua with tears in his eyes.

"I'm really touched to hear that," Rob confided. "I've been pretty hard-nosed about the whole question of hearing God's voice, and you know how I've argued with you whenever you talked about it. But today, for the first time in my life, I understand! I know for certain that HE told me to give you the money. I'm so blessed to be the answer to your prayer."

The Alexanders were astounded to receive money from someone as a result of prayer. Joshua thanked the King of kings for the gift, and then reminded Him of the $50 still needed. The Saturday mail brought nothing but more bills. How was the Lord God going to provide the balance?

When the phone rang on Sunday afternoon the two of them were surprised to hear the voice of their beloved friend Father Meinen calling from Eau Claire. They hadn't been in touch with each other since Christmas, but because it was the 22nd anniversary of his ordination as a priest, Myron wanted to share his joy with them.

They were about to hang up the phone when their friend stated offhandedly, "Oh by the way, I administer a caretaker fund for the parish and it has some extra money in it. I am being led by God to send you $100. Do you happen to need any money right now?"

For the second time in two days, the couple shed tears over the telephone. With a grateful heart Joshua mailed out the cheques - just in time.

Two days later an express envelope arrived from Eau Claire. It contained a cashier's cheque for $175. The priest and another friend had added some personal funds as an extra gift.

Joshua was taken aback to receive the additional $125 (not that he was complaining). He and Faith prayed to the Provider Himself.

His heart swelled when he heard the Lord say, *"The extra money is for you to fly up to Seattle for your interview this week."*

The next morning (Wednesday) Joshua packed his suitcase and made a reservation to fly to Seattle at 2:30 that afternoon. His wife was amazed. There had been no indication that he was about to be interviewed. She looked at the packed bag and prayed for a mighty miracle, then asked her husband to explain himself.

"My love, this is a perfect opportunity to exercise our faith and witness God's faithfulness. It's really quite simple. I have to have my interview (and job offer) in Seattle by tomorrow latest, otherwise I can't sign up for employment on Friday. And unless I sign up on Friday, the company can't arrange for the movers to come in time to pick up our stuff next Tuesday, which is the first workday after the Memorial Day holiday weekend. If you recall, Tuesday is May 31st, the day our lease runs out – the last day we can be in this house. *Ergo*, I HAVE to leave today or it'll be too late.

"That's why I reserved the flight. I'm sure the Lord has set it up this way to pull off a last-minute rescue again. I'm just going along with HIS plan. You'll see - He is so faithful!"

Faith tried vainly to follow his logic but gave up.

By 11 o'clock that morning, however, Joshua's faith had slipped a notch or two. He decided to call his recruiter ally in Seattle to find out what, if anything, might be happening.

"Dr Alexander, how good to hear your voice again. I thought by now you'd surely have accepted one of many other offers. It's very good of you to hang on, but unfortunately nothing has changed up here. Frankly, I have to advise you to GIVE UP on our company. The only possible lead I ever had for you was with a Mr Landis, but he's been away on a very long assignment. I'm really, really sorry."

Disappointed, the pair sat down again to pray. The Lord was unmoved. He had not changed His mind - the Alexanders would be moving to Seattle as promised.

The phone rang a half-hour later. "Hello, is this Dr Alexander? Oh good! This is Jerry Landis in Seattle. I'm glad to find you in." Joshua was speechless.

Landis continued. "I just got back to my office this morning after two months in Alaska and found your résumé sitting on the very top of my in-basket. I believe we have an excellent match for your qualifications. I've just this moment cleared it for you to come up for an interview, in spite of our hiring freeze - if you're still interested. You are? Oh, that's great.

"There's only one hitch," he pressed on. "With the long weekend coming up, the ONLY day I can see you is tomorrow. Could you possibly leave San Diego on such short notice? It means flying up this afternoon..."

"No problem at all, Mr Landis," grinned Joshua, finding his voice.

"Really? That's excellent! I'll tell Personnel to phone you at once with the details. They'll take very good care of you. I look forward to meeting you tomorrow..."

Joshua hung up the phone with a howl of triumph and hugged his wife with all his might. The promised call came in from Personnel and the couple celebrated over a lunch of soup and liverwurst (plus three courses of thanksgiving) before driving to the airport.

At the gate before boarding his flight Joshua poured out his heart in praise: *"Who is like You, Lord Jesus? What great things You've done - how great You are! Now Lord, please bring us to your flock in Seattle as You promised, and glorify Your Name..."*

Joshua allowed his pocket New Testament to fall open in his hands as he prayed, and his eyes now fell on the words[21]: **'By faith the people passed through the Red Sea as on dry land... By faith the walls of Jericho fell.'**

God's Plan Unfolds

"See, I have placed before you an open door that no one can shut."
(Revelation 3:8a)

In Seattle the next morning, Joshua was astounded to hear that interviews had been scheduled in three different technical areas. He felt he was dreaming when, by one o'clock, he had THREE job offers in hand at the highest salary each group could afford (since they were competing for him). The company's hiring freeze had been overridden, and of course there were no technical questions. The door was as wide open as every previous door had been tightly shut.

Joshua had not expected to have to choose among three outstanding job offers. In prayer, the Holy Spirit clearly directed him to accept the position in solar energy development, and he duly signed up for employment on Friday to start work on June 1st. The company arranged for movers to come on Tuesday the 31st and the Alexanders vacated their house just in time. It all went 'exactly according to plan'.

The Almighty Father had fulfilled His promise to provide a job in Seattle, and in so doing He met all of the family's needs. He demonstrated His mastery over every detail of their life by lifting them out of an impossible situation at the very last moment when they were down to their very last pennies.

"My soul will rejoice in the LORD and delight in His salvation. My whole being will exclaim, 'Who is like You, O LORD? You rescue the poor from those too strong for them...'"
(Psalm 35:9,10)

---

[21] *Hebrews 11:29-30*

9

Diamonds in the Rough
(August 1977 - June 1978)

"As you come to Him, the living Stone - rejected by men but chosen by God and precious to Him - you also, like living stones, are being built into a spiritual house to be a holy priesthood, offering spiritual sacrifices acceptable to God through Jesus Christ."
(2 Peter 2:1-5)

Eight weeks after their arrival in Seattle the Alexanders were still praying about how to find the 'flock' God had promised. *"Heavenly Father,"* Faith prayed, *"how shall we recognise this church? What do You consider to be important in a church?"*

The answer came in four short words: ***"Acts two forty-two."*** She turned to the second chapter of the Acts of the Apostles and meditated on verse 42: **"They devoted themselves to the apostles' teaching and to the fellowship, to the breaking of bread and to prayer."**

The next morning Joshua was about to leave for work when he heard something from Heaven. It seemed trivial yet it caught his attention. He shared it with his wife as they kissed goodbye: "The Lord just said that the letters ***'ABC'*** are significant to the church He has chosen for us. I don't know what it means. When I asked Him to clarify, He said (as usual), ***'Trust Me!'***"

During the course of the day, a colleague at work suggested to Joshua that he might like to try a nearby Baptist church. At about the same time, a neighbour dropped by their home and told his wife about this same Baptist church. On the strength of these two 'witnesses', the Alexanders visited the church the next Sunday morning. The children were directed to their respective Sunday-school classes and their parents went to the pastor's introductory class on Christian foundations.

Faith and Joshua were electrified to hear the pastor teaching on the New Testament Church and its hallmark - the practice of Acts 2:42. He emphasised that the four aspects of this verse were equally important to that Baptist church. Moments later he mentioned that the church was part of the American Baptist Convention.

Joshua nudged his wife's elbow and smiled happily. Faith, catching on that the church was an 'ABC' church, almost laughed aloud for joy. They were 'home'.

ABC might as well have stood for 'All Believers Church' since the Alexanders enjoyed fellowship with Christians of almost every background (including even a few Baptists), united in a common desire to know, follow and serve the Lord Jesus. Every Sunday the worship services included prayer, systematic Bible teaching, Communion and fellowship. This vibrant community wholeheartedly embraced the Alexanders as 'part of the family', and on September 16th - Joshua's fifth anniversary of entering God's Kingdom - he and Faith were baptised by full immersion.

A Christmas Surprise Party

"Trust in the LORD with all your heart and lean not on your own understanding; in all your ways acknowledge Him, and He will make your paths straight."
(Proverbs 3:5-6)

The new job in Seattle brought the family some longed-for financial stability, but things remained extremely tight. At least Joshua could now cover the monthly interest payments, and in some months he even made a tiny dent in the loan balance. The couple tried not to think how many years it would take to pay off their debt mountain at this rate.

In mid-December Joshua travelled to Washington DC to represent his employer at a three-day conference. While he was gone Faith had a disconcerting thought, that he would hear about another job during the trip.

Fantastic Adventures In Trusting Him

As soon as he returned home (late at night, and before he had even shut the front door) Faith questioned him as gently as she could: "What happened on your trip, honey? Anything significant?" Her weary husband put down his suitcase and kissed her. He shrugged and shook his head.

"Think, Joshua! Wasn't there ANYTHING unusual?" (She did not want to lead him but could not help herself.)

He sat down heavily. "Well yes, there was," he said at length. "I met a colleague at the conference who recently left our company to work for a new research institute in Colorado. He cornered me at breakfast yesterday and virtually ordered me to apply for a job there. It was actually quite embarrassing."

"Darling, I thought something like that had happened - let's pray about it, please? Right now? I believe it's important."

In prayer, Joshua was surprised to hear the Lord directing him to send his résumé to Colorado. He updated it next morning and mailed it with a cover letter. At the end of the day the couple prayed again because they had a strong sense that God had more to say. Joshua's conversation with the Lord was truly startling.

"Lord Jesus, assuming a job does come out of this application, will You want us to leave here at the end of the school year, early next summer?"

"No, not in the summer."

"Oh? Then when, Lord?"

"Do you trust Me enough to cross the mountains in winter?"

"Yes I do, but You know how Faith is, Lord - she hates going by car through mountains, especially in the snow and ice..."

"You leave her to Me. Are YOU willing to trust Me for the trip to Denver with your family, crossing the Rockies in winter?"

"Yes Lord, I do trust you."

"All right then. I want you to leave Seattle on My birthday."

"WHAT? On Christmas Day? That's only five days from now! You're saying we should leave for Denver without any job offer in hand? Can You possibly mean that, Lord?"

"Yes, that's exactly what I mean. Just trust Me and I will lead you."

Diamonds in the Rough

Joshua forced himself to share this unpalatable news with his unsuspecting wife. "...And that's how it went, my love. Quite a bombshell, isn't it?" He looked at her hollow-eyed, seeking any flicker of encouragement in her face, but it was pale with shock.

Faith stared back at him, her mind racing. At last she found her tongue. "But this means that you'd have to come back to Seattle after the children and I are settled in Denver, doesn't it?" (He nodded.) The enormity of this idea crushed her like a dead weight.

"Oh, Joshua, this is dreadful! And I've just realised something else: if you quit your job in Seattle within the first year, you'll have to reimburse the company for all the moving expenses they paid for. Isn't that right?"

"It is," he nodded miserably.

"Are you certain this is what the Lord is saying? To leave for Denver... this week?"

Joshua got up from the sofa and began pacing the room. "Yes, sweetheart, I'm as certain of this as anything I've ever heard from the Lord." He turned to face her. "Don't you have ANY confirmation in your heart? If not, I must be dreadfully confused. God has always given us complete unity and agreement in these things."

His wife looked down at the floor and passed a trembling hand over her forehead. "Well..." she frowned unhappily, "yes, I have to admit my spirit does witness and confirm everything you have said. Still, we've got to keep praying. Maybe this is only some kind of test? You know, to see if we're willing?"

She raised her eyes after a few moments and groaned, "No, this is for real! *O God, what have we done to deserve this? We've only just settled here and now You're having us move AGAIN?*" She buried her face in her hands.

Joshua came and stood by his sobbing wife, gently stroking her head. "Do you think you could stand being out there in Denver, alone with the children?"

"I don't know..."

"But surely it won't be more than a couple of... well, a FEW weeks at most, before a job comes through. Then I'll pay the company back somehow. Maybe my salary will go up or something?"

His wife straightened up and she put on a very brave face. "If God is sending us, He must have a good reason for it, and He'll give us the grace to see it through. He always does." She clasped his hands in hers.

Joshua recovered a little of his optimism. "You're right. And if it is NOT His idea, we'll trust that He will stop us from going! OK then, assuming that we are leaving, let's make a list of everything that needs to be taken care of." He found a pen and paper and sat down to write.

"There! That's quite a handful even for God to pull off in a few days." He handed Faith the list and sat back with a long sigh.

"Joshua, we have to agree, if all these things have been accomplished in the next four days, by this Saturday, we'll leave on the fifth day - Christmas Day. (Oh, Lord, what an idea…)

"But if even ONE of these items has not been taken care of, we'll have to conclude that NONE of it is of the Lord – and that we've been misled. Then we'll stay put. All right?"

"All right. Yes, that's good, but with one more proviso: before we go ahead with anything at all, our pastor has to agree that this move is of the Lord, and He has to give us his witness in the Holy Spirit and also his blessing," said Joshua with sudden relief. He even felt a little enthusiasm now that they had a working strategy.

He looked at her with curiosity. "By the way, sweetheart, CAN you stand driving over all those mountains in winter?"

She gave a nervous little laugh. "The Lord knows what a coward I am - but He seems to have done a miracle in my heart, rather like the time when He changed your heart about getting a technical job. I have His peace, and I'm sure He'll keep us perfectly safe."

The Alexanders' pastor was most obliging: he came over that same evening even though it was getting quite late. After some discussion and prayer with the couple, he confirmed (with regret) that the Lord was indeed calling them to leave for Denver, and at once. He blessed them in prayer and gave each of them a warm hug, full of compassion.

By Saturday (Christmas Eve) the Lord had successfully helped the Alexanders to deal with every item on their list: terminating their lease; finding homes for eight newly weaned puppies; selling their car, furniture and freezer; and buying a reliable used station wagon with a trailer-hitch. The car belonged to their Christian neighbours who asked if they might also adopt the Alexanders' dog (the last item on the list, and the one causing the most heartache).

Late in the evening, Joshua was wrestling with the leftover bits and boxes of their household, trying to cram them into a rented trailer. He looked up and saw a family from their church arriving with armloads of gifts. Christmas had not been cancelled after all! The whoops and shrieks and claps of delight from the seven-, five- and three-year-olds as they opened their packages were like music to the ears of these thoughtful friends (not to mention the parents).

After the Christmas morning service, this church - where the Alexanders had worshipped for a mere four months - surprised them with a goodbye party and presented them with a cash gift that was more than enough to cover their travel expenses. These precious friends embraced the family and sent them off with prayers for God's guidance, protection and blessing.

As the car and trailer heaved out of the church parking lot, five-year-old Ricky cheered his sorrowing parents with the words, "God ALWAYS takes good care of us. I know everything will work out okay in Colorado - the Broncos are such a great football team!"

The trip was far from ordinary. Although the weather had started out quite clear, huge storm clouds and snow flurries were soon chasing after the Alexanders. They pushed on as far as they could, well up into the Blue Mountains of Oregon, and stopped for the night in Pendleton.

By early Monday morning it was clear again, but while they were checking out of the motel the desk clerk remarked, "It's REAL good you're gettin' along now 'cos there's one BIG blizzard comin' up fast outa the west – it's expected here later today! You couldn't-a timed it better, 'cos we just got through havin' three days o' BAD freezin' rain."

The Lord had assured Joshua and Faith that He would provide them with a window of good weather, but this was cutting it very fine.

On the third day, however, the travellers experienced gale-force winds along the interstate highway in Wyoming. They were confronted by a massive overhead sign fluttering like a handkerchief in the wind, repeatedly flashing the message: "WARNING: SEVERE WINDS AHEAD! TRUCKS AND VEHICLES WITH TRAILERS AVOID NEXT 100 MILES."

Without a word, Joshua slowed down and stopped on the hard shoulder just ahead of the next exit. Looking out of the side windows he and his family were shocked to see the roadside bushes and reeds being completely flattened by the violent wind.

"Joshua, what are we going to do?" moaned Faith, pointing to the map. "Leaving the interstate will mean adding hours and hours of extra driving to our journey."

"I guess so," he muttered, "but we can't risk losing the trailer in this windstorm. Just listen to it howling." The heavy station wagon and full trailer were lurching back and forth from the buffeting of the wind. The children clutched anxiously at their parents from behind the front seat.

"But didn't the Lord promise to keep us safe on this trip? He asked us to trust Him," insisted Faith. "Let's pray and ask Him what to do."

"Okay guys, let's pray... *Lord Jesus, which way should we go? What should we do? Please tell us.*" They all waited silently on the Lord.

A gentle response came at once to Joshua's heart: **"*I'm going straight on. What about you?*"**

He swallowed. *"You're continuing on the interstate, Lord Jesus? I guess we'll follow You then..."* He shared this leading with the others.

"The Lord was telling me the same thing," chimed in Faith, "and He also reminded me about how He calmed the wind and the waves in the Gospels. We'll have to ask Him to do that for us now..." She eyed her husband uncertainly. The children were speechless, wondering what would happen next.

"No, I believe He wants US to do it - He wants us to command the wind - and then He will let loose His divine power. Remember how He rebuked the disciples for not having enough faith?"

Joshua took a deep breath and cried: *"WIND! We command you to be STILL until we reach Denver, in the authority and name of our Lord, Jesus Christ!"*

The others all shouted, *"Amen!"*

He reached out his hand and put the car in gear. "All right then, let's get going..."

"Dad!" squealed Jacqueline who was almost eight years old. "Look out there at the bushes - they're all standing straight up! God answered our prayer real fast - it's a MIRACLE." The whole family shouted with relief and joy as they sped off down the deserted highway.

The Lord had indeed gone ahead of them. That entire day there was not another breath of wind, even when they rolled into Denver late at night.

The Alexanders located a rental house next day. It backed onto a large park in Arvada, an attractive north-western suburb of Denver. The landlord offered to let them move into the house the same evening, even though he still had a few things to finish up.

Joshua went to visit his ex-colleague at the institute. This man rose to the occasion and gave him a tour, after getting over the shock of seeing Joshua walk in unannounced. He introduced him to three department heads, each of whom had job openings. During the visit, however, Joshua's heart almost failed him when he overheard someone say that literally thousands of applications were pouring in to fill just a couple of dozen positions.

"What have I done?" he thought to himself in horror.

Joshua flew back to Seattle on the first day of 1978 after a wrenching farewell from his wife and little ones. They had no idea how long they would be apart, nor where Joshua would even be living - without family, home or even a car. He went straight from SeaTac Airport to the Sunday evening church service by taxi, and reported how wonderfully the Lord had cared for them all.

At once a friend took him in for a few days. After that the pastor and his wife invited him to move in with them, offering him the use of a car that had just been donated to the church. Joshua thanked the Lord for having planted him in this exceptional fellowship with such loving and generous people.

Along with the divine provision, Joshua's daily life was full of difficulties and challenges: a job that was now obviously going nowhere, an uncertain future, a greater-than-ever financial burden, and of course the unremitting pain and constant embarrassment of being cut off from his family. Too often he was approached by (well-meaning) brothers who pointed a finger at his strange situation and attributed it either to stupidity or to a major unconfessed sin in Joshua's life.

He repented of everything he could think of, and surrendered himself to the Lord's will.

"With My Whole Heart!"

"The prayer of a righteous man is powerful and effective."
(James 5:16)

Faith had settled the children in a local school in Arvada and was doing her best to create a normal family life for them. She too was having to bear up under enormous pressure from without and within.

Early one February morning, Faith was impatient for her husband's regular call from Seattle. Her heart was bursting. "Oh Joshua, at last! Something wonderful happened and I've been longing to tell you about it!"

Joshua's heart was cheered to hear his wife's lilting and musical voice. He was ready for some good news. "Oh sweetheart, tell me, I'm all ears," he laughed.

"It's so good to hear your voice. I've missed you so much..."

"Me too! But for God's grace, I'd really be a basket case by now. I feel the Lord's support all the time, day and night. It's so comforting to know that He is with us. So tell me, what happened?" His voice was eager.

"Well, first the bad news. I woke up around four this morning with one of the worst migraine headaches of my life. My head was pounding and I felt terribly nauseous. I was desperate to talk to you and have you pray for me, but I would have woken up the pastor's whole household if I'd called. Anyhow, when I tried to move I just felt worse."

"You should have called. They don't mind - especially when prayer is needed - and we all could have prayed for you," he chided gently.

"Well yes, you are right, but I was even too ill to get out of bed and use the phone. I was so weak. I just lay low and felt really sorry for myself. I felt very alone, very needy. The children were asleep downstairs and I was groaning and moaning, thinking, *'If only I had someone to pray for me!'*

"Suddenly there was Andy at the foot of my bed! I couldn't believe my eyes. Joshua, do you realise this was only the second time in his life that he has woken up and come to me during the night? Do you remember the first time, when he came in and said, 'Jesus loves you, Mommy'?

"I was so amazed to see him standing there. Then he announced, 'Mommy, I'm hungry. Get up and make me breakfast!' He looked like a little soldier waiting for me to get up and serve him. He's never done anything like that before.

"I managed to whisper, 'I'm so sorry but Mommy is very ill. I can't get up. I'm sorry, I can't make you any breakfast right now.'

"Andy came round the bed to me and asked, 'You're ill, Mommy? You can't make me breakfast?' He looked at me with his wide brown eyes. He thought deeply about this. Then he said, 'I guess I'll have to pray for you to get better.'

"He closed his eyes for a moment or two and opened them again. 'Are you better now, Mommy?'

"I answered him the truth. 'No darling, I'm very sorry. I still feel awful. I can't help you.'

"Andy was quite hurt. 'You mean, Jesus didn't heal you?'

"'No, He didn't. I'm sorry, Andy, not this time.'

"'Well then, I'll just have to pray for you... with my whole heart!' He looked at me with great concentration. Then he knelt down by the bed and buried his head in his little hands. I could hardly believe my eyes, he was rocking back and forth on his knees, clasping his head, mouthing words silently to Jesus. He was praying for me with all his heart and soul and strength.

"Then it happened! A lightness filled my body. My head stopped throbbing, the nausea vanished - and I felt fine. The Lord had come to my rescue. I sat up in bed and pulled Andy into my arms. 'Oh my little angel, thank you. The Lord has healed me! I feel fine now.' I was laughing. 'It's a miracle. Jesus heard your prayer. Thank you, thank you!'

"'Really, Mommy? Jesus healed you?' he asked happily.

"'Yes, darling. I feel totally well again - I'll get up now and make your breakfast.'

"But Andy shook his head and said, 'Never mind, Mommy, I'm not hungry any more...' and he went downstairs and back to bed."

"What a precious story," exclaimed Joshua. "Glory to God! How touching that Andrew prayed for you with his whole heart."

"Afterwards I was thanking and praising the Lord, and the scripture **'The prayer of a righteous man is powerful and effective'**[22] came floating into my

---

[22] *James 5:16*

heart. *'But Andy isn't a man, he's only a child. He's not even four yet,'* I thought. Then I remembered the words of our Lord: **'I tell you the truth, unless you change and become like little children, you will never enter the kingdom of heaven.'**[23] I think the Lord was saying that we need to depend on Him completely, like little children. Only then will we be powerful and effective in His Kingdom..."

Joshua and Faith hung up reluctantly. Nevertheless, during this time of trial they were beginning to understand that their Father's purpose was to separate each of them to Himself so they might come to a new place of utter dependence on Him only – not on one another.

The winter weeks dragged by, cold and bleak. Faith had pinned her hopes on Joshua's birthday in March as a very significant day. She looked forward to it because she was sure the Lord had promised - even before they had left Seattle - that they would be reunited by Joshua's 35th birthday.

All hope was extinguished, however, when Joshua called in distress early on his birthday (a Friday) to say there was no possibility of his joining her and the children - the money was simply not there.

She longed for him, mourning her dashed hopes as she wandered up and down the aisles of a grocery store later in the day, having a pity-party with the Lord. *"I really, really thought You said that we'd be together again by today, Jesus. Sometimes I think we're just fooling ourselves and that it wasn't Your idea at all for us to be separated like this."* Despite her deep disappointment, she bought extra food, drink and 'goodies', hardly aware of what she was doing.

She and the children were snuggled up together in the family room that evening, watching the film *Black Beauty*. A sudden loud knocking on the front door made them all jump anxiously. They knew practically no one; it was well after dark; and they were all too aware of recent burglaries on their cul-de-sac.

"Mommy, don't open it!" little Ricky cautioned her. "Ask who it is first. Be CAREFUL."

"Right," assured his mother with a quick squeeze. She went to the door with the three children padding nervously behind her.

"Who is it?" she stammered.

A deep voice intoned: "It's... your... husband..."

---

[23] *Matthew 18:3*

Diamonds in the Rough

"Wha... husband?!" Faith struggled to open the door against the desperate crowding and cheering of the children. There he was, his arms full of flowers and gifts and a grin as wide as the Rockies.

"JOSHUA! My love, this is so wonderful! Why didn't you tell me you were coming?" she gasped, laughing and crying at the same time. The children went wild with joy and tried to grab an arm or a leg of their Daddy, not willing to let him go.

At last the pandemonium died down and their surprise visitor told his tale: "This afternoon my boss came in and actually ordered me to come to Denver to attend a conference. The person scheduled to go had cancelled at the last minute. So here I am, for more than a week - all expenses paid!

"I rushed about getting signatures, tickets and money, and booking a rental car – it was so tight that I had to pack my suitcase in a taxi on the way to the airport. I managed to catch the last flight into Denver tonight with only three minutes to spare. I would have missed it if I'd stopped to phone you.

"Once I arrived in Denver I thought, *'Wouldn't it be great to surprise everybody?'* It certainly has been."

"Ooh, the Lord is so faithful - I was SURE He had promised me that you'd be coming today. But wait here, just for a minute..." She ran laughing into the kitchen and soon returned with a birthday cake full of lighted candles, and a jug of lemonade.

"Happy Birthday To You," she sang, the children joining in with whooping and joyful commotion. It was a precious start to a reunion that lasted nine days (with occasional breaks for obligatory attendance at the conference, of course).

Joshua also visited the institute to follow up on his application. He was devastated to learn that each of the hoped-for openings had been filled. There were no other prospects.

He and his wife tried to grapple with this grim situation. They had to admit that the Lord had never actually promised a job - they had simply assumed that He would provide one. The crisis was all the more poignant because they were finally reducing their debt by tiny increments. Being unemployed again would plunge them into penury, maybe even bankruptcy.

What could they do? Surely the Lord wanted them back together as a family, but just as surely Joshua would have to keep on working in Seattle until early June to avoid having to pay back his prior moving expenses. After that he could rejoin his wife and children in Denver - but what would they live on?

Fantastic Adventures In Trusting Him

They committed their bleak future into God's hands, and immediately experienced the precious comfort and peace of the Holy Spirit assuring them of God's complete faithfulness.

The following Sunday Joshua was on an almost empty flight back to Seattle. He gazed out over the clouds with profound sadness in his heart. The prospect of spending three more months away from his wife and children gave him extreme pain.

Unexpectedly the Spirit of Jesus called to him: ***"Joshua, can you surrender everything to Me?"***

"I thought I already had, Lord," he responded with surprise and a tinge of reproach.

"No, you haven't, My son. There are still things in your life that you are holding onto as your own. I want you to give up EVERYTHING you have. Are you willing to go down to nothing? Can you go down to the point of having nothing to call your own - except My love? Can you trust Me that much? Can you lose your very life in Me?"

Such a heavy burden weighed upon his heart that he bowed over in his seat. He wept as he recognised one thing after another that was an idol or a false security in his life. When he considered his wife and children and forced himself to count the cost of giving them up as well, his heart broke. Yet he recognised that the cost of giving up everything and everyone was nothing in comparison with the infinite price that Jesus had already paid for his salvation.

"O my Lord and my God, forgive me," he grieved. *"I give it all up to You. Please bring me to absolutely NOTHING, so that whatever happens in my life from now on may come from Your hand, and may bring You glory, dear Jesus, because You've purchased me. I trust in You completely. Please, Lord, look after my loved ones - be a Husband and a Father to them..."*

As Joshua surrendered everything to the Lord the heavy burden suddenly vaporised. An overwhelming, incomprehensible peace cradled and comforted his heart and soul.

Walking on Thin Ice

"Surely the Sovereign LORD does nothing without revealing His
plan to His servants the prophets."

(Amos 3:7)

Joshua visited a friend's house in Seattle a month or so later with several others from the church. They had gathered to hear from a man with a divinely anointed gift of prophecy who was visiting their area. By the end of the evening, everyone had been prophesied over except Joshua. The prophet called him out from the back of the room and laid his hands on him. He spoke as follows:

"Has your heart been able to contain what the living God has done? Have I not filled your life with good things? Have I not given you the treasure in your heart? So give it forth and glorify My Name, and do not withhold what I give...

"You will continually grow strong in the Lord, and you will be as JOSHUA. Yes, says the Lord, your path will seem strange. You will be walking, as it were, on thin ice. You will ask, 'Will it sustain me and keep me?'

"But I tell you that I have made the way. Even though all the vultures of the air will try to ensnare you and put you into bondage, I say to you that you will walk in My Word and be endued with the Presence of the Lord in everything you do.

"Has not My word declared that you are called by My name? I have called you as an ELECTOR, as one who will speak out and see the elect of the Lord stand up in the move of God. I have surely given you an enduement, a gift of laying on of hands so that others would receive of My Spirit.

"In Me is an everlasting well of water springing up into everlasting life, in which you cannot even plumb the depths of My love. The love of the Lord shall always be in your heart. Surely, says God, you will walk forward and know that My courage and My strength are with you, and that the glory of My Kingdom is upon your heart.

"Yes! Everything I am saying shall be done in My Name, and surely you will SEE, even more completely, the work of the Lord, for the Lord your God has done it. For I the Lord your God shall work it in you, and I shall give you

*even the **BLUEPRINT AND THE PLANS OF MY CHURCH**... Surely it shall be unfolded before your eyes, and you will rejoice in it."*

The prophecy astounded Joshua, and later Faith also when she read the transcript, particularly his being called by name and being promised the 'blueprint and plans' of the Church. Yet the reference to 'walking on thin ice' was familiar enough, and reassured them that the prophecy was from God. Its larger meaning eluded them, but the sense of God's love and His many unusual promises caused the Alexanders' life to be infused with new hope.

God now bared His holy arm. A call from the institute informed Joshua that a new position had been created a whole year ahead of schedule and that he was at the top of their list of candidates. After two paid interview trips (and jubilant visits with his family) he was offered a starting date of early June.

Oddly enough, at the same time his company in Seattle offered him a better-paid management position, but Joshua had to decline it. God had already 'planted' him in Denver.

After five interminable months of separation from his wife and children (and feeling only half-alive), the family was reunited on June 2nd.

The church family gave Joshua an emotional farewell and presented him with a beautiful card inscribed, *'To the Denver Apostle'*.

> **"And the God of all grace, who called you to His eternal glory in Christ, after you have suffered a little while, will Himself restore you and make you strong, firm and steadfast. To Him be the power for ever and ever. Amen.**
>
> *(1 Peter 5:10-11)*

10

Father's Heart
(August 1978 - September 1980)

"God our Saviour... wants all men to be saved and to come to a knowledge of the truth."
(1 Timothy 2:4)

Joshua walked home from work one day in August for an *al fresco* lunch by the pool of their new home in Applewood, a suburb of Denver. He casually mentioned to his wife that 'some poor sucker' from his group would soon have to move to the Arabian Desert to oversee a multi-year demonstration program of solar energy technology.

Faith froze with her mouth full of cantaloupe. Managing to swallow, she stared at her husband in shock. "No, this can't be happening. Not AGAIN! Early this morning the Lord was telling me that He was going to take us to a thirsty place, and had me read Psalm 63. It starts, '**O God, You are my God, earnestly I seek You; my soul thirsts for You, my body longs for You, in a dry and weary land where there is no water.**' Doesn't that sound awfully like Arabia? Could WE be the 'poor suckers' who'll have to go?" She spoke with great agitation.

It was Joshua's turn to gawk, motionless, unable even to swallow. After a long silence, he recovered his speech. "No-no-no-NO!" he said angrily. "We just GOT here. How could the Lord even think of moving us anywhere else, let alone the desert?" The subject was dropped like the hottest of hot potatoes.

He called his wife from work the following morning with an unusual lilt to his voice. "Guess what, sweetheart? You know how nervous I was at the mere mention of going to you-know-where? Well, I woke up today praying that IF the Lord wanted us to go there He would change my heart because it was like stone. That was barely two hours ago. Now I have such an overwhelming desire to go to the Middle East that I'd actually feel disappointed if we didn't go. Isn't that a most amazing thing? I suspect He really IS calling us to go there."

"I think you're right - He's been working in my heart as well. In fact, I'm just on my way over to the library to borrow all the books I can find about the Middle East and Islam..."

The couple consumed every book the library had to offer on these subjects. As they read, the Lord stirred their hearts with love and compassion for the Moslem people. It was not merely a desire to identify with them; it was also a growing burden to pray and intercede for them to come to know the whole truth about Jesus Christ as revealed in the Bible.

The Lord was giving Joshua and Faith 'missionary hearts', and they began preparing themselves for the possibility of going to the Arabian Desert. They even located a British boarding school for missionaries' children (in Wales), in spite of having no outward sign that they would be sent.

An outsider was unexpectedly brought in to manage the Arabian Program because of its high political profile. He immediately selected Joshua as his choice for the resident position in Arabia and began to negotiate terms with him. Meanwhile, Faith began packing up the household (yet again) and planning the complex logistics of the relocation.

A few evenings later Joshua heard the Lord say, *"Forgive your new boss."*

He thought this development very odd. *"But Lord, he hasn't done anything for me to forgive..."*

"Just forgive him from your heart."

He obediently poured himself out in forgiveness for his new supervisor.

The following morning this man confronted him, declaring (without explanation) that Joshua was no longer a candidate for the resident position. Joshua was shocked and confused, but to his surprise he found no judgement rising in his heart. The Holy Spirit had prepared him well.

He and Faith refused to believe that this abrupt U-turn could be God's will. They prayed in faith and searched the Scriptures for guidance, but the heavens were 'like brass'. As the days and then weeks went by, they gradually came to their senses and realised that their Heavenly Father had never said anything about sending them to Arabia. That presumption had come out of their misinterpretation of Scripture and their misunderstanding of God's purpose.

In fact the Father's purpose was simply to transform the Alexanders into 'world Christians' by the ministry of His Spirit. The couple's new missionary hearts began to burn with a desire to go with God's truth to anywhere He might send them - either in person or, at the very least, in prayer as 'intercessors'.

The Cutting Edge

"Do not make light of the Lord's discipline..."
(Hebrews 12:5)

The flimsy paper gown crinkled against Faith's goose flesh as she leaned down to pick up her Bible. *"Perhaps the Lord will speak to me out of His Word and warm me up,"* she murmured to herself. *"This doctor's office is freezing."*

She held the Bible and closed her eyes. *"Lord, I am so needy. I long to hear something from You. Please guide me to a passage in Your Word that I can hang onto."* She opened the Bible prayerfully and focused on the verses[24] where her right thumb was resting: **"Let us throw off everything that hinders and the sin that so easily entangles, and let us run with perseverance the race marked out for us. LET US FIX OUR EYES ON JESUS, the author and perfecter of our faith, who for the joy set before Him endured the cross, scorning its shame, and sat down at the right hand of the throne of God."**

She read and re-read the passage, her mind riveted on the words. One of her favourite worship songs welled up in her heart:

> 'Turn your eyes upon Jesus,
> look full in His wonderful face,
> and the things of earth will grow strangely dim
> in the light of His glory and grace.'

God's presence filled her with peace as she savoured the words, repeating them again and again: **"Fix your eyes on Jesus... Fix your eyes on Jesus..."**

---

[24] *Hebrews 12:1-2*

"Oh yes, Lord, thank You. I will fix my eyes on You."

The door opened abruptly and Dr Wilson appeared with her chart. They were strangers to one another, one of the inevitable consequences of repeated moves.

After the usual exchange of small talk, he got to the point. "I see here on the chart that you have a swelling in your abdomen which you have been aware of for a few months and which appears to be getting larger. Will you show me where it is?" (Faith pointed to her left side.)

The doctor manipulated the area and said, "Yes, there's definitely a mass here." A puzzled look crept over his face as his skilled fingers interpreted what lay hidden. "I'd say it's at least the size of a grapefruit." He stepped away from the table pensively. "We'll have to do some tests - quite a few, actually - to determine what this is. It could be any number of things. Can you get over to the hospital right away if I'm able to arrange an appointment?"

Although surprised by this unexpected urgency, Faith complied willingly since she had no other plans. Before she left the office she was given three different appointments, including one with a surgeon the following day. The Lord's prescription, to keep her eyes on Jesus, was perfect. Instead of anxiety and panic, she was filled with peace. She decided to treat this new chapter of her life as an adventure. She was determined to enjoy this foray into the medical arena.

After a full spectrum of diagnostic tests, the origin of the 'culprit' remained a mystery. Surgery was scheduled within the week, and a massive fluid-filled cyst (nearly a foot in diameter) was removed. It had invaded the entire left side of her abdomen and had pushed every organ out of shape and position. Evidently the cyst had been there from birth, only recently had it increased in size. It was not connected to any organ system, however.

A few days after coming home from hospital in early 1979, Faith began experiencing excruciating pains throughout her body. These waves of pain were caused by a huge pocket of air or gas trapped under her left lung (the aftermath of surgery). Nothing would assuage the pain, neither painkillers nor special foods. Not even being anointed with oil and prayed for by the church elders had any effect. The initial discomfort from the operation had been nothing as compared with this new stabbing pain under her heart. The days and nights were filled with agony, although the condition itself was not serious.

She propped herself up and prayed, *"Lord, I love You... and I know You love me. What are You trying to tell me? Please show me..."*

She reached for her Bible, which opened again to the same passage in Hebrews given before her operation: **"Let us throw off everything that hinders and THE SIN THAT SO EASILY ENTANGLES, and let us run with perseverance the race marked out for us. Let us fix our eyes on Jesus, the author and perfecter of our faith, who for the joy set before Him endured the cross, scorning its shame, and sat down at the right hand of the throne of God."**

As she re-read the familiar words it was now the phrase **"the sin that so easily entangles"** that jumped out so forcefully from the page.

"SIN, Lord?" groaned Faith in consternation. *"Me? Us? What do You mean? Have we been such unrepentant sinners that You have to subject me to this?"*

"Keep reading, My child," she heard in response.

She looked at the page again and read: **"Do not make light of the Lord's discipline, and do not lose heart when He rebukes you, because THE LORD DISCIPLINES THOSE HE LOVES, and He punishes everyone He accepts as a son."**[25]

"I didn't realise Your love includes discipline, Lord... You obviously love us a lot!" (She could not resist the irony.) But then she thanked her Heavenly Father from her heart for His discipline and felt a little encouragement as she continued to read: **"God disciplines us for our good, that we may share in His holiness. No discipline seems pleasant at the time, but painful. Later on, however, it produces a harvest of righteousness and peace for those who have been trained by it."**[26]

The voice of her Shepherd now spoke. ***"Yes, Faith, I do love you, and you are very special to Me. But you and Joshua have been most disobedient, and I had to get your attention because you have ignored what I have been saying. I have been telling you to write down your stories! There is so much I want to do in others' lives through your testimony, and you must take this seriously. Your stories do not belong to you alone.***

---

[25] Hebrews 12:5-6
[26] Hebrews 12:10-11

"But it is not just you who have been disobedient; My whole Church is being disobedient! I am going to have to remove the huge tumour of pride from My Body as well. It will be very painful, but essential for My people. You must all recognise that the sin of pride has caused My Body to become ill and out of shape, like yours.

"So rededicate yourselves to your task. You will find fulfilment and joy in writing if you discipline yourselves and obey what I say."

Faith was appalled. She prayed, *"Oh my God, please forgive us! We've always assumed this writing was 'optional'. Writing is so impossible - well, difficult - for us. We've been thinking (and hoping) that we weren't hearing You correctly. Anyway, Lord, our life is so full of failure and instability - how can writing about that encourage anybody? Just look at our debts... and our doubts! Besides, what will everyone think of all the crazy things we've done, and the endless moving?"*

"Sit down and write, and I will help you. Don't give up so easily. You haven't written anything since you left Eau Claire three years ago. It's time to get busy again."

When Joshua came home from work, his wife shared this sobering news with him. Sinking onto the edge of her bed, he held his head between his hands and prayed, *"Oh God, You've let her suffer but it's all my fault. I have been so selfish and lazy... and disobedient... and proud."*

He turned to Faith. "We think we're so great because we can hear His voice, and then we ignore what He says. We are lower than the insects - at least they get on with their work."

The next morning all her pain was gone.

A Birthday Blessing

"...Your Father knows what you need before you ask Him."
(Matthew 6:8b)

Jacqueline's ninth birthday was fast approaching. Faith, still very weak from her operation and in bed most of each day, began to fret about how to make the day special for her little girl. Jacqui had specifically requested a pink satin jacket and her mother was determined to find one. A couple of days before her daughter's birthday in mid-March, Faith ventured out to a nearby shopping mall. She shopped for only five or ten minutes before having to sit down and rest, sweat pouring down her face. After several pathetic and fruitless attempts, she returned home in defeat. (Having so little money to spare, she was careful not to buy anything other than what her daughter had asked for.)

She poured out her heart in prayer: *"Oh Lord, I wanted so much to find that pink satin jacket. Now I have NOTHING for Jacqui. Why is life so hard? I'm really disappointed. I feel so useless,"* she sobbed into her pillow. *"Lord Jesus, would You please do something for her? I have no strength left."*

The day arrived, but there were no presents for the birthday girl whose mother was still out of commission and whose father was working on the Arabian project almost around the clock.

Just before the children were due home from school, about 2 p.m., the doorbell rang. It was Jan, an old friend from Arvada whom Faith had not seen in some months. In her arms she was holding a big brown paper bag.

"Hi, Faith, how are you doing?"

"I'm still pretty shaky, I'm afraid, but I'm so happy to see you. I've missed you. Come on in - let's go back to the bedroom if you don't mind." Jan followed her down the hallway.

When Faith had settled herself on the bed, Jan placed the bag gently on her knees. "There's a little story behind this," she remarked with a mischievous smile. "I was halfway out the door when I had a thought that perhaps there were a few things in our closet that you could use. So I went back in, and these are the things I found..."

"Oh dear Jan, thank you, how thoughtful of you. I do love surprises!" Sitting up carefully, Faith peered in the bag. On top was something shiny and pink. Her heart leaped with hope.

It was a brand new pink satin jacket, in Jacqui's exact size.

Her eyes filled with tears. "Jan, Jan, you have no idea what this means to me," she cried, reaching out to hug her friend. "It's Jacqui's birthday today and all she wanted was a pink satin jacket. And you brought it to us. Thank you, thank you!"

The whole family recognised this gift as coming from the Lord's hand, the fruit of Jan's obedience. It was a beautiful token of God's loving heart.

Pruned Back

"The Lord disciplines those He loves..."
(Hebrews 12:6)

Time slipped by until it was almost summer, yet the Alexanders had not written another word. Sadly, they continued in their disobedience. They should have known better.

After the removal of Faith's cyst, a pathologist had determined that some of its cells were borderline cancerous. Even though the mysterious cyst had not been attached to her ovaries (or anything else of significance), Faith was now being advised to have a complete hysterectomy (removal of her ovaries and uterus) to evade the quiet killer, ovarian cancer.

Faced with whether to undergo another major abdominal operation, she consulted the Divine Physician while waiting for a final consultation with her earthly surgeon.

The Lord whispered, *"Look up Isaiah 18:5."*

Turning to the scripture she read: **"For, before the harvest, when the blossom is gone and the flower becomes a ripening grape, He will cut off the shoots with pruning knives, and cut down and take away the spreading branches."**

Faith was amazed at this extraordinary confirmation of a total hysterectomy. Having always made a practice of asking God to confirm His direction through the Bible, she had been quite dubious about finding an answer to this specific question, but here it was. The Holy Spirit was displaying His ability to speak through the Bible on every vital issue.

The surgical operation, her second in four months, was a delicate one because her previous scar had to be re-opened and closed. Joshua begged the Lord to be merciful and take away any pain this time around, and He did. The recovery, although quite lengthy, was virtually free of pain.

Father

Healing the Broken-Hearted

**"My grace is sufficient for you, for My power is
made perfect in weakness."**

(2 Corinthians 12:9)

The insistent ringing of the phone abruptly ended Faith's late-afternoon nap under the shady back porch. She was extremely weak from the operation just ten days before, and didn't want to talk to anyone.

"Sorry darling," whispered her husband, "I tried to put her off, but she says it's an emergency and insists on talking to you." He wrestled with lengths of tangled cords.

"Emergency? Who is it?" quizzed Faith, but he merely shrugged.

"Hello?" She adjusted herself carefully in the lounge chair while trying to prop up the phone so as not to put pressure on her tender abdomen.

"Hello, my name is Louise, but please call me Lou," began a pressured, well-modulated contralto voice. "Someone gave me your name. I don't remember who exactly, but they thought you could help me."

"Really?" murmured Faith, contemplating the 15-inch-long gauze bandage that ran down her front like a giant zipper. *"What can I possibly do for her?"* she mused. *"I'm the one who needs help."*

Trying to focus, she continued, "Uh, what kind of help are you needing, Lou? I'm not in the best of... um... shape right now, myself. I've only just come home from the hospital."

"Yes I heard that, but I'm desperate. I keep thinking of killing myself. I've been to psychiatrists and psychologists but nobody seems able to help me. My doctors tell me I'm manic-depressive... You are a counsellor, aren't you?"

"Well, I'm a trained clinical psychologist, but I'm not licensed to practise. Besides that, Lou, I believe the only person who can solve these problems is the Lord Jesus Christ. I have no confidence in anyone or anything else."

"Yes, that's what I heard about you, and that's exactly what I want. I WANT TO KNOW JESUS. Would you pray for me?" Lou's strong voice was pleading and insistent.

"How can I possibly turn her down?" thought Faith.

Lou continued relentlessly: "My mother is dying of cancer, and my second husband has cancer as well... and I just found out that my daughter and her boyfriend, who are both on drugs, are going to have a baby... Please, help me!"

"Well... my husband and I can pray for you. When do you want to come over, Lou?"

The voice brightened and cried, "I live at the top of the hill. I'll be down in five minutes!"

"See you... soon, then," replied Faith, but Lou had already hung up. "Isn't that just like the Lord?" she smiled wryly at Joshua, who took away the phone set. "He is amazing. I haven't counselled anyone in... I can't remember how long. But now that I'm flat on my back He brings me someone from who-knows-where with a ton of problems. That's God's timing for you, perfect as usual." She sighed, closing her eyes in resignation.

Joshua helped his fragile wife straighten herself out. A close friend who had come all the way from San Diego for two weeks to help the family dragooned the children into gathering up and stowing away the deadly minefield of toys and junk lurking inside the front door. They all sensed something unusual was about to unfold, even as Louise came sweeping into the house.

God's timing was indeed perfect. Faith's weakness provided the perfect springboard for their encounters. One of Louise's greatest problems was her tendency to manipulate and control others, but she had no opportunity to exercise her dominating personality. Whenever she appeared on the doorstep, Faith had only enough strength to pray with her but not enough to counsel her.

They worked out a routine that lasted about six months. Lou would appear several times a week but would only stay for five or ten minutes, long enough to sit or kneel down with Faith (and Joshua when he was home) and wait on the Lord to speak 'words of life'. God was always faithful to do so.

Frequently the words were so heavy that they would have crushed most people, but for Lou they were 'manna from Heaven'. She treasured and pondered each word in her heart. Week after week, huge progress could be seen in her attitudes and lifestyle. Even with all this improvement, however, the mere sight of Lou coming up the pathway made the Alexanders want to hide under their beds - her afflictions were so overwhelming.

Louise eventually asked if, in addition to these individual prayer times, she might come to a regular Bible study and bring along some of her friends. This was promptly arranged and soon a little group was meeting twice weekly to study the book of Ephesians.

Rebuilding Louise's life required vital Christian fellowship, Bible study and group prayer in addition to the private prayer sessions. To Faith it was somehow reminiscent of Acts 2:42. The Holy Spirit seemed to take Louise apart - 'separating the wheat from the chaff' - with each individual word (*rhema*, in Biblical Greek) that she was given privately. The Holy Spirit then put her back together and strengthened her using the other activities based on the written word (*logos* in Greek).

Medical science offers no cure for manic depression, treating only its symptoms with drugs. Today, however, Louise is totally healed. After becoming a widow, she went through seminary training and she is now a pastoral counsellor. When last heard from, she was leading a happy and fully restored life. Her daughter married the boyfriend, who found work. They came off drugs and their baby boy was born healthy.

It is only in weakness that we can lean totally on God. It was thanks to - not in spite of - Faith's weakness that Louise was able to meet so consistently with her Saviour and be healed. God's victory was decisive, and it was the Alexanders' privilege to be eyewitnesses of Lou's complete restoration.

It also encouraged them to complete their writing assignment over the following months, in obedience (finally) to the Lord's command.

God's Idea from Heaven

"See if I will not throw open the floodgates of heaven and pour out so much blessing that you will not have room enough for it."
(Malachi 3:10b)

Joshua and Faith went to hear Dr Yonggi Cho of Korea speak in mid-April 1980 at a large church in the Denver area. They eagerly attended the evening sessions.

On the third evening this remarkable man of God declared, "When God opens the floodgates and the windows of Heaven to pour out a blessing, it is not cash that He pours out (even though that is what we're hoping for) but rather an IDEA. It's when we take hold of His idea that we allow blessing (and cash, if needed) to overflow in our life."

For over seven years (realised Joshua with sudden conviction), he and Faith had been waiting for the Lord to pour down enough cash to melt away their mountain of debt. They had suffered tremendous discouragement following Faith's illness and two major operations the previous year. Healthy again, Faith had still needed months of recuperation. The medical and other expenses had of course been loaded onto their never-ending burden of debt.

The couple seemed further than ever from being financially free, but armed with Pastor Cho's intriguing advice to ask God for His idea, Joshua returned home determined to do precisely that.

He prayed: *"Loving Heavenly Father, all these years we've been praying for You to solve our problems, instead of asking You for Your idea and Your purpose. Please forgive us, Father. Only You can make our life fruitful and useful, and a blessing to others. If You would please show us YOUR IDEA, we will take hold of it and run with it, and we will know that we are in the centre of Your will. Amen."*

Day after day Joshua prayed along these lines. By early May he had become quite desperate for some response from the Lord. Kneeling on the floor one evening with a heavy heart and with eyes red from weeping, he felt crushed and humiliated.

At last, after three weeks, the voice of the Master spoke softly to his heart: **"Look up Psalm one hundred and thirteen, verses seven and eight."**

He wiped his eyes and found the passage in his Bible: **"He raises the poor from the dust and lifts the needy from the ash heap; He seats them with princes, with the princes of their people."**

He blinked a few times and re-read the verses in wonder before running to the kitchen to share them with his wife. The couple rejoiced in the Lord as they hugged each other. Even though they had little understanding of the significance of these verses, a supernatural faith from the Holy Spirit was rising in their hearts - something not experienced for months. The persistent feelings of discouragement and uselessness fled away. Surely nothing would now prevent God's idea from coming down from Heaven.

The following week Joshua was flying home from a solar energy technology conference in Texas. It was his older son's eighth birthday, and he remembered how an angel of God had foretold Richard's birth. It had been a momentous beginning to their spiritual odyssey. *"Whatever could be next?"* he wondered wryly. *"What will God do with our life now?"*

Father's Heart

He tried to concentrate on the government report on his lap, *The Export Potential of Solar Energy Equipment*. He was uncomfortably wedged between two other business travellers on the full plane. Joshua checked his watch, almost an hour and a half to go. His heart warmed at the prospect of celebrating Ricky's birthday later that afternoon.

Reading the document, Joshua reviewed the familiar list of unmet basic needs of millions of poor people around the world - for safe water, nutritious food, cooking fuel, vaccines, sanitation, housing, and so on. He knew the stark reality: that unless an effective strategy could be found to provide these needs in an appropriate and cost-effective way, many more millions of people would suffer the same deprivation. His heart pained him as he read the litany of human misery.

The three questions that had been on Joshua's mind for many days now confronted him yet again: *"Could solar energy provide an answer for these multitudes? Could it be THE answer? Could it be GOD'S answer?"*

Joshua put away the document and began to pray. A strange weightlessness came over him. He was no longer conscious of his body or even of being on the airplane. A beautiful light surrounded him - he was 'in the Spirit'. The sense of Jesus' presence became overwhelming, and the peace, love and glory of God embraced and filled his whole being. It was the beginning of a divine encounter unlike anything Joshua had ever known.

A vision began to unfold. He was in outer space looking back at the rotating Earth, which completely dominated his field of view. An unusual golden glow girdled the planet. It was bright yellow and very broad, encompassing all of Africa and the Middle East, Latin America, South Asia and the Pacific Islands - a vast region lying approximately between latitudes 40 degrees north and 40 degrees south of the equator. Thousands upon thousands of tiny black dots were visible under this golden glow and were scattered all throughout the tropical and subtropical land areas of the Earth.

"Lord Jesus, what are all those dots, and what is that golden glow?" As soon as he posed the question, God's answer came directly into his spirit, which he realised was somehow fused with the Lord's Spirit.

"The 'dots' represent over one million remote villages, each with hundreds, even thousands of people - people who have been forgotten by the rest of the world and who are still waiting to hear of My atoning love and sacrifice for them. They are the poorest of the poor, in body, soul and spirit. They are without help, without hope, without the Holy Spirit.

"The golden glow represents the 'Solar Belt', the region where the sun shines so strongly that the people see it as their enemy. The sun would be their friend if they could only make use of its power to supply the necessities of life that they so desperately lack, which you in the West take for granted..."

As Joshua gazed at this vision of the Earth, he suddenly understood what the Lord was saying. *"Oh yes! These forgotten, remote villagers who've never heard Your Name - the ones who are the poorest of the poor - they're the ones who have all this solar energy! So by using the sun's energy to meet their physical needs, we can bring them Your Gospel for their spiritual needs!"*

As soon as he grasped this concept, he found himself 'zooming in' by the power of the Holy Spirit to one of the million villages he had seen as black dots. Standing in the middle of the village, he was confronted by a horrifying and heart-rending scene.

The village was completely devastated and its people were in utter despair. Men, women, children and animals were staggering and crawling about, dying from thirst, starvation and disease. Many dead bodies were lying on the ground, unburied. There was no clean water, no edible vegetation, no means left to support life.

It dawned on Joshua that this village was one of a million like it. He cried out in pain and anguish, *"Lord!... Lord! How can these poor people be helped? There are so many of them. They are so far gone. How can You - even You - help them, Jesus? You must help them, You MUST... Please, please, help them somehow!"*

There was no response from the Lord. Joshua remained standing there, his heart filled with an overwhelming compassion he had never felt before.

Out of the corner of his eye Joshua caught sight of a team of young people marching into the village. Each of them carried some kind of technical equipment under one arm and carried a Bible under the other arm. They set up the equipment, which began supplying electricity for pumping water from underground and for linking the village into a global satellite network. (Joshua was also shown these satellites: they were broadcasting the Gospel into each of the million villages in its own individual language.)

The young missionaries gave water to the people, prayed for the dying (they recovered) and prayed for the dead (they rose up). They then made their home in the village. This aspect was the most touching to Joshua, who marvelled at the love of these young people for the poor villagers.

Next, each young team member sat down on the ground with a group of villagers and, empowered by the Holy Spirit, began to teach them from the Bible. Before very long, the love and forgiveness of God and the truth and power of the Gospel became so evident to the villagers' minds and hearts that they ALL came into God's kingdom, repenting of their sins, rejoicing and giving glory to their Heavenly Father.

The scene suddenly changed: the village was now miraculously transformed. Joshua was seeing a place overflowing with prosperity. The devastating poverty had been completely erased!

"Lord, how is this possible? How can You - even You - have done this?"

The vision slowly began to dissolve and fade. Joshua realised that it was not a physical reality he was seeing - at least not a present one. Rather, he had seen a prophetic view of the future in which terrible drought and famine would affect the whole of the less-developed world, and in which God's awesome love and power would be displayed by His young 'technical missionaries'.

The Lord then explained to Joshua the details of His divine strategy and how to implement it. He concluded, ***"I want to heal these poor ones who are suffering in spirit, soul and body, and make them WHOLE. You will need a million dollars to start this - a million dollars for a million villages. Everything will be in place within one to two years... In My time I shall do this quickly!"***

Joshua found himself 'back' in his seat, stiff and trembling, his face wet with tears. Shortly he heard the captain announce the start of their descent into Denver airport. After looking at his watch Joshua realised he had been 'out' for over an hour.

"Won't he be surprised?" thought Faith happily as she waited for her husband to appear at the arrival gate. She had finally steeled herself to negotiate the 'Denver Mousetrap', a complex and dangerous freeway interchange on the way to Stapleton [the old airport]. She thanked the Lord yet again for the clear, dry roads.

When Joshua appeared at the gate, a huge smile lit up his face on seeing her. She smiled back and wondered, *"Why does he look so different? Wow, he's shining like a light bulb!"*

They hugged and kissed each other between words. "Darling, you look like Moses coming down from the mountain," she laughed. "What happened up there? You've been with the Lord!"

"You can tell? It's visible?"

"Yes, you're surrounded by light!" she insisted. "What happened?"

"That's amazing..." He looked at his wife with wonder in his eyes. "I'm so thrilled you came to meet me, my love - today of all days. It's awesome to find you here, waiting for me. I'll explain in a moment. Yes, something amazing DID happen to me up there, and I'm exploding to tell you about it, but there's something I have to find out from you first."

"Oh? What's that?"

"Tell me what the Lord said to you today."

"Today? Hmmm... Oh yes, there was something, but it was so odd I really didn't think it was the Lord..." She smiled apologetically.

"Okay, okay, but what did He say?" His hands were trembling as he held hers.

"Well, I was getting ready to come and pick you up and was combing my hair at the mirror. I thought I heard, **'You will be working with three organisations,'** and then I heard their names." (She listed the three names.)

"YES!" Joshua whooped with delight. "Those are EXACTLY the same names He told me. I asked Him for a special sign to confirm that what had happened on the plane was really from Him, not some weird hallucination or something. He told me you'd be waiting here and that He'd already spoken to you about these three names. Isn't He wonderful? You even repeated them in the same order, hallelujah! Come on over here and let's sit down - I've got something tremendous to share with you..."

As Joshua finished telling about his experience he said, "It was a real vision, an open vision, like we read about in the Bible. I can hardly believe it, even though I saw it myself."

Faith was overwhelmed. "Joshua, this must be God's idea from Heaven that you've been desperately praying for. But it's so colossal, so inconceivable. It's so much more than just an idea - it's a global programme... a global strategy to help millions - no, billions - of people."

He grimaced and ran a hand through his thick brown hair. "I know, I know. But what can I say? I'm absolutely sure it was from the Lord after the wonderful confirmation He gave us. And He told me to follow Him and trust Him implicitly." He shook his head slowly. "Faith, this is a 'Mission Impossible' if ever there was one. Who will even believe it?" He rubbed his eyes.

"But Joshua! Don't you REMEMBER?" She brushed tears away and put trembling hands around her husband's neck. "Surely you remember? It was exactly seven and a half years ago this month..." He looked blank.

"It was what the Lord said, through Deborah. I can recall the words as if it were yesterday: *'You're going to be on an airplane. Not "Mission Impossible", but "Mission POSSIBLE" - and "Mission COMPLETED!"'*

"This vision IS from God," she declared quietly but firmly, "and He will DO it."

'Mission Impossible'

**"'Not by might nor by power, but by My Spirit,'
says the LORD Almighty."**
(Zechariah 4:6)

Joshua shared his vision with their closest friends including the much-loved pastor of the Denver church they were attending. Their reactions, after initial shock, ranged from despair at the immensity of the vision to enthusiasm for its simple strategy.

One friend exclaimed, "It's as if the Lord has revealed the **blueprint** of how He plans to build His worldwide Church before He returns." Another friend said, "You'll need the courage of Joshua in the Bible to go forward with this vision." These comments resounded in his heart as he recalled the prophetic words spoken over him by a stranger two years before in Seattle.

A couple of weeks later Joshua was again out of town on business travel and was sitting alone in an empty, closed meeting room, having arrived an hour early for a Sunday evening service. He was praying.

He almost jumped out of his skin when he heard an audible voice just behind his head repeating the name, *"JOSHUA! JOSHUA!"*

He spun around, but there was no one there. He tried to recover. *"Lord, was that You?"* he gasped.

The Lord replied (no longer audibly but to his heart), *"Yes, My son. I called you 'Joshua' by name because you are going to lead the way into a land of promise. Don't be afraid! Be full of courage and know that I have given you the land, and that I am sending you. Now, get ready and GO! I am with you and will never leave you. Only believe in Me and trust Me, and GO."*

Joshua phoned his wife after the service to tell her about this amazing encounter. "Faith, I'm sure the Lord means for us to 'go' not just spiritually but physically." Taking a deep breath he added, "I believe He wants us to leave Denver and go out to California, and begin working out this vision. What do you think of that?"

There was a long silence on the line.

"Faith...?"

"Yes, I'm here..." Her voice was faint and sombre. "Joshua, I can't say I'm at all thrilled to hear this. We'll have to pray hard and long about it. It's really scary."

"I know." After more silence he reiterated, "I didn't imagine it, sweetheart. The Lord called me *'Joshua'* by name - and this time it was out loud!" He waited for her comment but she said nothing. "It will take a lot of effort to communicate this vision to the Church," he went on, taking a deep breath. "I believe God wants us to start in California."

"Oh darling, just think about it!" Faith's voice was choking. "Quitting your job and living on faith will be SO much tougher this time around. The kids are five years older than when we left Maryland. Ohhh, Joshua..." The drawn-out sigh betrayed her profound weariness. They had moved house ten times in the previous eight years. She hardly needed to raise the obvious questions... What would they live on? And what about their huge financial obligations?

"We'll have to pray it through," she said with resolution. "We must ask the Lord to confirm your vision through His Word, and through other believers. And of course He'll also have to confirm whether or not He wants us to leave Denver." They hung up with heavy hearts.

Over the next several days the Holy Spirit directed the couple to various scriptures that gave specific and powerful confirmation of the vision:

"See, I am doing a new thing!... I am making a way... I provide water in the desert and streams in the wasteland, to give drink to My people, My chosen, the people I formed for Myself that they may proclaim My praise." (Isaiah 43:19-21)

"The poor and needy search for water, but there is none; their tongues are parched with thirst. But I the LORD will answer them; I, the God of Israel, will not forsake them. I will make rivers flow on barren heights, and springs within the valleys. I will turn the desert into pools of water, and the parched ground into springs... so that people may see and know, may consider and understand, that the hand of the LORD has done this, that the Holy One of Israel has created it." (Isaiah 41:17-20)

"Some wandered in desert wastelands, finding no way to a city where they could settle. They were hungry and thirsty, and their lives ebbed away. Then they cried out to the LORD in their trouble, and He delivered them from their distress... Let them give thanks to the LORD for His unfailing love and His wonderful deeds for men, for He satisfies the thirsty and fills the hungry with good things." (Psalm 107:4-9)

"The revelation awaits an appointed time; it speaks of the end and it will not prove false. Though it linger, wait for it; it will certainly come and will not delay." (Habakkuk 2:3)

"There is no wisdom, no insight, no plan that can succeed against the LORD." (Proverbs 21:30)

As for their leaving Denver and paid employment to live once more in total dependence on Him, the Lord showed them:

"Cast your bread upon the waters, for after many days you will find it again." (Ecclesiastes 11:1)

"If you spend yourselves on behalf of the hungry... then your light will rise in the darkness... The LORD will guide you always; He will satisfy your needs in a sun-scorched land and will strengthen your frame." (Isaiah 58:10-11a)

Greatly encouraged, the couple asked the Lord to provide them with 'Godly counsel' and to speak to them through spiritually mature believers. God's answer came at once.

"Faith, listen! I have some amazing news," laughed Joshua. (He was calling from his office.) "They're sending me to Italy to represent the Department of Energy at an international solar energy conference. I have to leave this weekend. It's the opportunity we've been praying for. You MUST come along so that we can visit Britain on the way and go to the Bible College of Wales together. Who better to ask for discernment about the vision before we go any further with it? The question is, can you find someone to look after the children at such short notice?"

"Yes I can, because a friend just offered that at church yesterday, out of the blue! But can we afford my ticket?"

"Darling, how can we afford for you NOT to go? We'll charge it of course, because I believe it's vital that you come along to hear what they may say in Wales. We're in this thing together, aren't we?"

"All the way, my Joshua!"

He made reservations to London on the last possible connection leaving Denver that Friday afternoon, flying on to Italy Sunday. He also booked a rental car so they could visit the Bible College of Wales on Saturday.

When Faith arrived at his office in a taxi to pick him up that Friday, she had to wait and wait because his travel authorisation had still not come through from Washington.

"Lord Jesus," she reminded Him, *"we've got to catch this flight or we'll miss the opportunity to go to Wales. Please move the officials to approve the trip!"* After nearly half an hour Joshua came running out with everything finally in order. They caught the plane with two minutes to spare and praised God for having overcome the spiritual opposition.

Death and Resurrection

"I tell you the truth, unless a kernel of wheat falls to the ground and dies, it remains only a single seed. But if it dies, it produces many seeds.
(John 12:24)

Joshua had visited the Bible College once before and he pointed out a large empty pedestal opposite the entrance. It bore only a simple inscription: **Jehovah Jireh ("The LORD Will Provide"**, Genesis 22:14). He pulled on the old doorbell, and soon the Alexanders were engrossed in conversation with two friends from Joshua's previous visit.

These two dear brothers listened carefully to the account of his vision, then excused themselves to take time for individual private prayer.

About an hour later they returned and found the Alexanders walking in the gardens. The men's faces were wreathed in smiles as they joined the couple and, taking each by the arm, they began to walk with them.

After some moments the older man (Dr Priddy) asked, "Joshua and Faith, do you have any idea what the Lord has entrusted to you?" The couple looked at him in surprise.

"NOT ONLY is this Vision from God but it is an outworking of the Vision given 45 years ago to Rees Howells, the Founder of the College, before either of you was even born. It is very much in line with what the Founder saw. In fact I was here on that momentous day...

"Mr Howells called it *'The Every Creature Vision'*.[27] He had been praying about the Great Commission given at the end of Mark's Gospel (**'Go into all the world, and preach the Gospel to every creature'**). All at once the Holy Spirit visited him with a Vision of the whole world. He inspired him to believe that God could accomplish what was impossible for man - and in a single generation. The Holy Spirit then asked him to take on the great burden of interceding for this Vision, which is why the Bible College has been, ever since, a house of prayer for all nations."

Faith glanced at her husband: his eyes were brimming with tears.

The younger man declared, "We've been praying this past hour and we find we're in complete agreement: this Vision you saw is from the Lord. God bless you for coming here to share it with us. It is so encouraging for us to hear that the Lord is on the move. We will be interceding for you."

The couple were introduced to Sister Gladys, a recently retired missionary with a lifetime of rich experience with God. They sat together as tea was being served and she listened attentively to their stories and especially to Joshua's Vision.

After he had finished speaking Gladys confided, "Now, I want to tell you children something very important about God's WAYS." She made sure she had their full attention before continuing. "Whenever God prepares to do something - anything - He first tells us what it is, so that we will get it started. But then He allows it to die, and He buries it. But in His good time He always resurrects it. And finally He brings about the outcome.

"You see, it's a process: first the word... then the death and the burial... then the resurrection (how we praise Him for that, hallelujah!)... and only THEN the outcome. Remember, it's the outcome that is important, but also

---

[27] *For more about* The Every Creature Vision, *see* Rees Howells: Intercessor *by* Norman Grubb (CLC 1997).

remember that no outcome is ever possible without the unavoidable steps of death, burial and resurrection.

"So don't be surprised, beloved, when (not if) your vision goes into the tomb and stays there for five, ten, maybe even twenty years." (Joshua's heart sank.) "But you can always count on God to resurrect whatever belongs to Him. His word never returns to Him void. If this vision is from the Lord - and I'm sure it is! - you will see its fulfilment, the outcome. And then you will know that it was by God's doing only, NOT by man's. It is something impossible for man to do, anyway..." She put a comforting hand on Joshua's arm and looked at them both with great compassion, seemingly aware of the extent of suffering and travail that would be coming into their life.

"Sister Gladys," swallowed Joshua, "those are such hard words. You see, I feel such great urgency in my spirit to get on with this work. It's a burden I simply cannot ignore. At the same time, I accept what you say... I've heard about the 'death of a vision' and I understand that it has to die, regardless of anything I do. I just pray it won't be as long as you think before God resurrects it - so many millions of people are suffering already. Please, please, keep us in your prayers."

The precious people at the Bible College promised to pray and intercede faithfully for the Alexanders before God's throne, and in this way *Jehovah Jireh* provided them with a powerful spiritual 'covering'. As yet, the couple had no inkling of what they would have to endure over the next years for the sake of the Lord and His Heavenly Vision.

Seated With Princes

**'The LORD was with him; He showed him kindness
and granted him favour...'**
(Genesis 3f9:21)

The couple travelled on to the solar energy conference in Genoa. Joshua unexpectedly was called upon to give the keynote speech the opening morning. He was followed by the energy ministers from several North African and Middle Eastern countries.

As a consequence he found himself being sought out by several high officials from these arid countries. Joshua and his wife were given seats of honour with these men at the lavish banquets provided by an enthusiastic Italian government. Faith seized the opportunity to ask these officials about the 'number-one problem' in their countries.

The answer was, invariably, "We can get the technology, we can get the money, but we can't find the PEOPLE - people willing to come and work in our villages, people able to train and develop our nation."

"Your Excellency, your nation is Moslem. What if the only people willing to come and help you are Christians, coming in Christ's Name?" Joshua would ask.

"We would welcome them, Dr Alexander! We MUST have this help..."

Joshua realised that God was fulfilling the Bible verse that had been given to him by the Holy Spirit barely a month before: "**He raises the poor from the dust... He seats them with princes.**"

Throughout the summer Joshua was sent on business trips all over the USA. Wherever he went he shared the "40/40 Vision" (so named because the Solar Belt extends between latitudes 40N and 40S) with the people selected by the Holy Spirit. As a result doors were opened, relationships were forged and people invited him to speak. He received such encouragement and was showered with so many confirmations that he was left without any doubt that what he had 'seen' was the Lord's prophetic Vision - and that it would definitely come to pass.

Into the Deep End

"We are fools for Christ..."
(1 Corinthians 4:10)

The family left Denver with the blessing of their pastor, their church fellowship and their friends. Each of the Alexanders had an inner assurance that God would faithfully care for them as His children as they headed out to Los Angeles, where Joshua had unexpectedly been invited to work with a missions group.

Without any prompting, their church fellowship and some other loving friends began sending Joshua and Faith a few hundred dollars a month. Selling their furniture had also raised some cash. They still had a little credit left, and Joshua had the possibility of some consulting work in the future. Otherwise the day to day survival of the five Alexanders lay entirely in God's Hands, yet again.

"**The LORD's unfailing love surrounds the one who trusts in Him.**"
(Psalm 32:10b)

11

The Refiner's Fire
(September 1980 - March 1983)

---

*"He will be like a refiner's fire or a launderer's soap.
He will sit as a refiner and purifier of silver; He will…
refine them like gold and silver."*
(Malachi 3:2b-3a)

"Our God is a consuming fire."
(Hebrews 12:29)

Almost as soon as the Alexanders arrived in Los Angeles, they discovered that the enthusiastic invitation from the missions group had been made without proper authorisation. It was in fact null and void. Nevertheless, two rooms on campus were made available to the family on a temporary basis and they moved in. In contrast to Joshua's earlier visit there, vanishingly little interest was shown in the 40/40 Vision. The family felt out of place, bewildered and discouraged. Two weeks passed without any glimmer of what to do or where to go next. Joshua began to fast on only water. He and his wife prayed earnestly for God's direction.

After seven days the Lord finally spoke to Joshua: *"You may stop fasting now and leave. Go south over the mountains and into the Valley."*

After making some inquiries, Faith said, "What could that mean, Joshua? The San Fernando Valley is the only valley that anyone around here has heard of, but that's to the north." She pondered for a few moments.

"I just remembered something!" she exclaimed, looking intently at her husband. "Didn't our friends back east give us a name to contact somewhere in Orange County? That's south of here, isn't it? Why don't we ask them about a 'Valley'?"

Joshua found the number, dialled and introduced himself. "We're friends of the McNeils in Virginia and we're moving south of Los Angeles with our three children - though we don't know exactly where yet. I was wondering, can you recommend a Christian school in your area?" (He was surprised to hear this question come out of his mouth.)

"Well, we think the best one is in the Valley."

"The VALLEY?"

"Yes, the Capistrano Valley - San Juan Capistrano."

With relief and thanksgiving, the family packed up their things and within a day or so had said goodbye to Los Angeles.

Less than two hours drive to the south, over the San Joaquin Hills and into the Capistrano Valley, they came to the bright and beautiful Mission town of San Juan.

The couple found a cosy little townhouse ready for occupancy at a reasonable rent, and (as the Lord had directed) the children were enrolled in the Christian school. Curiously, the Alexanders hardly ever heard the area referred to again as 'the Valley'.

The Upgrade

Before a month had elapsed, Joshua was engaged by his former employer as a consultant to support a three-day meeting in Boston. The day before his return to California he received a distress call from his wife.

"Oh Joshua, I'm afraid our car has given up. I couldn't get it to start so I had it towed, and the station mechanic said it would cost a lot more to repair than it's worth. What should we do? We can't live in California without a car, and we can't afford to buy another one."

"Don't be anxious, honey, our Good Shepherd has already provided the solution. Only last night I was talking to our friend Dale in Denver and he asked me if we might need a car. He knows someone who wants to donate her extra car to a 'worthy missionary cause'. Dale had already told her about us, and the car is sitting there. All I have to do is pick it up in Denver. Isn't that wonderful?"

"How sweet of the Lord. And what incredible timing, provided you can use your ticket to fly into Denver instead of LA. Can you?"

"Sure enough. I'll be home a day or so later than planned, but with a CAR. Glory to God..."

The Lord showed His sense of humour as well as His timing. The car turned out to be a recent Datsun sedan - the same make as a station wagon the Alexanders had given away at the Lord's command some years before. God simply recycled the blessing precisely when needed, but with an upgrade (this car was five years younger).

After Joshua arrived home in the shiny blue sedan, he asked for a second opinion about the old Plymouth and found that it only needed a minor repair after all, which was quickly done.

"So what do we do now? The Plymouth has a clean bill of health. Since we don't need two cars, shouldn't we sell the Datsun?"

"A wonderful idea, Faith. That way the children can stay in their school, we can afford to pay the rent, we can keep up our interest payments... and we can even eat!"

Poverty versus Prosperity

"As the heavens are higher than the earth, so are My ways higher than your ways and My thoughts than your thoughts."
(Isaiah 55:9)

Jehovah Jireh was their faithful Provider, but at the same time the couple suffered a string of humiliating rejections by Christians, even by some who had earlier embraced the Vision with enthusiasm. Joshua's message was no longer welcomed, though it (and he) had not changed. He no longer had the same credibility in people's eyes because he was no longer employed. It did not matter to them that he was unemployed out of obedience to the Lord.

The couple had become 'non-persons', without 'market value'. The 40/40 Vision for these southern Californians was an embarrassing intrusion into their comfort zone. It was something quite irrelevant to most individuals, most churches and sadly most ministries. For the Alexanders, life in the 'Valley of Opulence' (as they called it) with nothing to call their own, was simply hurtful.

They learned what it was like to walk in the shoes of the poor and to be ignored by the rich. They also found out who their real friends were. Fewer than a handful of precious people who wholeheartedly responded to the 40/40 Vision and who were mostly hard up like themselves.

The two of them felt betrayed and cried out to their Heavenly Father for comfort. *"My dear children,"* He replied, *"don't you realise that everything in your life has come from My hand? You need to experience poverty to identify with the poor, and you need to experience rejection to identify with the forgotten, rejected ones. I am teaching you to identify with the people in the million remote villages.*

"Your life has now become a daily intercession on behalf of the poorest of the poor - those souls that I have called you to serve and bless. So give yourselves to prayer, and spend yourselves on behalf of the hungry."

Their situation became transparently clear by this word of wisdom. They obediently gave themselves to daily prayer on behalf of the world's helpless and hopeless people, pleading with the Lord to deliver them, heal them and restore them. The suffering and devastation of the remote villagers, already shown to Joshua in the 40/40 Vision, caused them great heartbreak as they interceded for them before God's throne of grace. Each day they identified a little closer with those who were on God's own heart and felt more of His pain and compassion for the poorest of the poor.

Faith and Joshua used every opportunity to alert individuals and organisations to the coming global famine. They tried to encourage them to grasp this great opportunity to fulfill 'the law of love' as expressed in the New Testament: **"This is how we know what love is: Jesus Christ laid down His life for us. And we ought to lay down our lives for our brothers. If anyone has material possessions and sees his brother in need but has no pity on him, how can the love of God be in him? Dear children, let us not love with words or tongue but with actions and in truth."** (1 John 3:16-18)

It was like trying to awaken Sleeping Beauty, however. Only the kiss of the Prince of Peace, Christ Jesus Himself, would have any effect.

The day after Christmas the couple prayed for a specific word of reassurance from Father. He pinpointed Jeremiah 29:11-14 [written to the House of Judah while exiled in Babylon]:

"For I know the plans I have for you," declares the LORD, "plans to prosper you and not to harm you, plans to give you hope and a future.

Then you will call upon Me and come and pray to Me, and I will listen to you. You will seek Me and find Me when you seek Me with all your heart. I will be found by you," declares the LORD, "and will bring you back from captivity and restore your fortunes. I will gather you from all the nations and places where I have banished you," declares the LORD, "and will bring you back to the place from which I carried you into exile."

The Holy Spirit filled their hearts with divine faith to appropriate these promises for their own life, and He wrote the verses on their hearts to comfort them in their own 'exile'.

The couple remembered that in Eau Claire their Good Shepherd had promised one day to free them from their indebtedness. Was He now saying that one day he would take them back to the place where their spiritual odyssey and financial 'captivity' had first begun – Maryland?

Out of the Frying Pan...

"Many are saying of me, 'God will not deliver him...' But You are a shield around me, O LORD."
(Psalm 3:2-3a)

After six exasperating months in southern California, the Alexanders' resources and support all dried up at once, as if by divine intent. Without money to pay for rent or school fees, the Alexanders gave notice on their house and withdrew the children from school as of the end of April 1981. They prepared to move out without having any idea where to go.

A Chinese missionary couple with four children (and a fifth on the way) had recently made friends with the Alexanders. In spite of their own pressing needs the Lees began to bring bags of groceries and spiritual comfort to the family almost weekly. During April, Joanna Lee - without having any idea that they were without support and were facing huge bills and loan payments - quietly took Faith aside.

"Dear sister, I want you to have this." Joanna removed a heavy Chinese 24-carat gold bracelet from her wrist and pressed it into Faith's hand. "Sell it, please, and pay your bills. The Lord told me to give it to you because He wants you to have it." They embraced each other in tears. The gold price was high enough (and the bracelet heavy enough) for the Alexanders to realise several hundred dollars from the sale, covering the month's obligations in full.

On Easter morning, the family were worshipping in a church service when a stranger sitting behind Joshua touched him on the shoulder and whispered, "I have a scripture verse for you: Revelation 3:8. The Lord Jesus loves you and will never forsake you."

He opened his Bible and read: "**I know your deeds. See, I have placed before you an open door that no one can shut. I know that you have little strength, yet you have kept My word and have not denied My name.**" Joshua bowed his head and wept.

In the final days of April, the Alexanders heard about a Christian community that had been struggling to control its sky-high electricity costs. Joshua was urged to offer the group his technical help, so the couple drove across the Santa Ana Mountains to a remote part of Riverside County. Once at the community ranch, he described the 40/40 Vision to the leadership.

"Brother Joshua, why don't you use this ranch as a 'pilot village' for the Vision? Pray about it! We could become independent of the electric company, and you could test out your ideas for implementing God's strategy with solar and wind equipment... Of course, you're all welcome to move here whenever you like - we have plenty of room."

The sprawling, ramshackle ranch seemed appropriate enough for modelling a third-world village, it seemed to Joshua. He and Faith prayed and got a definite go-ahead from the Lord. The five of them moved in on the last day of April with everything they owned stuffed into the back of the old Plymouth wagon. It was their only option and they accepted it gratefully. God had provided them with a safe haven; the Alexanders had been rescued once again.

They little suspected that the ranch would become the graveyard of their hopes and dreams.

...Into the Fire

"Unless the LORD builds the house, its builders labour in vain."
(Psalm 127:1)

Life on the ranch was an exhausting and constant trial for the Alexanders and during their six-week stay they learned an enormous amount about how to accomplish nothing at all. Even though the Lord was with them, His anointing was not.

Everything Joshua tried came to naught. Everything Faith tried came to naught. And the children? Jacqueline, now 11, stayed part of each week back in San Juan with friends in order to continue her gymnastics training (all the while wishing it were the whole week). Rick and Andy kept each other company and tried to stay out of the way of the ex-prisoners (some of them former murderers, thieves and drug-addicts) who were working on the ranch for their rehabilitation. Faith 'home-schooled' the children each morning; their afternoons were spent with the animals, the boys feeding the pigs and Jacqui helping with the horses.

One day after lunch the two small boys decided to take a long walk to 'get away from it all'. Hours later they found themselves far away, without any idea how to find their way back to the ranch. After some panicky minutes, nine-year-old Ricky stopped and prayed, *"Father we're lost! Please show us the way home, in Jesus' Name..."* The Lord was gracious and immediately pointed them in the right direction. They made it back just before dusk, to the immense relief of their father and mother. Richard never forgot that providential answer to his prayer.

After a month at the ranch, Joshua heard the Holy Spirit calling him to fast for an indefinite period. Instead of joining the others at mealtimes, he adopted the practice of walking around the perimeter of the property twice daily, interceding for the Lord's people and purpose.

One evening while Joshua was out on his walk, Faith left the children to finish their supper in the main building and went back to her room. She lay down, limp from the unremitting heat and emotionally at the end of herself.

"Oh Lord," she wept, *"when is this agony ever going to end? Everything we've tried has failed. We have no money or credit left. We're in the middle of nowhere. And now our car won't even start. On top of it all, we've had no direction from You since You sent us here, in spite of Joshua's fasting already for two weeks...*

"I don't see ANY sign that Your Spirit is with us to work out the 40/40 Vision here. Quite the contrary, Lord - all our efforts have been futile. Without the power of Your Spirit, the 'streams in the desert' will never flow anywhere, and transformation will never happen.

"Lord, what has it all been FOR? What have we accomplished these six weeks - actually, in these nine months? It's pitiful. The Vision is NOWHERE. Why did You ever show it to Joshua? I just don't understand You, Lord. You've brought us nothing but pain and grief..."

"My daughter," came an unexpected but gentle reply to her heart, *"what you have been experiencing is as nothing compared with MY pain and MY grief - My pain over the downtrodden, abandoned millions, and My grief over the complacency of My people who refuse to listen to My voice..."*

Joshua entered their little cabin some time later. His wife and children were now lying together on the bed, commiserating with one another. They looked up at him with long sorrowful faces.

He smiled at them encouragingly for a few moments. "My dear suffering family, I have good news," he declared. "The Lord finally spoke to me. He said, *'Your time here is over and you're released. You have learned what you came for. But keep on fasting and praying, and trust Me. Now pack up the car and leave early in the morning, and then you'll see what I shall do.'*"

"Oh Dad, you mean we can finally get OUTAHERE?" cried Jacqui with sudden joy. The children all clapped and shouted, "At last, at last!" and hugged their father and mother with relief.

"Thank You, Lord Jesus," Faith prayed. Then she stood up with a frown. "But Joshua, where can we go from here?"

"That's no problem. I just phoned the Lees and they welcomed us to stay with them for as long as we want."

"Oh what generous hearts they have. God bless them! What would we have done without them?"

"Okay children," said Joshua softly, "go into your room and get all your things together, and Mommy and I will pack up in here. Then get to sleep right away so we can leave very early - just as soon as it's light." The children skipped out into the little adjoining room to pack under Jacqueline's oversight. "...And pray that the car will start!" their father called after them.

"Darling, please come outside for a minute..." He took Faith's hand and very quietly led her outside into the gathering darkness. He pointed at the horizon. "I didn't want to scare the kids, but do you see over there?"

"FIRE!" she gasped. "The trees - they're all on fire."

"Yes, and it's headed this way. I caught sight of it on my walk, just after the Lord told me that we could leave. I stopped in to tell the leaders about the fire, and they tuned in the radio. It is really big, and the wind is blowing it along very fast. It's out of control.

"While I was with them I let them know that we are leaving tomorrow morning. It didn't seem to surprise them, and they were quite nice about it. So I said goodbye for us all.

"The fire is getting closer all the time - can you see? The wind is blowing it straight towards us. At this rate we will all have to leave, maybe before morning. We must pray for the wind to change direction so the ranch will be saved." He held his wife tightly in his arms.

After they had prayed, Faith took a deep breath. "Darling, I really think it's time to give up... on the Vision, I mean. It's got to die."

"Die? It's already DEAD. I realised that tonight. I was asking Father why everything had failed so utterly and why the Vision had come to nothing. All He would say was, *'I'm simply answering your prayer...'* Sweetheart, what do you think He meant?"

She looked at him steadily in the gloom for a long moment. "You can't figure it out, can you? You prayed that He would bring you to NOTHING."

"Oh, that..." Joshua gulped.

"Yes, that. We have only an old car to our name and we have nowhere to call home. Your Vision is dead. We owe tens of thousands of dollars. And now we're escaping from a forest fire in the middle of a wilderness, like refugees - that is if, by a miracle, the car starts. Yes, Joshua, I'd say that He's answered your prayer all right."

"I'm so sorry, my poor girl." He held her in his arms and kissed her. "But since we're into 'true confessions', I happen to recall a certain night back in San Diego when the Lord asked you if you'd be willing to go penniless and homeless and ragged and barefoot down a dusty road... What did you tell Him then?"

"Oh yes, you're right, Joshua," she moaned. 'I said I was willing - and I did mean it! But dear Lord, does that mean the car won't start and we'll have to WALK out of here?"

He laughed at her irony. "Has He ever let us down, Faith? He said *'Pack up the car,'* so I am SURE it'll start. You see, things could be worse! And haven't we learned a tremendous lot here?"

"I suppose we have." She leaned her head on her husband's broad shoulder. They watched the bright orange glow in the distance. It was now evident that the fire was moving to their right, and they could feel a breeze blowing on their left cheeks. They looked at each other with relief.

The wind had changed. God had saved the ranch.

At dawn the family climbed into the loaded wagon and prayed for another miracle as Joshua put the key in the ignition. (He had tried it dozens of times in the past few days but the lock had always jammed.) The key now turned easily in the lock and the engine sprang to life.

Joshua kept the car running until they pulled into the Lees' driveway several hours later. The next day the lock was jammed again. A tow-truck had to take the car away to be repaired.

Faith watched sadly as the old green wagon was towed away. *"How symbolic of the Vision,"* she thought. *"It died out there in the wilderness, just as Sister Gladys predicted."*

"Saved... as one escaping through the flames."
(1 Corinthians 3:15b)

Dragging Around a Dead Body

**"The LORD Himself goes before you and will be with you;
He will never leave you nor forsake you. Do not be afraid;
do not be discouraged."**
(Deuteronomy 31:8)

The Lees' house was overrun with 'uncles' and 'aunties' - their extended Chinese family. Most weren't even related to Timothy and Joanna but all were made welcome in Christ's Name. The Alexanders were embraced, fussed over and made as comfortable as possible, but the added strain of five more persons on the household (particularly on the plumbing) was soon evident.

They knew they had to move on, but to where? As they prayed about it, Faith had a flash of memory. She promptly telephoned an acquaintance at Camp Pendleton (the Marine base between San Juan Capistrano and San Diego).

"Hello, is this Tom Diamond? It's Faith Alexander. Some weeks ago you and Pam bought some of our furniture, just before we left San Juan... That's right, we met you there at the church.

"Well, I just recalled your mentioning that if we were ever in a pinch you might be able to book us into a trailer on the Base for a week or two. Could you please find out if there's one available? Oh thanks, and here's our number..."

The next evening, however, all five Alexanders were squeezed around Tom and Pam's dining table (along with the four Diamond children) in their very modest house on the Marine base. Lifting his glass of water, Joshua toasted his hosts: "Tom and Pam, you are the greatest! How can we ever thank you for inviting us into your home like this?"

"It's our pleasure, but you don't need to thank." Tom smiled radiantly. "After I found out from the office that there were no free trailers, I started praying about how to help you guys.

"The Lord simply said, *'Whose house is it, Tom?'*

"*'Yours, of course, Lord,'* I replied.

"Then He said, *'I want you to share the house and everything I have given you with the Alexanders.'* So please make yourselves at home, as if it's your own place."

"You precious people, may the Lord bless you," Joshua cried. To his children he added, "Isn't it wonderful when people are obedient to God's voice?"

"Oh it's no more than His due," added Pam with obvious sincerity. "This really IS the Lord's house, not ours. Please stay as long as you want..."

"We've been wondering, Joshua," said Tom. "How could you have survived here in Orange County for so many months without a regular income? We just can't imagine it."

Joshua shrugged as he sipped water and watched ten mouths devour Pam's delicious lasagne. "Tom, it was truly by the grace of God," he sighed, and began relating the whole tale of humiliation, rejection and failure, ending with the final six weeks on the ranch.

"It... was... AWFUL," droned Jacqueline, Richard and Andrew like the chorus in a Greek tragedy.

"It really makes you wonder about Orange County, doesn't it?" Pam grimaced, dishing out a third helping of lasagne to each of the seven children around the table. "Most of the people here, even the believers, are so self-absorbed that they have no idea what the rest of the world has to face."

Faith nodded her agreement, but then laughed. "You know, Pam, your lovely lasagne reminds me of a story. Some friends from Denver arrived quite unexpectedly one day at our house in San Juan, just when we had practically no food in the house and no money left. I asked the Lord, *'How am I going to feed everyone?'*

"Within a few minutes the doorbell rang and there was the postman with a gigantic box. It was a VERY late Christmas present from an American friend of Joshua's in Italy. She'd sent us, more or less as a joke, every possible variety of Italian pasta filled with meat or cheese."

"And that's what you served for dinner?" asked Pam, giggling.

"Not just dinner! We ate practically nothing else for breakfast, lunch and dinner for the next two weeks." They all howled with laughter.

That night Joshua had a visitation - not a visitation from God, but from the fleas that were usually resident on the Diamond family pets. (Fleas are unavoidable in that part of California.) The poor man had hundreds of bites the following morning. His wife, though sleeping in the same bed, had not been touched.

Groaning and unable to stop scratching, Joshua lamented, "Why is my blood so irresistible? It must be because I'm fasting…" Just then the family dog ventured into the bedroom. Joshua looked at it closely. Was he seeing a grateful look on the dog's face?

"Darling," he added wryly, "I just realised what Jesus might say about us right now. **'On that night two people will be in one bed; one will be BITTEN and the other left.'"** [After Luke 17:34.]

After a week on the Marine Base, the Alexanders heard the Holy Spirit speak to them in prayer: *"Your intercessions have been accepted - it is done! Joshua's fast is over…"* (He had taken in nothing but water for 20 days and had lost 30 pounds.)

These words from God's Spirit made Faith and Joshua appreciate what God had granted them through their experience of poverty and hunger, a much deeper compassion for the poor and hungry, and a much closer identification with them. Furthermore, the couple had now gained a vital position of intercession[28] from which to pray for the poorest of the poor, and perhaps one day to alleviate their suffering.

---

[28] *For a full explanation of this concept, see* Rees Howells: Intercessor *by Norman Grubb (CLC 1997).*

Faith joyfully welcomed the news that her husband was to start eating again. "Joshua, don't you think it's now time to return to a normal life? We can't go on forever without an income," she volunteered.

He raised his eyebrows. "You mean I should go out and find a... job?"

"Yes, darling, preferably with a salary. Have you forgotten? The 40/40 Vision is dead! Or are you trying to breathe life back into it?"

"A job!" he frowned heavily. "But Faith, what if the Lord raises up the Vision again? You know nothing is impossible with Him... I should be available in case He does, shouldn't I?"

"Joshua, it's DEAD! You need to work again, if only to keep paying our debts. We have five mouths to feed and three growing children to clothe... What's wrong with working in a job, anyway?" she implored with tears now rolling down her cheeks. "Didn't God just tell us that our intercessions had been accepted? Then we've won! It's been a VICTORY, not a defeat.

"And anyway, wasn't the 40/40 Vision all about lives being transformed when people started to produce an income and prosper? People and nations have to have an income or they die - and so shall we. Please darling, can we just get on with our life now?" She gently put her arms around him and murmured, "It's not your responsibility any more, it's God's."

Deliverance!

A phone call made to an old friend in San Diego revealed that she was about to leave on vacation, and she offered the Alexanders her empty apartment for the month of July. They returned to their favourite city and Joshua began to pound the pavement for a job. The very first engineering company he walked into made him an immediate offer.

"This is too easy," he thought. *"It can't be God. Besides, the work isn't up my alley at all."* But after drawing a blank with 21 other firms, he bowed to the inevitable and accepted the position, supervising an industrial laboratory in support of high-reliability electronics manufacturing.

The return to 'normal' life was astoundingly rapid. Without much hope of finding any place to call home, the couple came to look at a beautifully furnished rental house overlooking a canyon in *Tierrasanta* ('Holy Land'). When the owners heard that the pair had been 'sort of missionaries', they refused to take any deposit (there was none on offer), AND reduced the rent, AND delayed payment of the first month's rent... all without any prompting.

The Alexanders moved in with little else than the clothes on their backs to find the cupboards and refrigerator stocked with food. A swimming pool, Jacuzzi and tennis court were only a few steps away. The family's wounds began to heal as each member experienced the Spirit's restoring power.

To crown it all, Faith's younger sister offered them a loan of $1000, allowing minimum payments to be mailed out to each of their many creditors. Amazingly, not one of their payments arrived late. In fact, on looking back the couple recognised that their Lord had been faithful to supply their needs for nearly nine years without a single payment being a day late or a dollar short.

Day of Burial

"Any of you who does not give up everything he has cannot be My disciple."
(Luke 14:33)

About five months later, just before the end of 1981, Joshua was shocked to get a telegram 'out of the blue' from UNIDO (the United Nations Industrial Development Organisation). He was being offered an immediate assignment in Central Africa to create a solar energy program for rural village needs. (This 'UnidoGram' was the unexpected result of a casual enquiry made by Joshua two years earlier.) It seemed to be offering the ideal pilot project for the 40/40 Vision - at UN expense.

After days of intensive prayer over the Christmas break, the couple still lacked peace that this assignment was from the Lord's hand. "Faith, why can't we get CLARITY? We've waited on the Lord, we've searched the scriptures, we've sought Christian counsel from our elders, but NOTHING. Meanwhile, our friends are completely sure that I should accept and go! They don't seem to understand what we mean about having complete peace. How can we proceed without the Lord's peace?" (She shook her head in silence, exhausted by their ordeal.)

Joshua's face was drawn. "There's this shadow of doubt. Is it from anxiety? Or is it because the invitation is NOT God's will?" He wrung his hands. "I have to tell UNIDO my decision tomorrow. Should I presume that God has 'raised up the Vision' because the project seems so pertinent, and accept? Or should I risk missing God's best by turning it down?

"Maybe I should just accept. After all, isn't 90-percent certainty pretty good?" He grimaced at once, convicted by the shallowness of his words. They weren't spoken in faith, nor were they energised by the precious gift of faith so often enjoyed by the couple in past times of crisis.

"Joshua, perhaps the Lord will show us something tonight, in our Bible study meeting," suggested his wife with a helpless shrug.

The meeting began as usual with prayer, singing and worship, and eventually they all turned to the New Testament letter to the Hebrews. The Alexanders had been leading a systematic study of this book for several weeks, and they were about to continue from the middle of the 11th chapter (the so-called 'faith' chapter).

Joshua read aloud from verse 17: **"By faith Abraham, when God tested him, offered Isaac as a sacrifice. He who had received the promises was about to sacrifice his one and only son, even though God had said to him, 'It is through Isaac that your offspring will be reckoned.' Abraham reasoned that God could raise the dead..."**

He had to stop reading about Abraham's obedience to God on Mount Moriah because the Holy Spirit had come on him so strongly. The words swam in front of his eyes: **'God tested him... Isaac as a sacrifice... received the promises... raise the dead.'**

The Spirit of Jesus spoke gently to his heart: *"Give up the African project, Joshua! It is NOT My will for you. Please offer it to Me as your 'Isaac'. Sacrifice it, even though it appears to be My vehicle of promise, and exactly what you have longed for and prayed for to start the Vision. But believe Me when I say that in My perfect time, I WILL raise the dead..."*

Joshua bowed his head. In that instant he saw all his dreams, plans and struggles pass in front of his eyes, and now he recognised them for what they truly were - futile. He gladly surrendered and abandoned them, together with the UNIDO African project.

Something supernatural occurred at that moment, an enormous weight, one that Joshua was not even aware of carrying, came off him and seemed to fall away. It was the burden of the Vision. As he sat there with his eyes closed, the Spirit showed him a remarkable thing. The floor opened up and the burden fell away from his shoulders into an abyss under his feet. It fell deeper and deeper until it was out of sight, and the floor closed up again. Joshua was free!

The Vision, already dead for several months, had at last been buried. It was now God's Vision, because only God could resurrect it from its deep tomb. It was in its proper place, where it would have to stay (he remembered Sister Gladys' words) 'for five, ten, maybe even twenty years.'

Joshua recalled what the Lord had said at the end of the 40/40 Vision: **"Everything will be in place within one to two years."** The words had given him great faith and courage to persevere in the face of great difficulties. Now, at last, he understood what the Lord had really meant; that everything to do with the Vision would be in the TOMB (dead and buried) within one to two years. The Lord of course was right on schedule - it was one year and eight months later.

Joshua shared some of this shattering yet liberating experience with the group that evening and declared, "So you see, we're NOT going to Africa. The Lord asked me to sacrifice the project to Him, even though it was the vehicle of promise that we've been waiting for so long - our 'Isaac'. It's all over now."

But it was not. Next morning, Joshua went cap in hand to his employer to be reinstated (having previously given tentative notice for the African posting). He was thoroughly humiliated by his managers. A far more devastating situation followed, however. The problem arose with two young believers (hitherto good friends of theirs) who strongly desired to take over the Alexanders' house. Presuming that the family was definitely leaving, and ignoring Joshua's warning to wait, they had given notice on their own apartment without telling him. Now they were all packed up and ready to move in!

There was a sudden confrontation. The Alexanders, feeling somewhat responsible for these young girls, decided to move out of their house anyway. When the girls realised that they would be putting a family of five out onto the street, they bitterly refused the offer and left.

The next thing Joshua and Faith knew was that the church leaders had 'excommunicated' them, apparently without cause. Furthermore, their closest friends were told that if they had anything to do with the family they also would be excommunicated. There were no letters, no calls, no visits by the elders. Only one friend had the courage to tell them the situation. Otherwise nothing.

As soon as this injustice was revealed to them, the couple fell on their faces. *"Dear Father, what have we done? We were just trying to be obedient to You, the best we could. Perhaps we shouldn't have said anything to anyone* until we were sure of Your will. Yet Your Word says that plans succeed with many advisers[29]... We are so sorry about this mess, Lord."

"Little children, I am with you. Don't seek to justify yourselves. Say nothing, and let Me be your vindication. Humble yourselves under My Hand, and in due time I will lift you up."

About ten days later, a letter arrived from a friend at the Bible College of Wales. To Faith and Joshua it was a love letter from the Lord Jesus Himself:

"Except by way of the Throne, our last contact was when it seemed that the Lord was giving you an opening into central Africa. I heard that the Lord actually used that Africa 'opening' to lead you into a real **Mount Moriah** *experience (Genesis 22:2). Bless you both, and the precious children! How my heart has gone out to you all!*

"Rest assured that I still believe that the Vision was from the Lord and still stand with you in faith. You have rightly let it all go from your hands - but into His Hands. You could do no else when that was the way He took you. And I know that you sank everything that you had into it and it cost you mentally, emotionally and spiritually, as well as materially.

"I cannot help seeing that it was the way the Master went, the way of the Cross. He too gave His all and did not shrink from the highest price. But what an eternal outcome He will see! And somehow, in God's way and time there will be resurrection harvest from the sowing in death that has been yours. God's ways are inscrutable and I cannot guess how or when, but I know that a divine principle is involved which cannot fail.

"No doubt the Accuser says that you have been shipwrecked. Yes, but shipwrecked on God! - and now He is responsible for all further moves."

---

[29] *Proverbs 15:22*

The Arm of Flesh

"The sacrifices of God are a broken spirit; a broken and contrite heart, O God, You will not despise."

(Psalm 51:17)

For months the couple pondered their experiences of being brought to absolutely nothing and of being 'broken'. Why had it been so necessary to bring them down to zero? The verse[30] **'The Spirit gives life; the flesh counts for nothing'** gave them a clue: the 'arm of flesh' must be broken to permit God to do whatever He wants by His Spirit.

God's promised 'Isaac' (the work of His Spirit) must never be pre-empted by an 'Ishmael'[31] (the work of the flesh). The Holy Spirit needed to break Joshua and Faith. The 40/40 Vision could only come to life by God's resurrection power, NOT by any human strength or exertion. And without His resurrection there would be no outcome (in the words of Sister Gladys, again).

The pair discovered the same inescapable pattern in the Old Testament stories of Abraham, Joseph, Moses, Gideon, Jonah, David, Daniel... the list seemed endless. In every instance the Holy Spirit had spoken words of faith and power into situations of human helplessness, bringing freedom and life out of captivity and death.

Joseph had languished for years in prison and Moses had endured 40 years in the backside of the desert before the Lord exerted His resurrection power. How long would the Alexanders have to wait? Only the Father could know the timing, and though unfathomable, His timing is perfect.

"Let him who walks in the dark, who has no light, trust in the name of the LORD and rely on his God."

(Isaiah 50:10)

Zeros to Zillions

Late in November 1982, around Thanksgiving, the Alexanders were ending a family prayer time together. The children raised the subject of their endless financial difficulties. Jacqueline, nearly 13 and in junior high school, suddenly

---

[30] *John 6:63*
[31] *Genesis 17:17-22; 21:1-14; and Galatians 4:28-31*

confronted her father: "Are we going to be as poor as church-mice forever? I thought you said the Lord would take care of our debts?" She gave him a stricken look.

Joshua's heart contracted in sudden pain. He responded with compassion. "Sweetheart, God has promised to take care of the debts, and He always keeps His promises. But because He wants us to depend on Him alone, He hasn't allowed us to put our trust in anything or anyone else. He has kept us tied up in debt so we won't be able to run off whenever we get the urge and start something without Him. Your mother and I are sure He'll be coming to our rescue soon, though."

"I do hope you're right, Dad," she sighed.

"You'll see Him do it... As a matter of fact, the Lord has shown me something rather interesting about the 'zeros' in our life."

"Zeros, Dad? What do you mean?" asked Richard with a look of concentration.

"Our zeros are the parts of our life which have come to nothing, Ricky. Our finances, our careers, our plans and our ambitions have all come to nothing. We have no possessions, no investments, no property, no roots even. We don't have a city we can call 'home' with friends and neighbours nearby. We have no worldly security in things like savings, pensions or life insurance. These are all things that people consider important, even essential, but we don't have ANY of them. They are our zeros.

"The reason we have so many zeros is that when we decided to put our trust in God, we gave Him the OK to strip these things out of our life and bring us to nothing. We knew He wanted us to trust Him and depend on Him, and not to look to any other provider. You know the song, *'Jehovah Jireh, my Provider'*, don't you? That's what it's all about."

"But it isn't WRONG to own a house and live in the same place your whole life, is it?" asked Jacqui.

"Of course not, no. It just isn't what Father intended for us. He has a different plan for everyone. For us He planned lots and lots of zeros so He could show us His greatness. And we have a bunch of zeros s-o-o-o long!" Joshua stretched his arms wide and made a zero with each hand.

"We're just a bunch of zeros, then!" cackled Andy, provoking hilarity.

"That's right, a bunch of zeros... but there's a twist. Listen: you know how the Bible says that Jesus is the 'Living One'? Tell me, what happens when a lot of zeros follow a '1'?"

Jacqui looked at him with renewed interest. "The One makes the zeros... valuable. I get it! If we follow Jesus, the Living One, then all our zeros get to be worth something."

"A-Plus, princess!" applauded Joshua. "That is how our lives become valuable - in God. A million is worth much more than a thousand not just because of the extra zeros, but thanks to the one that goes in front of them. We live for Christ, the Living One, the Holy One, the Resurrected One - and that's why our zeros have value, because of HIM."

Ten-year-old Richard broke in, bright-eyed: "Then, with all of our zeros, wow! - we must be worth billions, trillions... zillions in God."

"So suddenly we're zillionaires?" trilled Faith, making them all laugh. "Nothing is too difficult for God... He asked us to give up everything to follow Him, and in return He has given us the greatest Treasure of all. It's worth more than silver, gold, houses, land, life insurance, anything and everything. You see, the Treasure is Jesus Himself - and knowing Him! He is our Heavenly Treasure, and He is the One who turns our zeros into zillions. All we have to do is give Him our whole heart. We have nothing to worry about because the Lord is with us, and He is faithful... He will certainly keep His promises!"

"Promises, promises..." chanted the three children together, giggling.

"We're going to see a miracle soon," smiled their father. "The Lord promised to deliver us from all our debts and restore our lives. The same power that raised Jesus from the dead will deliver us." He hugged his wife and children, and prayed inwardly, *"Oh Lord, please do it soon."*

The Hand of God

"It was not by their sword that they won the land, nor did their arm bring them victory; it was Your right hand, Your arm, and the light of Your face, for You loved them!"
(Psalm 44:3)

A phone call came for Joshua a few evenings later from a former colleague in Maryland. "Hi Joshua, it's Larry. How would you like to work for your old company again?"

"Oh Larry, you're putting me on as usual," he laughed.

"No, really I'm not. There's a major new program starting up and I told our vice president that you might be available. They need you on the West Coast team that oversees the work, Joshua. I just thought you'd like to know that he's ordered the LA office to recruit you with an offer you can't possibly refuse!"

Joshua started work in Los Angeles in March 1983, on his 40th birthday. God had restored his career and given him a substantial salary increase as well.

"I am the LORD, the God of all mankind. Is anything too hard for Me?"

(Jeremiah 32:27)

12

His Glorious Riches
(July 1983 - August 1986)

"**My God will meet all your needs according to His glorious riches in Christ Jesus.**"
(Philippians 4:19)

The summer in Los Angeles was sparkling. One mid-July morning Faith was by the open windows, curled up on the sofa with her Bible. The net curtains swished gracefully in the cool breeze coming off the Pacific Ocean only a mile away. She became aware of the presence of the Lord Jesus.

"*How would you like to live in England, Faith?*" The beloved, familiar voice made her heart sing.

"*England, Lord?*" she replied in wonder. "*That would make a change! Yes, I'd love to. How will You manage that?*"

"***Trust Me! You'll be there exactly nine months from now...***"

She picked up the phone and called her husband at work. "Guess what the Lord asked me just now?"

"Darling, you know I can't guess. Just tell me, okay?" There was an edge of apprehension to his voice.

"He asked, '*How would you like to live in England?*'"

"England? Oh, surely NOT!" he replied in a strangled voice.

Fantastic Adventures In Trusting Him

"Why? What kind of attitude is that?" she protested in surprise. "Isn't there a chance your company would send you to work over there?"

"I can't see it at all," he answered shortly. "We already have enough people in the UK office. Besides, the engineer working over in Stevenage is a real 'Anglophile'. I'd say he was immovable. But I'll ask," he added to pacify his insistent wife.

Joshua called back an hour later. "You can forget about England," he declared. "There's just no way the man will come back of his own accord for at least two years. I'm afraid you're up the creek on this one, my love." Then he lost patience and blurted out, "I don't want to hear another word about England, okay?"

Faith was distressed at how abruptly - even harshly - he had hung up. *"That just isn't like him,"* she thought. But she kept her peace, in spite of being certain that the Lord had spoken.

After two long weeks, she couldn't restrain herself from taking the matter one little step further. *"Lord Jesus,"* she prayed, *"would you please confirm our going to England from Your Word?"*

"Acts twenty-two twenty," came the immediate reply to her heart.

She turned to the verse and read, **"And when the blood of Your martyr Stephen was shed, I stood there giving my approval and guarding the clothes of those who were killing him."**

She also read the next verse: **"Then the Lord said to me, 'Go; I will send you far away to the Gentiles...'"**

She moistened her lips and swallowed. This confirmation was too wonderful not to share. She hovered uncertainly by the phone for quite a while before dialling her husband.

Joshua sighed when he heard his wife remind him about England. When she read him the verses, he asked in confusion, "I don't get the point. What's so significant about the death of poor Stephen?"

"Darling, don't be silly. Concentrate! If your firm sends you to England, where will you be working? In Stevenage! What could be more precise?"

There was silence on the line. "All right, I surrender," he chuckled. "I admit that's persuasive. And I am willing to go if the Lord wants to send us. I just can't imagine how He'll ever do it."

His Glorious Riches

"Joshua, you don't have to imagine it, you just have to BELIEVE it, because He has spoken!" She relished having the last word.

When the $1400 rent was due at the end of September, Joshua did not have it. His expenses in Los Angeles were double what they had been in San Diego, and financially he and Faith were struggling as desperately as ever.

"Please do something, Father," he prayed, *"or I'll be forced to default either on the rent or on the banks..."*

A thought came to his mind and he decided to call the landlord to explain their situation. Before he even had an opportunity to speak, the man exclaimed, "I'm so glad you called! I was just about to look up your number to tell you that I need to sell the house, and to make you an offer. If you're willing to stay in the house and show it to prospective buyers, I won't ask you for any more rent. Your deposit will cover the next two months' rent anyway, but after that I'll let you stay rent-free until the house sells..."

Joshua hung up the phone in a daze. "Sweetheart, the Lord has done it again, and just in time as usual. More than that, I see that the house being put up for sale is really a token from the Lord that we ARE going to England in April - just as He told you."

The house was sold in December. Believing that they were indeed leaving for England, the Alexanders sold off most of their furniture and moved into a little furnished apartment on a temporary basis.

At about that time Joshua's supervisor was unexpectedly offered, and took, early retirement. The company ordered the 'immovable Anglophile' back to LA at once, because he was being promoted.

Of course Joshua was offered the position in Stevenage. He also received an unexpected bonus. The company decided to change their policy and pay him a lump sum to cover the transatlantic moving costs of an average family of five, without requiring receipts for the actual costs. Now Faith's skill in moving house (20 times at least) came into its own and paid off handsomely. She pared the household down to a minimum and negotiated the shipment herself, reducing the cost of moving their essential items 6,000 miles to Europe to a paltry $350.

When the lump sum payment came, it was for an astonishing $15,000, allowing them to pay off almost a third of their total debt.

The family flew into London's Heathrow Airport in mid-April. It was Good Friday, precisely nine months after God had given Faith His invitation to live in England. They moved straight into the furnished house that Joshua had already found and rented on a previous visit (having described it to his wife as 'a real beauty').

Faith was appalled as she went through one room after another: the carpets, the walls and the furniture all seemed to taunt her, shouting, *"Look how ugly we are!"*

She slipped into the kitchen to be alone. *"How could Joshua have rented us this house?"* she bristled. *"Father, I hate it! It's really horrible! Why did You allow him to put us here?"*

"Faith, don't worry about it! You'll be out of this house in three months."

"I should be that lucky," she thought bitterly, rejecting the words. *"How could that possibly be the Lord?"*

She tried to pull herself together. She glanced out of the kitchen window at the exquisite daffodils, tulips, weeping willows, shaped conifers and heather bushes framing an immaculately clipped lawn. *"Hmmm. Well, I suppose I'd better keep my eyes on the beauty outside, and not on the mess inside,"* she muttered to herself.

Her husband came in and put his arms around her. "You don't like it, do you." (He had seen her wiping her eyes.) "I'm really sorry, darling. I can't understand it. The house was SO different when I saw it. All these nasty purple and green overstuffed chairs must have been in storage, gathering dust until the previous renters moved their own stuff out." He waved his hand in disgust. "But it's my fault too for not looking carefully at the carpets and the walls. All I saw was the structure, and the central heating, and the number of rooms. It's still exceptional for an English house..." Joshua held her face and looked into her eyes. "I do feel bad for you, honey. Can you ever forgive me?"

She was distraught at the prospect of living with the cacophony of clashing patterns and colours, and found it unusually difficult to forgive her husband. It took weeks before she could walk from one room to the next without her senses being jarred. She felt disappointment, even betrayal. When they had been dirt-poor their homes had always been tasteful and pleasant. Now they were locked into a two-year lease and not even allowed to make the slightest changes to the vile decor.

It was a Sunday evening following seven weeks of hard work when Faith announced to her family that they were officially 'settled'. Joshua was full of admiration and praise for his wife, who had been able to cover up most of the ugliness and make the house much more welcoming.

At nine o'clock next morning, however, there came a telephone call from the leasing agent. "I don't know how to tell you this, Mrs Alexander. I have bad news, I'm afraid. The owners of the house just called me from Singapore to say that they're being transferred back to England.

"I am very, very sorry, but I'm obliged to inform you that they are invoking their 'diplomatic lease-break' clause. You'll have to find somewhere else to live, I'm afraid. It's one of those things. I'm terribly sorry."

Faith made appropriate clucking noises not to give away her true feelings of elation and relief. The Lord had spoken, after all.

The couple found nothing else to rent - not even to buy - in their price range. There was one house, though it was much too expensive of course. Faith dragged Joshua to see it only out of curiosity because she had seen pictures of the interior in an estate agency window. It was breathtakingly lovely. The owners had spent a fortune upgrading it, using the most prestigious interior-decorating firm in London, but this expense had not been included in the selling price.

The couple fell in love with it, and as an anniversary surprise Joshua found a lawyer and put in an offer on the house.

"Joshua, have you gone insane? We can't possibly afford this house," protested Faith. "We don't even have money for the down payment, do we?"

"No we don't, but let's not worry!" he laughed. "Nothing is binding in this funny old country until the so-called 'exchange of contracts', and that can take weeks. Something might happen by then. If not, we can just drop out without it costing us anything at all."

"What 'contracts' are those?" she asked with perplexity.

"I don't exactly know, but the lawyer said that if we like the house we should make a verbal offer and figure out the rest later. He said he could find us a 90-percent mortgage at least. And as for the down payment, darling ... we'll just have to see."

"That's really how it's done here? How PECULIAR..."

Their offer was accepted and the whole family went over to see the house. The children adored it, wandering around as if they were in a dream. They also spent time chatting with the owners about their favourite sports, soccer and gymnastics.

Joshua was duly approved for a 95-percent mortgage, but within a day or so the official mortgage interest rate suddenly jumped up by two whole percentage points. After some agonising, he called up his lawyer and told him to withdraw the offer. With so many bank debts still needing to be paid off, he could not handle such a high monthly payment. Quite apart from that, he had been unable to put together the down payment.

The estate agent called him to try and salvage the sale, admitting that seven other sales had been cancelled that morning because of the interest rate shock. Then he got to the point. "Dr Alexander, the house owners have just called me with a unique proposal. Evidently they are very taken with you, especially with your children, and they really want you to have their house."

"Well it's mutual, but we can't afford the monthly payments..."

"Yes, they understand that. So they want to offer you, at the completion of sale, the cash equivalent of all the extra interest you'll have to pay over the next two years. It would be an outright gift to you, at 'settlement' as it's called in America. A very generous offer, don't you think?"

Joshua's head was reeling. He made a mental calculation. "Why, that amounts to... over 5,000 pounds – 8,000 dollars! Umm, is this a real offer? I mean, can it work like that?"

"Oh yes certainly, although I've never heard of it being done before."

"This is astonishing... Okay! My lawyer will be calling you again."

He gently replaced the phone, dazed and smiling. "How wonderful of God!" he crooned as the others gathered around him. "A gift of $8,000, with no strings attached." Feeling weak in the knees, he sat down. "Do you know what this means? The sellers are putting up over half the down payment. What a God we have - He's actually GIVING us that house."

"THAT'S AWESOME!" sang out Jacqueline and Andrew in ecstasy. After 24 hours of distress at losing the house of their dreams, this U-turn was truly spectacular.

"But Dad," protested 12-year-old Richard with a most sober look, "I still don't see how we can afford that fancy house. I thought you said we didn't have any money?" He was determined to maintain the position of 'financial controller' to keep his parents from going down the tube again.

Joshua put his arm round his son's shoulders and gave him a loving squeeze. "You're right, Rick, we don't have the money. But the Lord has it, and He is providing it ALL! I found out something else yesterday, right after withdrawing the house offer, but I didn't have the heart to tell you in case it got your hopes up again for nothing.

"But now it's a different situation. Listen to me, children. My company has offered us up to $9,000 to cover temporary living expenses while we're in between houses, to spend as we please! That's because we moved straight into the rental house when we first got here and I didn't claim any of these costs before."

"That's fantastic, Dad," they said in unison with shining eyes.

"Yes. We can use most of that money to buy the house, because our friends the Dysons have offered to let us housesit while they're on vacation next month.

"So you see," he continued, grinning, "with this additional gift of $8,000 we'll have the whole down payment and the costs, and STILL have something left over to buy furniture with..."

"Of course, we'll have to be careful with expenses," chimed in their mother, "but we've had lots of practice, haven't we? I'm sure we'll manage."

"And remember, dear Ricky, all our credit cards have been paid off (and cut up), leaving only the banks and our personal loans to be paid off. *Jehovah Jireh* is taking care of us!" Joshua cried. "He promised He would, and He IS. Hallelujah!"

A few days before moving-day, the house owners drove up in a brand-new cream-coloured Rolls Royce and whisked Faith and Joshua from their temporary lodgings to the most elegant restaurant in town.

As the *hors d'oeuvres* were being served George ventured a question. "What makes you people so different? There is something special about you and your family. Your children are so lovely and you are all so... so alive. We want to know what it is. What makes you tick?"

George and Beth were spellbound to hear the stories of God's guidance and provision, and especially how the Lord Jesus had revealed Himself to them as the Risen Saviour.

It was George's turn by the time the dessert trolley came around. "I'm so glad you told us these remarkable stories. I admit they made the hairs on the back of my neck stand up," he laughed. "But I have to share the strange thing that happened to me. Two days after we offered to cover your extra interest payments, a man came to our door and out of the blue offered me a full-price sale immediately - for cash."

Joshua and his wife gasped at the same time. "Why didn't you take it?"

"It was all rather amazing," said George as he ran fingers through his wavy blond hair. "I told the man that the house was already promised to someone else, and that was it! I just couldn't accept his cash. Everything in me wanted YOU to have the house. We were so taken with your children, you see.

"But now I'm realising that it was God who constrained me to give you the money and then make sure you got the house. He USED me - as His instrument - to bless you! And do you know something? I don't even mind." He sat back and roared with laughter.

Within two months of buying the house, the official interest rate plummeted back down as suddenly as it had risen. The Alexanders' monthly mortgage payment, which was on a variable rate, was adjusted downward to BELOW what Joshua had originally budgeted. The financial pressure was totally relieved and that beautiful house - so generously provided by God Himself - served to heal all the pain of the past, especially for the children. The endless penny-pinching denials faded into distant memories as the Lord now showed the Alexander family an open-handedness they had never experienced in the past.

God Keeps His Promise

"Is the LORD's arm too short? You will now see whether or not what I say will come true for you."
(Numbers 11:23)

After working in England for a year, Joshua qualified for a company-paid 'home leave' benefit. To his delight, the firm allowed him to take the benefit without having to travel 'home' to Los Angeles. (They had no home there anyhow.) Instead, the family enjoyed three weeks of vacation in Greece: a luxury cruise to several islands in the Aegean, sandwiched between two weeks at a Club Med resort - at absolutely no personal cost.

On their return from this unforgettable holiday, the couple became aware of a strange feeling of restlessness in their spirits. They sought their Lord in prayer.

He spoke to both of them: ***"The time has come to put this house up for sale. Then you will see what I shall do."***

"Joshua, can you believe it? He wants to move us out of this wonderful house after only a year! Is this ever going to end?"

"Our Father God knows best, my poor darling. Maybe we'll be leaving England sooner than we think. Anyway, we have to face the fact that this is HIS house. He paid for it, after all. Will you miss it terribly?"

"We'll all miss it, Joshua. You know that." Her eyes were full of tears.

Joshua listed the house with an estate agency, and was informed that house prices had appreciated by more than 10 percent in that year alone. Within four weeks a buyer came along, and the proceeds from the sale ($30,000) enabled the Alexanders to pay off every last remaining debt. Joy at being debt-free even outweighed the regret over leaving the beautiful house.

The Alexanders marvelled at God's wisdom and His sovereign power. He had led them into debt by persuading them to buy a lovely house that they could not possibly afford, and now He had delivered them out of debt by enabling them to buy another lovely house that, likewise, they could not possibly afford. Only God could have worked out a project of such perfect symmetry to achieve His purposes.

God had fulfilled His promise to restore their fortunes in His own way and in His own time. The spectre of financial ruin that had stalked them for exactly 13 years since November 1972 had been banished.

Their debt had been finally, totally - divinely - forgiven.

Deep Revelations

"He reveals deep and hidden things; He knows what lies in darkness, and light dwells with Him."
(Daniel 2:22)

The Alexanders moved into a plain little rental house only a short walk from Joshua's office. It was not much different from the house in Maryland where Faith had first heard the Lord's voice. In fact, they had barely settled in when God began speaking to her about an entirely different matter, one that had caused her years of inner anguish.

It started with a divine revelation early one frosty morning in November. Faith was dreaming and next to her in the dream was the Lord – His presence was unmistakable. Together they watched a scene unfold.

Some dancers were preparing themselves offstage, each one was writing something on a large white card. As the half dozen or so dancers made their way onstage she recognised them to be members of the non-denominational church that the family was now attending.

Music started in a minor key. The dancers moved slowly around the stage in a circle, holding the cards against their chests to conceal what was written. One by one, however, they began to reveal the cards to each other. Faith strained to see the writing but it was a blur.

"What do those cards say, Lord?"

"The dancers have written down their sins on the cards, and they are now confessing them to one another."

It was a confessional dance. *"How humiliating!"* she thought, feeling her cheeks burn and her body become tense as she watched, appalled. She couldn't imagine confessing her sins in public, or even aloud for that matter. For years she had pressed them down and as far out of sight as possible.

Next the dancers bent down and laid the cards with their inscribed sins at their feet. A sense of great expectancy was in the air. Dramatically the music modulated and changed from minor to major. The dancers picked up their cards, which somehow had been transformed. The tempo accelerated and the dancers were whirling and rejoicing around the stage. They sang songs of victory and praise as they lifted their 'changed' cards high above their heads.

"Do you understand?" the Lord whispered in her ear. **"The new cards symbolise the grace and truth I have given them. Each of them has embraced My answer to their sin, and now they are free!"**

"Surely You aren't serious, Lord? Your people confessing their sins in a public confessional dance? This is too heavy for me..."

Faith opened her eyes to escape, but could hear the Shepherd's voice calling after her, **"You will know the truth, and the truth will set you free..."**

That same evening she described her dream to a small Bible study group. There followed a lively discussion of the scripture, **"Therefore confess your sins to each other and pray for each other so that you may be healed. The prayer of a righteous man is powerful and effective."** (James 5:16)

Some reacted with grateful acceptance of this Biblical prescription for healing, others with complete ignorance. They all wanted to be healed, but none of them was keen on the confessional aspect of the dance. God would have to move powerfully by His Spirit to get those hearts confessing and feet dancing.

Before going to sleep that night, Faith posed the inevitable question that had been brewing in her heart throughout the day. *"Lord, what sin do You want me to confess?"*

His answer came in the form of a second dream in the early hours of the morning. Again the Lord was by her side. She recognised the scene - the hallway of her favourite childhood home in Spokane, Washington. There she was at nine years old, stretching up to reach a moneybox on the top shelf of the linen cupboard. For the second time in two nights Faith felt herself blushing in a dream. This episode had been buried and forgotten for over thirty years.

"Guilty, guilty," she exclaimed, acknowledging her sin. *"Yes, I am definitely guilty."* She had stolen repeatedly from her oldest brother's moneybox to support a butterscotch-sundae habit at the corner drugstore. What was worse, the money was not his – it belonged to the high school drama club.

Abruptly the scene changed. *"What's all that commotion?"* wondered Faith. She saw herself cowering behind her bedroom door, listening to angry voices coming from the hallway. Her parents were furious with her brother but he was insisting on his innocence. Her heart raced with fear at the prospect of being found out, but no one thought of accusing her. Her secret was safe. Her brother took the 'rap', paying back the missing money out of his paper-route earnings.

*"**You know the gruesome headaches you've had all these years?**"* came the familiar voice. (Faith nodded, bewildered at this new tack.) *"**They began the same year. By stealing, you gave Satan a foothold in your life, and you have paid dearly for your guilt. That is the price of unconfessed sin.**"*

She saw herself lying in bed with a cold washcloth over her eyes, suffering one of her many crippling headaches. It was a stunning revelation from the Lord - in three years of psychotherapy this sequence of events had never surfaced.

*"**My child, you are no different from Adam and Eve, back in the Garden of Eden. After they sinned, they hid from God, they hid from the truth, and**"*

they hid from their own sinfulness. You have been hiding from the truth all these years. That is why the thought of confession is so painful to you!

"You have also been hiding from your brother, because this sin built a wall between you and blocked your relationship. The only way to tear down the wall is to confess your sin to him and ask for his forgiveness.

"Satan is very proud of the walls that he builds to divide people – especially My people. He uses unconfessed sin and unforgiveness as his raw materials..."

"You are so amazing, Lord!" she prayed, now fully awake. *"You have certainly changed my attitude these past 24 hours."*

Faith immediately got up and began to write a letter to her brother, asking for his forgiveness. Writing letters had always been difficult for her in the past, but she noticed her pen flying across the page, the words coming easily and fluently. Signing the letter, she remembered what the Lord had promised: **"You will know the truth, and the truth will set you free."**

A few days later, on November 21st, she was sorting through some old Christmas cards and found one dated 1977. It was from Father Anthony, the parish priest who had instructed her before she entered the Roman Catholic Church. With a jolt Faith realised it was exactly 23 years to the day since he had baptised her.

A whirling cloud of guilt and pain overwhelmed her. *"No, no, this is ridiculous. Stop it!"* she told herself. But recriminations kept coming to taunt her. In light of her recent dreams about confession, she began to tremble at what might be coming.

She wanted no part of it, but before she could dodge the thought there came a whisper, **"It's time to make a good confession. You didn't leave the Catholic Church honourably. You need to make a good confession..."**

Remembering her past failures at confession, Faith prayed in anguish, *"No, Lord, I can't. You know I can't. It's too painful for me. Please, anything but that. Confession terrifies me. Please, no, no, no!"*

Waves of uneasiness poured over her. It was one thing to write a letter to her brother, but the thought of returning to a Catholic priest for confession - no, never again! She really hated the thought of 'making confession' and was filled with anxiety and panic. Surely this latest prompting was some neurotic residue from the past? Surely it could not be the Lord? She tried to quash the voices that were bombarding her and not listen to them.

"I don't want to hear another word about this!" she declared with authority, then relented a little, *"...unless that really was You, Lord."*

The Struggle for Freedom

"If you hold to My teaching, you are really My disciples. Then you will know the truth, and the truth will set you free."
(John 8:31-32)

As Christmas drew closer, Faith found herself longing to spend it with her family and friends in the USA. She had not seen them in five years and the pull of her heart 'homeward' was becoming irresistible. *"But isn't my place with my husband and children, caring for them during the holidays?"* she wondered. She sounded out the children about all of them going together to Ohio for the Christmas holidays.

"No way, Mom!" they replied with one voice. "We all want to go skiing. You go off to Ohio and we'll go to Switzerland with Dad!"

Faith's heart was severely divided. Joshua encouraged her to 'pray it through'. She knew that he wanted her to be obedient to God's will, but he was clearly hoping they would all be going together to enjoy the little apartment he had booked in Crans-Montana. Faith had no desire for the 'high life' and was still dithering two weeks before Christmas. She longed to have specific guidance from the Lord but only sensed vague inner promptings.

At the Sunday morning service the pastor's wife, Wendy, approached her. "I think I have a word from the Lord for you, Faith," she began shyly. "He seems to have been telling you to do something, but you can't believe it's really Him, yet it IS! So be at peace, and do it."

Reassured, she booked the trip with the wholehearted encouragement of her family. The airline had grossly overbooked the pre-holiday flight, however, so when Faith arrived to check in she was 'bumped' along with some 200 other passengers. There was complete chaos at all the desks so she wandered off to find a telephone. She called home.

Jacqueline answered. "Mom, just go back to them and ask for compensation! And get them to book you on another flight..."

The Provider, Jehovah-Jireh, now showed His hand. After Faith had waited in line again, the airline representative readily agreed to both her requests. She was reimbursed in full for the round-trip fare, and was given free passage (and the last seat) on another flight leaving a few hours later.

Her 'welcome home to Ohio' was delightful, and Faith was pampered, loved and appreciated. Each evening she spent with the Lord, discovering new truths in the Bible about righteousness. Sleep seemed almost irrelevant because of the great gift of having so many hours alone with God. She remembered with a smile the scripture the Spirit had given her just before leaving England: **"In His presence is fullness of joy."** (Psalm 16:11)

Faith decided to contact Father Anthony several days later. She was very fond of him and grateful for the tremendous support he had been to her at a very painful time in her life. One day in the mid-1960s, however, he had arranged a meeting with Faith and her parents. The priest had explained kindly but firmly that she had become too attached to him and that it was not a healthy situation. His parting words to her had been, "Come back and see me when you are married and have three children!"

Now 23 years later, they met again and exchanged stories of how the Holy Spirit had worked in their different lives with miracles, disciplines and an ever-deepening relationship with the Lord Jesus. As the visit was ending, Father Anthony encouraged Faith to write a book (having no idea about the Alexanders' on-going project).

Faith gathered up her scarf and gloves and muttered, "You have no idea how difficult it is, being obedient to the Lord in writing our stories…"

The priest quipped over his shoulder as he went to fetch her a calendar, "You'd better be obedient or I will give you a penance!"

A cold blade pierced her heart. *"The 'good confession'… Oh no, Lord! Was that really You speaking to me back in November? If so, then why didn't You remind me before I came to see him today? I'd completely forgotten and now it's too late - I'm on the way out the door. Help!"* Her cheeks were burning with guilt and confusion as she left.

For the next three nights she had no rest. Fear, condemnation and confusion tormented her in turn as she wrestled with the Accuser and agonised in the crucible of decision. Was it the Lord wanting her to go back to the priest, or just her imagination? Or was it the Evil One having a field day with her psyche? She questioned everything, particularly her motivation in wanting to see Father Anthony again.

Faith had not felt so miserable in years, weighed down with unresolved problems and pain. At her wit's end, she sifted through the notes she had made the week before. A scripture jumped out at her: **"Be clear-minded and self-controlled so you can pray."** (1 Peter 4:7)

"That's what I need, Lord," she wept, *"to deal with this irrational panic. Please help me to be clear-minded and self-controlled so I can pray, and hear Your voice."*

The Lord answered her prayer. As her mind cleared, Faith realised she needed to submit this struggle to the Word of God that **"judges the thoughts and attitudes of the heart."** (Hebrews 4:12)

Faith began to search the scriptures in earnest, holding the shield of faith close to her heart to resist the Devil's repeated attacks. The Holy Spirit gave her passage after passage: **"He who conceals his sins does not prosper, but whoever confesses and renounces them finds mercy."** (Proverbs 28:13) **"If we confess our sins, He is faithful and just and will forgive us our sins and purify us from all unrighteousness."** (1 John 1:9) **"God opposes the proud but gives grace to the humble. Submit yourselves, then, to God. Resist the devil and he will flee from you. Come near to God and He will come near to you. Wash your hands, you sinners, and purify your hearts, you double-minded."** (James 4:6-8)

She found it amazing that the scriptures favoured Confession so strongly. *"Then why am I so opposed to it?"* she prayed.

Silence.

"What's wrong with simply confessing to You in my own private prayer closet?"

Silence.

Anxiety and anguish began to overwhelm her. This wrestling with a silent Lord was agonising!

"I can see that Confession is a good thing, Lord Jesus, but surely I can just plead Your precious Blood and confess my sins to You alone? You are the great High Priest. Why should I confess to anyone else? And why would You send me to a Catholic priest? I don't even attend a Catholic church. I haven't been in one for years."

Silence.

"All right, all right, I give up! I'll go to Confession."

At once peace settled in Faith's heart. She did not dare to think or move. After a few minutes her heart stopped pounding, and she decided calmly and rationally that she was being hysterical. Ever so gently, with the tiniest shift of her mind, Faith reversed her decision. *"Maybe if I keep a really low profile God will not notice..."*

Wrong! Terror of the soul returned with a vengeance. She began to struggle yet again with the barrage of painful memories and accusations. They kept surfacing and Faith kept trying to press them down and hide them. In this maze of conflicting emotions and motivations she found it very difficult to discern God's will. *"Why is this 'island of conflict' raising its head? Why does it cause me so much pain? And what is it anyway?"*

In desperation she sat down and wrote a letter to the Lord, asking the Holy Spirit to illuminate the path He favoured. She put down everything she could think of, all the psychological and theological issues that were confusing her and causing her grief.

As she reviewed these ramblings, the Lord at last spoke unequivocally to her heart: **"Father Anthony is My special gift to you. I want you to go back."**

Once again the Lord embraced His daughter with peace. Faith came to her senses at last, perceiving that the Spirit of Jesus had brought her to Ohio for the purpose of blessing her, and had handpicked her former friend and counsellor to be the instrument of this blessing.

Nonetheless, she made a few conditions of her own. *"OK, I'll call Father Anthony, but I am not willing, repeat, not willing to tell him on the phone that I want to confess my sins. No way! Secondly, since I'm leaving in just a few days and he is so busy, You'll have to open the door if You want me to go through with this..."*

The Lord was well aware of Faith's weakness and reluctance, and had a ready answer: **"Just tell him that Satan has tried to sift you as wheat".**[32]

"What? Really, Lord? Isn't that a bit melodramatic?"

"It's the truth! Trust Me."

Faith made the call from a phone booth, barely able to speak. Father Anthony agreed to see her in two days. The die was cast.

---

[32] *Luke 22:31*

Set Free!

Faith felt strangely detached and calm driving across town to Father Anthony's church. She was determined to follow the Lord obediently through this 'Valley of Baca'.[33] *"This too shall pass,"* she encouraged herself, but her hands felt cold and clammy and she was trembling as she rang the doorbell.

"Lord, You promised to give me the words. I'm counting on You to bring me through this! Where are You?"

After the usual greetings, Faith sat down with growing anxiety. *"Lord, help! Where are You?"*

Meanwhile the Evil One was taunting her: *"What are you doing here, you fool?"*

Friendly and relaxed, Father Anthony walked around his desk and sat down opposite his reluctant visitor.

Faith swung her head quickly to the right and to the left. (Was this one last attempt to hide? The song *"Oh sinner man, where you gonna run to?"* flashed through her mind.) Her mouth was dry and she had no idea what to say. This WAS a big mistake, after all.

"Wwweeelll? What happened?" the priest asked with a quizzical yet compassionate expression.

Momentarily confused, Faith realised he must be referring to Satan having tried to sift her as wheat. Thanks to Anthony's comical expression, she completely relaxed (he was obviously a 'pro' at these things). Now the positive memories and trust in her friend made a way for the Holy Spirit to take over. Satan had had his day.

As soon as she began to speak, Faith became aware of the power of the Holy Spirit overcoming all her fear and self-consciousness. Her mind became quietly attentive to God's leading. Truth and wisdom were the guides as the two friends reviewed the past. They walked down the corridors of time, stopping along the way to unlock doors, open windows and clear away rubbish.

Finally they descended into the stronghold where the Evil One had established his headquarters. The searchlight of the Spirit exposed the poison that had infiltrated Faith's life. It had kept her from being useful in God's

---

[33] *'Baca' means 'trials' (Psalm 84:6).*

kingdom, separated her from Christian brothers and sisters, stunted her growth as a child of God and caused her to compete, argue and criticise.

"I know the sin in my life that really grieves the Lord's heart." Faith spoke slowly and matter-of-factly. "It is PRIDE." She lowered her gaze to the floor. The truth of this statement reverberated in her heart, and the enormity of her serious sin crashed into her like a shockwave. She was overwhelmed with grief and begged the Lord for forgiveness.

"Yes, Lord," she prayed, *"pride was the fortress that kept me from growing in the image of Christ. How many people have I hurt with my superior and arrogant ways? How could I have been so blind? I've confessed the sin to You before, Lord, but it never seemed as serious or real as it does now. Why have You walked and talked with me for all these years when my heart was so proud?"*

Faith noticed that her surroundings were changing. She seemed to be entering another world and everything both inside and outside her was stretched out in slow motion. Her perceptions became exquisitely sharp.

She discerned a thick transparent curtain hanging like a veil around her, about three feet away. She was alone with God inside this veil in some timeless dimension. Her body, mind and spirit were utterly still and transfixed by the holiness of God. His love caressed her like a mantle. It was as if the Lord had anaesthetised her body in order to do divine surgery on her spirit.

She was filled with awe and wonder at God's amazing holiness - it was all around her. She saw herself for the first time as a sinner saved by His love and grace. Redemption became real to Faith as never before. She was facing herself as a sinner - in the presence of a Holy God.

Glancing slowly to her right she discerned a dark, ugly green form floating away and downwards before disappearing. Her heart leaped. *"Was that real, or was it my imagination, Lord? Did you just kick the spirit of pride out of my life? Has it gone for good? Yes... I do feel different! Very, very different. Thank You, Lord, thank You!"*

There was no more fear, no more taunting voice, no more resistance. Quietness and peace filled her whole being. Faith's inner enemy had been routed and completely destroyed through the act of confession by the power of God. She suddenly recalled the scripture, **"So if the Son sets you free, you will be free indeed."** (John 8:36)

His Glorious Riches

Although this meeting had not been prefaced by any of the usual sacramental prayers, Father Anthony said softly, "Let's seal this with prayer." He reached over and put his hands on Faith's head and prayed for the Lord's forgiveness.

She got up to leave in a daze of wonder. All she could do was pray the scripture again and again: **"Holy, holy, HOLY is the LORD Almighty!"** (Isaiah 6:3)

Driving home she decided to celebrate by purchasing a worship tape. She could hardly contain her joy as she listened: **"Happy is the one whose sin freely is forgiven. His innocence has been declared by the Lord of Heaven."** (From Psalm 32:1-2)

A couple of days later she was on an airplane back to England, and the Lord highlighted a familiar scripture in the New Testament: **"Simon, Simon, Satan has asked to sift you as wheat. But I have prayed for you, Simon, that your faith may not fail. And when you have turned back, strengthen your brothers."** (Luke 22:31-32)

"...And when you have turned back, strengthen your brothers..." The line kept resounding in Faith's heart as the voice of the Holy One spoke to her: *"Obedience brings many blessings. Share freely what I have done for you. Exhort your fellowship to confess their sins to one another and forgive any grievances they hold in their hearts."*

Faith wondered how Joshua would react to her 'confession'. What would he think of her confessing to a priest? Would he be upset? She was amazed at his response.

"My darling, this is really amazing. The curtain that you experienced around you is described in the book of Hebrews![34] The Lord took you into the Most Holy Place behind the curtain and you were at the very mercy seat [35] of God. No wonder you were transfixed by His Holiness... What an extraordinary blessing! You must share your testimony with the church."

A few days later Richard approached his mother with great curiosity. "Mom, you seem very different since you got back from Ohio."

"Really? How do you mean, different?"

He pondered for a moment then offered a big smile. "You've grown up!"

---

[34] *Hebrews 10:19-22*
[35] *or 'atonement cover': see Exodus 25:17-22 and Hebrews 9:3-5.*

During the next several Sundays Faith stood up in the church gatherings and encouraged her brothers and sisters to get on with God's program of confession and forgiveness, reminding them how wonderfully she had been blessed.

As relative newcomers to the fellowship, the Alexanders were unaware of a long history of deep divisions among some of the members. One sister came over to Faith during worship and asked her to pray with her. They went out into the hallway and knelt down before the Lord. Jill began confessing the sins and hurts that had been keeping her captive.

When Jill had finished, the Holy Spirit whispered in Faith's ear: *"Now lay your hands on her head, just as Father Anthony laid his hands on yours, and pray for her. Tell her that by the authority the Holy Spirit is giving you right now, she is forgiven!"*

Initially shocked by this word, Faith realised that she must do exactly as the Holy Spirit had directed her. She laid her hands on Jill's head and prayed. Immediately her friend was healed and released, exactly as Faith had been. Over the following weeks Jill kept commenting, "It's like being born again... again!"

The good news raced through the town that God was setting free those people who would confess their sins to one another. Over the next weeks many more were blessed. One pastor called Faith to say that a woman had been praying for the infilling of the Holy Spirit for over a year without result. After being counselled to confess her sins, she was wonderfully baptised with the Spirit. The Lord was healing relationships among members of several churches, with many people asking each other's forgiveness.

Some days later Faith happened to read John 20:21, where Jesus appeared after His Resurrection to His disciples and said: **"'Peace be with you! As the Father has sent Me, I am sending you.' And with that He breathed on them and said, 'Receive the Holy Spirit. If you forgive anyone his sins, they are forgiven; if you do not forgive them they are not forgiven.'"**

"Joshua, look at these words," she exclaimed with excitement. "Jesus is telling us here what the requirements are for forgiving sins!"

"I see it, yes... We need to have been sent or commissioned by our Lord, and filled with the Holy Spirit. That's simple enough!"

"So why don't more Christians take this seriously?" bemoaned Faith. "How sad that so many churches have lost out on this practice. It's the heart of the Christian message! Confessing sins to one another brings such an extraordinary blessing. God doesn't want us to hide from each other or from Him. He wants us to hide together IN Him. Confessing our sins is God's way of renewing our minds and refreshing our hearts."

Joshua shook his head angrily. "How like the enemy to distort this truth, to make us shun the very process by which God brings us into health and wholeness."

No one actually did a confessional dance in that little fellowship of believers. Nevertheless, brothers and sisters began confessing their sins to one another, forgiveness was flowing and relationships were renewed. Hearts were dancing, if not feet. What a joy to be set free!

> **"God is light; in Him there is no darkness at all. If we claim to have fellowship with Him yet walk in darkness, we lie and do not live by the truth. But if we walk in the light, as He is in the light, we have fellowship with one another, and the blood of Jesus, His Son, purifies us from every sin."**
> *(1 John 1:5-7)*

Closing the Circle

"I will gather you... and will bring you back to the place from which I carried you into exile."
(Jeremiah 29:14)

In the spring, Joshua was informed that his foreign assignment was being terminated earlier than anticipated. He was to be relocated at the end of the summer. Against all expectations, the company decided to transfer him to their laboratories in Maryland instead of back to Los Angeles. The Alexanders looked forward to returning to Montgomery Village, the 'cow pasture' from where they had started their odyssey 15 years before.

Their loving Heavenly Father had a *grand finale* in store for them. Some friends living in France invited the family to spend part of August with them at a historic château in the sleepy Normandy countryside. Altogether there were eight children and five dogs and the time passed delightfully with endless games and escapades. Every evening a lavish formal dinner was served in the restored dining hall, with up to 24 people seated around the antique table.

On Sunday morning everyone woke up late. In spite of the drenching rain, they eventually got ready for church. Three full cars pulled out of the wrought iron gates and drove for nearly an hour to reach La Haye-du-Puits, a little town in the west of Normandy with a huge cathedral. Joshua dropped off his family at the side door of this giant edifice and went searching for a place to park the car. He returned with squelching shoes and dripping clothes and found Faith seated at the very back. The service was almost over, and from where they were sitting it was almost unintelligible.

Joshua whispered something and looked over at his wife. Her eyes were closed, her cheeks wet with tears. She was in another world, and was not responding.

Hundreds of people soon stood up and started to leave, but Faith did not move. Joshua went to find the children, and together with the other family they all waited patiently for nearly half an hour until Faith joined them.

Once they were back in the château, she drew Joshua aside. "God gave me a vision in there, a vision of His LOVE!

"No sooner had I found a quiet place to sit than I was taken up into the Lord's arms. The sense of His love was amazing. I was absolutely cocooned and protected in His love, and it seemed like I was separated from everything but HIM.

"Then He took me on a journey. The light got brighter and brighter, yet the sense of His love never diminished. He took me through many of the experiences we've had since we trusted in Him. As we reviewed the past, I realised what incredible love our Heavenly Father has for us - how He has lavished so much grace and mercy on us.

"I've never experienced anything like it. There were no words... just this amazing divine light and being wrapped in His love. It was so wonderful, such a gift of His love. What a taste of Heaven! I could have stayed there all day..."

A trip to the beach was organised on the final Saturday that the two families were to spend together. It was a perfect afternoon for playing in and out of the water, and eventually the friends sat down in little groups on the gentle, west-facing dunes. The sun was going down in a display of glorious colour that was mirrored in the glittering surface of the Atlantic Ocean.

The scene reminded Joshua of Faith's miraculous escape from sharks and the two of them began to tell their hosts, Rose and Philippe, all about it. Of course one story led to another, and before long their entire odyssey of surrender, rescue and restoration had been told.

"What fantastic adventures - the Lord is so faithful," rejoiced Rose. "He always keeps His promises!"

"Yes, He does," agreed Philippe, "and we have seen Him do some wonderful things in our lives also..." He gazed pensively at the beautiful sunset. The sun's final rays seemed to turn the ocean blood red.

"Joshua, I was wondering... What about your Vision?"

"It's in the tomb, Rose," he shrugged. "It must stay there until God raises it up. Still, I do know that whatever the Lord starts, He always finishes. I'm sure He will bring it to pass in His perfect time, whenever that is. He's never late, but He seems to miss an awful lot of good opportunities to be early!"

"That's so true!" added Faith after the laughter subsided. "We've learned that we can't force God's hand. Everything has its season. We need to keep our spiritual eyes and ears open to whatever God is actually doing. Right now we believe the Lord is preparing a whole army of believers to become one in heart and mind with Him. Then we'll see His resurrection power displayed on a massive scale..."

The two couples sat in silence as the colour drained from the sky and the twilight deepened around them. No one wanted to leave.

After a long while Rose looked up and murmured, "The Lord just spoke to my heart!"

There was a glisten of tears in her eyes as she continued. "I was giving God thanks for the incredible ways in which He draws each of us to Himself. As I was praying, He showed me the times in my life when He has carried me and comforted me in His arms. He encouraged me always to stay close to His heart. I told him I couldn't bear to move around the way you have, never staying in a home for more than a year or two..."

Rose laughed through her tears. "Then, in my spirit, I could see a Hand being held out forming a cup. I looked into it, and there was your family - all five of you!

"I heard the Lord say, *'They've made their home in the hollow of My hand... Their hearts belong to Me!'*"

> "I am the Good Shepherd… My sheep listen to My voice; I know them and they follow Me. I give them eternal life, and they shall never perish; no one can snatch them out of My hand."
> *(John 10:14a, 27-28)*

> "We proclaim to you what we have seen and heard, so that you also may have fellowship with us. And our fellowship is with the Father and with His Son, Jesus Christ. We write this to make our joy complete."
> *(1 John 1:3-4)*

Epilogue

Another Imaginary Audience in Heaven

"Well done, My good and faithful messengers - you have fulfilled My instructions to the last detail! Faith and Joshua now belong to Me and trust in Me. I have become their Shepherd and they are My sheep who hear My voice and follow Me."

"We thank you for the wonderful opportunity to have served You, our Sovereign Lord, and we praise and magnify your glorious Name! What is Your Majesty's will for them now?"

"It is time to shape their character. They must grow in integrity, faithfulness and wisdom. They must learn to recognise, confess and repent of the sins in their life, and to walk in the light as I am in the light. They must desire always to be clothed in My righteousness and to conform to the pattern of My Word, not to the pattern of their world.

"This will be a very hard process. They will have to undergo many difficult trials and tribulations, rejections and refinings in order that their precious faith may be purified as gold, and their 'old man' become of no account. I desire them to become 'priests' to one another and to their brothers and sisters, to carry each other's burdens as if they were their own, and to walk in repentance, humility and love at all times. Then I will be able to move and work through them without hindrance or resistance.

"They must become 'overcomers', depending on the power of My blood and the word of their testimony to come against the opposition of the enemy, *exercising My authority on Earth to loose and bind according to the moving of My Spirit.*

"*The Vision I gave to Joshua is a vital component of My purpose for the Earth. It is essential that you only allow it to be raised up when he and Faith have been sufficiently weakened that they will allow My Spirit to work through them without their help. Then they will see My glory begin to manifest in their life. When My time arrives, you are to release the promised seed funding through My chosen vessel.*

"*I have already prepared the people who will make up the missing parts of the blueprint I have given Joshua. You are to ensure that these missing parts - especially the technologies I have given My chosen technicians - will come into Joshua and Faith's hands by arranging 'divine appointments'. Your fellow messengers are already preparing the 'clean hearts' to work alongside Joshua and Faith and the 'clean hands' to provide them with My resources.*

"*It will be your task to bring them all together so that My work moves forward at the proper time. I shall provide you with special reinforcements because the opposition will be fierce and the battle will be long. But you will surely prevail!*

"*As you know, this is My time to bring revival to My people so they may be unified in My Spirit and purpose, loving one another as I have loved them. Then My saving love will at last reach to the uttermost parts of the Earth and the knowledge of My glory will fill the Earth as the waters cover the sea.*

"*First, however, I must remove the pride, prejudice, selfishness, complacency, greed and fear from My people by circumcising their hearts and setting them free. They must begin to move as one Body following their Head and as one Army following their Captain. They will do the 'greater things' that I promised after they are cleansed by My Blood and learn to exercise My authority.*

"*With your help I will make the way to display My love and bring My life to the remotest villages on Earth. Those who walk in My word and under My authority will harvest every people, tribe, nation and language for My name's sake as I open up the floodgates of Heaven and pour My Spirit out on all flesh.*

"*Then, at last, My house will be full!*

"*My purpose will NOT be thwarted. Godspeed…*"

Frequently Asked Questions

Faith and Joshua, why didn't you tell us more about yourselves?

"We wanted the spotlight to stay on the Lord as much as possible. The main point of the book is that God can speak to any of us if we'll take the time to listen and if we have the confidence that we can hear His voice. There's nothing special about us – it's the Lord."

What happened next? Will there be a 'Volume Two'?

"There were a lot more trials, tribulations, travels and moving on in the Lord! There will be a sequel but it's not written yet."

Do you still hear the Lord's voice so clearly?

"Yes, whenever He has something specific to tell us. Remember that the events in this book took place over a long period, 15 years, and often many months passed between those precious moments when He gave us His specific guidance. Most of the time the Lord directs us through His written word and by the peace and agreement He puts in our hearts. It's a process that requires faith and perseverance."

Have there ever been times when you made a mistake about God's guidance?

"Undoubtedly, but the Lord is able to redeem our mistakes. Only He knows what they were."

What do you do when God is silent?

"We ask Him why! There are different seasons in our lives, and when "the heavens are brass" we simply don't hear anything. Sometimes He's silent to discipline us. For example, if He has told us to do something and we haven't done it, He may get our attention by being silent. We have to go to Him in repentance and ask how we've offended Him. As soon as we get sorted out the communication is restored. At other times He's silent because there's nothing new He needs to reveal, or the timing isn't right. Then we need to be patient and persevere. It is very hard to bear, but He often gives us tokens of His love through His word and His people so as to comfort and encourage us."

What about the children? How did your moving around affect them?

"When we asked Richard this question some years ago he replied, 'The way I see it, I've lived more and had more experiences in my 16 years than most people have in 80. I feel privileged!' The three children gradually came to understand that the Lord knows everything best and that the things of this life are transient. Even though God called us to surrender everything to Him - including them - He always provided good schools and friends for each of them wherever He sent us as a family."

With hindsight, would you recommend your lifestyle?

"Spiritually yes, but physically no. The Lord is sovereign, and we cannot know what He has planned for us individually or as a family until we press in and ask Him. Even then, He is very gentle and tolerant with us if we can't stomach His 'program', and allows us alternatives. But if we surrender to His perfect will whatever the consequences, we will always experience His 'best'. We believe that God planned our life specifically to prepare us for something quite arduous but ultimately fruitful. The instability and moving around were tailor-made for us so we would let go of our worldly security, get out of our comfort zone and benefit from the variety of churches and locations He provided. The Lord knew that the five of us were resilient enough to handle this lifestyle. The continual hellos and goodbyes have been very hard, though – especially the goodbyes."

What is your attitude to borrowing money and living on credit?

"Again, the Lord is sovereign. If we live a life yielded to His sovereignty (and not ruled by principles, however true they may be), we must do whatever He tells us to do. If the only way to obey Him is by borrowing money, then we borrow; but as soon as we can repay, we repay. (It's the love of money and the reckless use of credit cards, in order to amass material things, that are unrighteous in God's sight.) After all, God asked Abraham to kill his son Isaac – isn't that more serious in human terms than using credit cards?"

What are the most important lessons you've learned about hearing from God?

"First that He loves us and cares about us, especially about our heart condition - He wants to set us free and make us whole. Second, He will always let us know whatever it is we need to know, and will never let us down. Third,

Frequently Asked Questions

He is a saving, rescuing God who enjoys 'snatching victory from the jaws of defeat' (we often call Him *Jehovah JIT* – Just In Time). Fourth, He wants us all to trust Him and become His disciples and eventually His co-workers. Fifth, His ways are not our ways, His thoughts are not our thoughts and (in particular) His timing is not our timing. His ways, thoughts and timing should be carefully studied in the Old and the New Testaments."

What about the "40/40 Vision"?

"We've waited nearly 25 years for 'God's time' to come, and are ready to start the company and launch the project just as soon as the Lord provides the initial funding. Back in 1980, the Lord said that we'd need a million dollars to start – 'a million dollars for a million villages'. We were awed but not surprised to find that the start-up phase of our recently completed business plan was going to cost exactly that amount."

Has the Vision stayed 'dead and buried'?

"In early 1995 the Lord announced quite unexpectedly that He was resurrecting the Vision. He gave us 'divine appointments' with key people, including inventors of technologies that will make this 'Mission Impossible' become 'Mission Possible'. Recently He has given us encouraging confirmations that He will release all the needed resources very soon."

What can I do to help promote the "40/40 Vision" and even get involved in it?

"Ask the Lord of the Harvest if you are to be part of the outworking of this Vision, and how. If this book has inspired you, please tell others about it."

How can I get in touch with you?

"Please write to us care of   faithandjoshua@yahoo.com

Fantastic Adventures In Trusting Him